theory of culture change

Theory of
CULTURE CHANGE

*the methodology
of multilinear
evolution*

JULIAN H. STEWARD

University of Illinois Press
Urbana   Chicago   London

preface

This volume sets forth certain concepts and methods needed to develop a general methodology for determining regularities in the functional interrelationships of cultural patterns and in the processes of culture change which have occurred independently among societies in different parts of the world. The Introduction presents a broad statement of the scientific objective and of certain heuristic concepts and procedures necessary to realize this objective. The first five chapters are primarily theoretical. Each elaborates a concept and method. The following seven chapters are slightly more substantive than theoretical in that they illustrate applications of the basic theory to selected cultures. Previously published essays form the basis of most of the chapters but in order to present a coherent and unified point of view, it has been necessary to revise these in some measure and to fill gaps with newly written chapters (2, 5, and 6).

Since the volume is primarily theoretical rather than substantive, it covers only a limited number of the many kinds of culture found throughout the world. The samples, however, present a sufficient variety of cultural types and levels to illustrate the kinds of phenomena, the problems and the methodological considerations that will be encountered in any study of culture change.

I. introduction

In cultural studies it is important to distinguish a scientific, generalizing approach from a historical, particularizing approach. The former attempts to arrange phenomena in orderly categories, to recognize consistent interrelationships between them, to establish laws of regularities, and to make formulations which have predictive value. The latter is more concerned with the occurrence of phenomena in time and place, the uniqueness of each constellation, and the ethos or value systems which characterize culture areas. The concepts and methods of the former must differ in part from those of the latter. My purpose in this collection of essays is to develop a methodology for determining regularities of form, function, and process which recur cross-culturally among societies found in different cultural areas.

Anthropology has been distinctive among the social sciences largely because of its historical and comparative approach to culture. Its task has been twofold: to describe the varieties of culture found throughout the world and to explain their development. Descriptive ethnology has produced a vast body of data concerning the customs of differing groups of mankind, and archaeology together with history has reconstructed the temporal as well as spacial occurrences of these customs. There is a wide difference of opinion, however, concerning what properly constitutes an "explanation" of culture. The many ways in which explanations are conceptualized involve fundamentally different points of view concerning the nature of culture development, and these in turn entail different ways of regarding culture facts. Historical or developmental explanations have, in general, been systematized in three different ways. First, the so-called "unilinear evolution" postulates that all societies pass through similar developmental stages. Since contemporary primitive peoples are presumed to represent stages in the development of more advanced societies, they are thought to exhibit a kind of arrested development. Second, in direct contrast to the unilinear evolutionists, the cultural relativists see cultural development as essentially divergent, and they focus attention upon features that distinguish societies from one another. Although they pay considerable attention to uniformities[1] or similarities which are caused by diffusion of customs within culture areas, they consider each area to be basically different from all others. Third, the position of multilinear evolution (Chapter 1), which constitutes the methodological position of the present collection of essays, assumes that certain basic types of culture may develop in similar ways under similar conditions but that few concrete aspects of culture will appear among all groups of mankind in a regular sequence.[2]

The cultural patterns and causal interrelations which may develop repeatedly in different parts of the world and thus constitute cross-cultural regularities are subject to both synchronic and diachronic formulations. In some instances, there are constellations of phenomena which occur repeatedly because certain phenomena presuppose others. The nexus between them is functional and need not be formulated in terms of historical change, time depth, or developmental process. These regularities are synchronic. In other cases, there is a succession of similar constellations which succeed one another in a regular and predetermined way because of developmental laws. These developmental regularities are diachronic and require processual formulations. Functional or synchronic formulations of regularities are illustrated in the case of dispersed family groups (Chapter 6), patrilineal bands (Chapter 7), and composite bands of hunters (Chapter 8). Diachronic formulations are illustrated in the case of the development of multi-

---

[1] For definitions of uniformities and regularities, see p. 88.

[2] I do not know the origin of the term "multilinear evolution." It has been used by Karl Wittfogel with much the same conceptual connotation as in the present volume. In "The Influence of Leninism-Stalinism on China," *Annals of The American Academy of Political and Social Science,* Sept., 1951, pp. 22-34, Wittfogel uses Marx's term, "pluralism."

clan societies (Chapter 9) and irrigation civilizations (Chapter 11).

Chapters 1 to 5 elaborate the heuristic concepts for determining cross-cultural types. Chapter 1 presents the general concept of multilinear evolution. It is an affirmation that significant cross-cultural regularities exist but a denial that such regularities must pertain to all human societies. The concepts set forth here are to be clearly distinguished from the views of L. H. Morgan, E. B. Tylor and other nineteenth-century writers and of V. Gordon Childe and Leslie White among contemporary authors. Whereas these writers have sought to formulate cultural development in terms of universal stages, my objective is to seek causes of culture change. Since "evolution" still strongly connotes the nineteenth-century view, I hesitate to use it but find no better term.

Chapter 2 develops a method for recognizing the ways in which culture change is induced by adaptation to environment. This adaptation, an important creative process, is called *cultural ecology*, a concept which is to be distinguished from the sociological concept, "human ecology" or "social ecology." The cross-cultural regularities which arise from similar adaptive processes in similar environments are functional or synchronic in nature.

But no culture has achieved so perfect an adjustment to its environment that it is static. The differences which appear in successive periods during the development of culture in any locality entail not only increasing complexity, or quantitatively new patterns, but also qualitatively new patterns. Consequently, in the comparison of the history of two or more areas in which the cultural ecological processes are the same, it must be recognized that a late period in one area may be much more like a comparable late or homotaxially similar period in another area than the earlier periods in either area. Cultural development therefore must be conceptualized not only as a matter of increasing complexity but also as one of the emergence of successive *levels of sociocultural integration*. This conceptualization is elaborated in Chapter 3. This concept of levels of sociocultural integration is useful in analyzing the internal structure of complex contemporary systems as well as in characterizing the successive emergence of qualitatively new levels in historical development. Chapter 4 illustrates the application of this concept to a national-level system.

The concept of *culture type* (Chapter 5) is based on the two frames of reference previously presented: cultural features derived from synchronic, functional, and ecological factors and those represented by a particular diachronic or developmental level. Cross-cultural regu-

larities are thus conceived as recurrent constellations of basic features
— the *cultural core* — which have similar functional interrelationships
resulting from local ecological adaptations and similar levels of sociocultural integration. The concept of culture type is confronted by the
apparent difficulty posed by the fact that forms, patterns, or structures
differ greatly. Since, however, similar functions may be served by
different forms while similar forms may serve varied functions, the
single concept of *form-function* is introduced.

Chapters 6 to 12 illustrate the methodology set forth in preceding
chapters through analysis of several culture types. These types are presented in successive chapters according to their level of sociocultural
integration. The lowest level, that of the Shoshonean Indians of the
Great Basin described in Chapter 6, exemplifies a society of hunters
and gatherers which functioned on a family basis. Because the cultural
ecological adaptations in this area precluded permanent multifamily
societies of any kind, the individual or nuclear family carried on nearly
all cultural activities.

Among the other hunters and gatherers, special cultural ecological
adaptations led to slightly higher levels of sociocultural integration.
Chapter 7 analyzes the particular conditions which brought about
patrilineal hunting bands in several widely separated parts of the
world. Chapter 8 shows how the somewhat different environmental
factors of northern Canada entailed an adaptation which created composite hunting bands in aboriginal times, while the post-European
development of the fur trade led to division of the country into family
territories.

Many primitive people are divided into several nonlocalized clans
which are functionally interdependent parts of villages or tribes. These
represent a higher level of sociocultural integration than localized
lineages, and they have probably developed from such lineages many
times in different parts of the world. Chapter 9 utilizes archaeological
and ethnographic data from the Southwest to reconstruct the processes
through which multiclan village organization developed independently
from localized lineages in at least three separate cases.

Although certain ecological adaptations produce patrilineal bands
or other social types and permit little if any social variation, there are
instances where the interrelationship between culture and environment
allows considerable latitude or potential variation in sociocultural
types. Where latitude is possible, historic factors may determine the
nature of the society. Chapter 10 shows how the environmental adaptations of the Carrier Indians of British Columbia first permitted

change in late prehistoric times from composite hunting bands to a system of localized, landowning moieties and social classes, when these people were influenced by the Northwest Coast, and second, allowed conversion in recent years into family units which own trapping territories and represent a special subculture of the larger Canadian sociocultural system.

In Egypt, Mesopotamia, China, Meso-America, and the Central Andes, comparatively complex civilizations developed on the basis of irrigation agriculture. Chapter 11 shows how in each of these areas fundamentally similar cultural ecological adaptations entailed a similar historical sequence which began with a simple village organization and finally reached a very high level of integration in militaristic empires. Despite many particulars in which these areas differed, the basic cultural patterns or forms, the functional interrelationships between cultural features, and the developmental processes were very much the same.

Chapter 12 briefly illustrates the application of the concepts of cultural ecology, levels of sociocultural integration, and culture type to a complex, contemporary society, Puerto Rico. In the study of Puerto Rico, which is being published in full in a separate volume, the author and his collaborators found these concepts to be indispensable tools of analysis.

An effort has been made to define the objectives and methods set forth in this volume as strictly as possible. That little attention is accorded many approaches now being developed in social science means simply that they are peripheral to the present purpose and not necessarily that their value is questioned. Thus, while culture and personality studies which are now greatly in vogue have great importance to problems of individual adjustment, I cannot see that they are relevant to the basic problems discussed in this volume. Personality is shaped by culture, but it has never been shown that culture is affected by personality. It is true of course that in a normative sense a previously molded personality may by resisting innovations retard culture change and by modifying new patterns give change a special direction. But these are short-range changes. In long-range cultural development the basic patterns and corresponding personality types are not perpetuated over centuries or millenia. In the course of time, culture develops qualitatively new patterns which cause and are not caused by new personality types.

Finally, I wish to stress that my delimitation of problem and method precludes all efforts to achieve universal explanations or formulations of human behavior. In view of what I take to be a very widespread interest among social scientists in making such explanations and formulations their ultimate goal, it is extremely important to be aware of the implication of this fact. Particular patterns of behavior found among one or more but not all groups of mankind must be explained in very different terms than behavior common to all people. In fact, particular patterns must be conceptualized differently than universals. The first constitute culture in its proper sense. The second constitute inherent human biological and psychological characteristics. The former are determined by history and by special local adaptations. They are super-organic. The latter are reducible to biochemical and psychological processes.

All men eat, but this is an organic and not a cultural fact. It is universally explainable in terms of biological and chemical processes. What and how different groups of men eat is a cultural fact explainable only by culture history and environmental factors. All men dance, but the universal feature of dancing is bodily rhythm which is a human rather than cultural trait. Specific movements, music, attire, ritual, and other attributes of dancing which have limited occurrence and give dances meaning as cultural facts are not subject to universal explanation or formulation. A formula that explains behavior of all mankind cannot explain culture.

It is difficult to conceive the kinds of understandings that Leslie White, an uncompromising culturologist, hopes to gain by dealing with culture in general rather than with cultures in particular. Yet White, like so many social scientists, seems to believe that a truly scientific formulation must explain all modes of behavior. I conclude this Introduction therefore by emphasizing that my own objective is to formulate the conditions determining phenomena of limited occurrence. The category of nature to which these belong is known generically as culture and is found among all mankind, but no cultural phenomena are universal.

II. concepts and methods

1

Multilinear Evolution:

Evolution and Process[1]

THE MEANING OF EVOLUTION

Cultural evolution, although long an unfashionable concept, has commanded renewed interest in the last two decades. This interest does not indicate any serious reconsideration of the particular historical reconstructions of the nineteenth-century evolutionists, for these were quite thoroughly discredited on empirical grounds. It arises from the potential methodological importance of cultural evolution for contemporary research, from the implications of its scientific objectives, its taxonomic procedures, and its conceptualization of historical change and cultural causality. An appraisal of cultural evolution, therefore, must be concerned with definitions and meanings. But I do not wish to engage in semantics. I shall attempt to show that if certain distinctions in the concept of evolution are made, it is evident that certain methodological propositions find fairly wide acceptance today.

In order to clear the ground, it is necessary first to consider the meaning of cultural evolution in relation to biological evolution, for there is a wide tendency to consider the former as an extension of,

[1] This chapter is adapted from "Evolution and Process," in *Anthropology Today: An Encyclopedic Inventory*, ed. A. L. Kroeber (University of Chicago Press, 1953), pp. 313-26, by courtesy of The University of Chicago Press.

and therefore analogous to, the latter. There is, of course, a relation-ship between biological and cultural evolution in that a minimal development of the Hominidae was a precondition of culture. But cultural evolution is an extension of biological evolution only in a chronological sense (Huxley, 1952). The nature of the evolutionary schemes and of the developmental processes differs profoundly in biology and in culture. In biological evolution it is assumed that all forms are genetically related and that their development is essentially divergent. Parallels, such as the development of flying, swimming, and warm blood, are superficial and fairly uncommon. These latter, more-over, are generally considered to be instances of convergent evolution rather than true parallels. In cultural evolution, on the other hand, it is assumed that cultural patterns in different parts of the world are genetically unrelated and yet pass through parallel sequences. Diver-gent trends which do not follow the postulated universal sequence, such as those caused by distinctive local environments, are attributed only secondary importance. Such modern-day unilinear evolutionists as Leslie White and V. Gordon Childe evade the awkward facts of cultural divergence and local variation by purporting to deal with culture as a whole rather than with particular cultures. But Childe (1951: 160) quite explicitly distinguishes biological from cultural evolution by stressing the divergent nature of the former and the operation of diffusion and the frequency of convergence in the latter. It is interesting that such history as is implied in cultural relativism is rather similar to that of biological evolution: the variations and unique patterns of the different areas and subareas are clearly conceived to represent divergent development and presumably an ultimate genetic relationship. It is only the complementary concept of diffusion, a phenomenon unknown in biology, that prevents cultural relativism from having an exclusively genetic significance, like that of biological evolution.

Analogies between cultural and biological evolution are also alleged to be represented by two attributes of each: first, a tendency toward increasing complexity of forms and, second, the development of superior forms, that is, improvement or progress. It is, of course, quite possible to define complexity and progress so as to make them charac-teristics of evolution. But they are not attributes exclusively of evolution; they may also be considered characteristics of cultural change or development as conceived from any nonevolutionary point of view.

The assumption that cultural change normally involves increasing complexity is found in virtually all historical interpretations of cultural data. But complexity in biology and culture differ. As Kroeber (1948: 297) states: "The process of cultural development is an additive and therefore accumulative one, whereas the process of organic evolution is a substitutive one." It is on the question not of complexity but of divergence that the relativists and evolutionists differ. According to the former, cumulative change follows parallel trends, whereas, according to the latter, it is ordinarily divergent, though sometimes it is convergent and occasionally it is parallel.

Although complexity as such is not distinctive of the evolutionary concept, an allied concept might be considered to distinguish both biological and cultural evolution from nonevolutionary cultural-historical concepts. This is the concept of organizational types and levels. Whereas relativism seems to hold that a rather fixed and qualitatively unique pattern persists in each cultural tradition, despite cumulative changes which create quantitative complexity, it is implicit in the evolutionary view that development levels are marked by the appearance of qualitatively distinctive patterns or types of organization. Just as simple unicellular forms of life are succeeded by multicellular and internally specialized forms which have distinctive kinds of total organization, so social forms consisting of single families and lineages are succeeded by multifamilial communities, bands, or tribes, and these, in turn, by state patterns, each involving not only greater internal heterogeneity and specialization but wholly new kinds of over-all integration (Steward, 1950, 1951). Thus evolutionism is distinguished from relativism by the fact that the former attributes qualitative distinctiveness to successive stages, regardless of the particular tradition, whereas the latter attributes it to the particular tradition or culture area rather than to the development stage.

This brings us to the question of progress, which is the second characteristic attributed to both biological and cultural evolution. Progress must be measured by definable values. Most of the social sciences are still so ethnocentric, especially in their practical applications, that value judgments are almost inescapable. Even the "Statement on Human Rights" (1947) offered to the United Nations by the American Anthropological Association clearly reflects the American value placed upon individual rights and political democracy. This or any other criterion of value, however, certainly does not imply evolution. In fact, the concept of progress is largely separable from evolution, and it may be approached in many ways. Kroeber, who is by no means an evolutionist, suggests three criteria for measuring progress: "the atrophy of magic based on psychopathology; the decline of infantile obsession with the outstanding physiological events of human life; and the persistent tendency of technology and science to grow accumulatively (Kroeber, 1948: 304). These values are not absolute in a philosophical sense; they are "the ways in which progress may legitimately be considered a property or an attribute of culture." By definition, then, it is possible although not necessary to regard progress as a characteristic of any form of cultural change, whether it is considered evolutionary or not.

We must conclude that cultural evolution is not distinguished from cultural relativism or historical particularism by any essential similarity of its developmental scheme with that of biological evolution, by the characteristic of increasing complexity, or by the attribute of progress. This is not to say, however, that evolution lacks distinctive features. The methodology of evolution contains two vitally important assumptions. First, it postulates that genuine parallels of form and function develop in historically independent sequences or cultural traditions. Second, it explains these parallels by the independent operation of identical causality in each case. The methodology is therefore avowedly scientific and generalizing rather than historical and particularizing. It is less concerned with unique and divergent (or convergent) patterns and features of culture — although it does not necessarily deny such divergence — than with parallels and similarities which recur cross-culturally. It endeavors to determine recurrent patterns and processes and to formulate the interrelationships between phenomena in terms of "laws." The nineteenth-century evolutionists are important to contemporary studies more because of their scientific objective and preoccupation with laws than because of their particular substantive historical reconstructions.

Cultural evolution, then, may be defined broadly as a quest for cultural regularities or laws; but there are three distinctive ways in which evolutionary data may be handled. First, *unilinear evolution,* the classical nineteenth-century formulation, dealt with particular cultures, placing them in stages of a universal sequence. Second, *universal evolution* — a rather arbitrary label to designate the modern revamping of unilinear evolution — is concerned with culture rather than with cultures. Third, *multilinear evolution,* a somewhat less ambitious approach than the other two, is like unilinear evolution in dealing with developmental sequences, but it is distinctive in searching for parallels of limited occurrence instead of universals.

The critical differences between these three concepts of evolution have not been recognized, and there is still a general tendency to identify any effort to determine similar form and process in parallel developments with nineteenth-century unilinear evolution and thus categorically to reject it. The Marxist and Communist adoption of nineteenth-century evolutionism, especially of L. H. Morgan's scheme, as official dogma (Tolstoy, 1952), has certainly not favored the acceptability to scientists of the Western nations of anything labeled "evolution."

Unilinear Evolution

There is no need to discuss the validity of the nineteenth-century evolutionary schemes, for their vulnerability in the face of twentieth-century archaeological and ethnographic research has been amply demonstrated. Although no effort has been made to revise these schemes in the light of new empirical data concerning the history of individual cultures — which itself is a somewhat remarkable fact — it does not necessarily follow that L. H. Morgan (1910) and his contemporaries (Tylor, 1865, 1871, 1881, 1899) failed completely to recognize significant patterns and processes of change in particular cases. The inadequacy of unilinear evolution lies largely in the postulated priority of matriarchal patterns over the other kinship patterns and in the indiscriminate effort to force the data of all precivilized groups of mankind, which included most of the primitive world, into the categories of "savagery" and "barbarism." The category of "civilization," however, involved a less sweeping generalization for the simple reason that civilization was thought of largely in terms of the Near East, the northern Mediterranean, and northern Europe. Other areas which achieved civilization, particularly the New World, were far less known and have been accorded less attention.

In other words, whereas the historical reconstruction and the deductions derived therefrom were largely wrong as regards early stages of cultural development because they failed to recognize the many varieties of local trends, the analyses of civilization contain many valuable insights because they are based more specifically upon developments which occurred first in Egypt and Mesopotamia and later in Greece, Rome, and northern Europe. Although comparisons with other areas, particularly with the Americas but also with India and

China, left much to be desired so far as forms, functions, and developmental processes of civilization in general are concerned, the conclusions may nonetheless be valid under limited circumstances. Thus Henry Maine's insights concerning the processes involved in development from a kin-based society to a territorial, state society undoubtedly throw light on cultural development in many areas, though not necessarily on all. Such categories as "kin-based" and "state" are too broad; distinctions between particular, though recurrent, types within these categories are needed.

There are probably many developmental forms and processes discussed by the evolutionists which have validity, provided that they are considered qualities of particular cultural traditions rather than universal characteristics of culture. The extremely illuminating analyses that V. Gordon Childe (1934, 1946) and others have given us of cultural development in the eastern Mediterranean and Europe probably would find certain rather precise parallels in other world areas if a truly comparative study were made. Significantly, however, Childe's approach to evolution on a wider scale has entailed a retreat into broad generalizations.

Universal Evolution

Universal evolution, which is represented today principally by Leslie White and V. Gordon Childe, is the heritage of nineteenth-century unilinear evolution, especially as formulated by L. H. Morgan, in the scope of its generalizations but not in its treatment of particulars. Aware that empirical research of the twentieth century has invalidated the unilinear historical reconstructions of particular cultures, which constituted the essential feature of nineteenth-century schemes, White and Childe endeavor to keep the evolutionary concept of cultural stages alive by relating these stages to the culture of mankind as a whole. The distinctive cultural traditions and the local variations — the culture areas and subareas — which have developed as the result of special historical trends and of cultural ecological adaptations to special environments are excluded as irrelevant. White (1949:338-39) states: "We may say that culture as a whole serves the need of man as a species. But this does not and cannot help us at all when we try to account for the variations of specific culture. . . . The functioning of any particular culture will of course be conditioned by local environmental conditions. But in a consideration of culture as a whole, we may *average all environments together* to form a constant factor which may be excluded from our formulation of cultural development" (Steward, 1949; italics mine). Childe reconciles the general and particular in much the same way. He writes that "all societies have lived in different historical environments and have passed through different vicissitudes, their traditions have diverged, and so ethnography reveals a multiplicity of cultures, just as does archaeology" (Childe, 1951:32). Childe finds that consideration of the particular is a "serious handicap if our objective is to establish general stages in the evolution of cultures," and, therefore, in order to "discover general laws descriptive of the evolution of all societies, we abstract . . . the peculiarities due to differences of habitat" (Childe, 1951:35). Diffusion must also be discounted, because any society must be in a position to accept diffused technological and social features. At the same time, while local developments within each general stage are largely divergent, the concept of evolution is salvaged by assuming that diffusion brings technological and social features to all societies, thus convergently re-creating the required patterns (Childe, 1951:160 ff). This rather involved effort to enlist diffusion in order to offset divergent evolution is based empirically almost exclusively upon Old World data. How Old World and New World parallels would square with such reasoning Childe does not say.

It is interesting that White's theoretical discussions make no reference to his own extensive and detailed studies of the Pueblo Indians and that Childe's superb knowledge of developmental patterns and processes which are disclosed in the archaeology of the Near East and Europe becomes almost an embarrassment in his theoretical discussions. Childe's insights into the cultural development of these two areas are most illuminating, but he merely confuses the two areas when he endeavors to fit them into simplified developmental stages.

It is important to recognize that the evolutionism of White and Childe yields substantive results of a very different order from those of nineteenth-century evolution. The postulated cultural sequences are so general that they are neither very arguable nor very useful. No one disputes that hunting and gathering, which is Childe's diagnostic of "savagery," preceded plant and animal domestication which is his criterion of "barbarism," and that the latter was a precondition of large populations, cities, internal social differentiation and specialization, and the development of writing and mathematics, which are characteristics of "civilization."

If one examines universal evolution with a view to finding laws or processes of development rather than examining it merely in terms of a sequential reconstruction of culture, it is also difficult to recognize anything strikingly new or controversial. The generalization that culture changes from the simple to the complex and White's (1943) "law" that technological development expressed in terms of man's control over energy underlies certain cultural achievements and social changes have long been accepted. Childe's transfer of the Darwinian formula to cultural evolution also will not evoke challenge. Variation is seen as invention, heredity as learning and diffusion, and adaptation and selection as cultural adaptation and choice (Childe, 1951: 175-79). It is certainly a worthy objective to seek universal laws of cultural change. It must be stressed, however, that all universal laws thus far postulated are concerned with the fact that culture changes — that any culture changes — and thus cannot explain particular features of particular cultures. In this respect, the "laws" of cultural and biological evolution are similar. Variation, heredity, and natural selection cannot explain a single life-form, for they do not deal with the characteristics of particular species and do not take into account the incalculable number of particular circumstances and factors that cause biological differentiation in each species. Similarly, White's law of energy levels, for example, can tell us nothing about the development of the characteristics of individual cultures. We may deduce from the data of both biological and cultural evolution that new organizational forms will appear in succession, but the specific nature of these forms can be understood only by tracing the history of each in great detail.

The problem and method of universal evolution thus differ from those of unilinear evolution. Right or wrong, the nineteenth-century evolutionists did attempt to explain concretely why a matriarchy should precede other social forms, why animism was the precursor of gods and spirits, why a kin-based society evolved into a territorial-based, state-controlled society, and why other specific features of culture appeared.

Multilinear Evolution

Multilinear evolution is essentially a methodology based on the assumption that significant regularities in cultural change occur, and it is concerned with the determination of cultural laws. Its method is empirical rather than deductive. It is inevitably concerned also with historical reconstruction, but it does not expect that historical data can be classified in universal stages. It is interested in particular cultures, but instead of finding local variations and diversity troublesome facts which force the frame of reference from the particular to the general, it deals only with those limited parallels of form, function, and sequence which have empirical validity. What is lost in universality will be gained in concreteness and specificity. Multilinear evolution, therefore, has no a priori scheme or laws. It recognizes that the cultural traditions of different areas may be wholly or partly distinctive, and it simply poses the question of whether any genuine or meaningful similarities between certain cultures exist and whether these lend themselves to formulation. These similarities may involve salient features of whole cultures, or they may involve only special features, such as clans, men's societies, social classes of various kinds, priesthoods, military patterns, and the like.

It may be objected that a limited formulation which postulates that some special feature — let us say a clan — has developed in two or more cultures independently for the same reasons cannot be considered evolution. We thus return to definitions. If evolution can be considered an interest in determining recurrent forms, processes, and functions rather than world-embracing schemes and universal laws, the many efforts to make scientific generalizations, whether they deal with synchronic, functional relationships or with diachronic, sequential relationships and whether they embrace few or many cultures, are methodologically akin to evolution. The nineteenth-century evolutionists were deeply interested in making generalizations.

THE METHOD OF MULTILINEAR EVOLUTION

Parallelism and Causality

An implicit interest in parallelism and causality has always been present in cultural studies, and it seems to have increased during the last two decades. It would be quite surprising, in fact, if anyone held so tenaciously to the logical implications of the relativist position as to claim that understandings derived from the analysis of one culture did not provide some insights as to form, function, and process in others. The difficulty is in raising these insights from the level of hunches to that of explicit formulations. Postulated parallels and recurrent cause-and-effect relations are regarded with suspicion. They may be questioned on empirical grounds; and the inherent difficulty of deriving cultural laws may be attacked on philosophical grounds.

The methodology of cultural studies thus remains predominantly that of historical particularizing rather than of scientific generalizing.

A genuine interest in parallels, however, has been clearly expressed by many scholars who have made outstanding contributions within the framework of the so-called "Boas school." Thus Lowie, who was unsparing of L. H. Morgan's unilinear reconstruction (Lowie, 1925), not only recognizes independent invention and parallel development in many features, such as moieties, dual systems of numbers, messianic cults, and others (Lowie, 1940:376-77), but he is quite prepared to accept a kind of necessity in cultural development to the extent that certain cultural achievements presuppose others. "If a tribe practices metallurgy it is clearly not on the plane of savagery; only stock-breeders and farmers forge metals" (Lowie, 1940:45). But he denies that cultures can be graded on the basis of metallurgy because the Africans, for example, were metallurgists but lacked other features of more developed civilizations. Although Lowie cannot accept Morgan's unilinear evolution,[2] he is in accord with most of the profession in accepting such generalizations as universal evolution has to offer, and moreover, he is something of a multilinear evolutionist. Who, then, is more of an evolutionist, Lowie or White?

American anthropologists have traditionally assumed that there were Old World and New World parallels in the invention of farming, stockbreeding, ceramics, metallurgy, states, priests, temples, the zero and mathematics, writing, and other features. It would perhaps be going too far to say that this makes them multilinear evolutionists. When the question of parallel cultural causality arises, these similarities are held to be only superficial or to represent convergent evolution, or else it is said that the historical and functional relationships involved are as yet too imperfectly understood to permit formulation in terms of cross-cultural regularities. Nevertheless, many persons have recognized such a deep significance in these parallels that they believe diffusion must have occurred between the hemispheres, while others have attempted to formulate Old and New World sequences in terms of comparable developmental periods.

Kroeber (1948:241) did not hesitate to conclude from the numerous parallels in different parts of the world that "culture relations

---

[2] Lowie, in a reply to White, stressed the fact that Morgan, Tylor, and others were forcing the historical data of particular cultures into unilinear schemes rather than dealing with the evolution of an abstract or generalized world culture. See Robert H. Lowie, "Evolution in Cultural Anthropology: A Reply to Leslie White," *American Anthropologist*, XLVIII (1946), 223-33.

or patterns develop spontaneously or from within probably more frequently than as a result of direct taking-over. Also, the types of culture forms being limited in number, the same type is frequently evolved independently. Thus, monarchical and democratic societies, feudal or caste-divided ones, priest-ridden and relatively irreligious ones, expansive and mercantile or self-sufficient and agricultural nations, evolve over and over again." Elsewhere, I have called attention to statements by Lesser, Boas, Kidder, and others that cross-cultural understandings in terms of laws, regularities, or parallels — those who object to calling these "laws" may use some other term — are a major objective of anthropology (Steward, 1949, 1950). This list could be extended to include a substantial portion of the profession.

The determination and analysis of parallels as a methodological objective of multilinear evolution need not be carried out on a purely cultural level. Leslie White (1949: Chapter 14) has argued so cogently in favor of understanding cultural change in strictly culturological terms that the impression may stand that culturology and evolution are synonymous. It is beyond the scope of this paper to argue the matter. But I must insist that White's elimination of both the human and the environmental factors is an aspect of his concern with culture rather than with cultures. I have endeavored in various studies to demonstrate how cultural-ecological adaptations — the adaptive processes through which a historically derived culture is modified in a particular environment — are among the important creative processes in cultural change (Steward, 1938). There are certain problems in which man's rational and emotional potentials are not a zero factor in the equation. Thus Kluckhohn (1949:267) suggests: "If a tribe's customary outlet for aggression in war is blocked, one may predict an increase in intratribal hostility (perhaps in the form of witchcraft) or in pathological states of melancholy resultant upon anger being turned inward against the self." This psychological attribute of human beings which channels aggression in certain ways may be a significant factor in the formulation of certain cultural parallels. For example, among the Iroquois and their neighbors, war captives were adopted as members of the captor's family, then tortured and killed. Raymond Scheele (1947) has suggested that this pattern provides a means of diverting latent hostilities against kin to members of an alien group. A similar pattern is found among the Tupinamba of South America and among tribes in other parts of the world. Although the psychological premises and the cultural manifestations may be open to question, the data suggest a useful cross-cultural formulation of certain modes of behavior.

The kinds of parallels or similarities with which multilinear evolution deals are distinguished by their limited occurrence and their specificity. For this reason, the outstanding methodological problem of multilinear evolution is an appropriate taxonomy of cultural phenomena.

Cultural Taxonomy

Any science must have precise means of identifying and classifying the recurrent phenomena with which it deals. It is symptomatic of the historical rather than the scientific orientation of cultural studies that there are few terms designating whole cultures or components of cultures which may be employed cross-culturally. "Plains culture," "East African cattle culture," "Chinese civilization," and the like designate culture areas which are conceived as unique patterns and complexes of elements. A great many sociological terms, such as "band," "tribe," "clan," "class," "state," "priest," and "shaman," are used to describe features which are found repeatedly in generically unrelated cultures, but they are much too general even to suggest parallels of form or process. The most precise terms designate very special technological features, such as "bow," "atlatl," or "ikat weaving." Such features, however, generally imply no large patterns, and the only inference ordinarily drawn from their distributions is that diffusion has taken place.

The present status of cultural taxonomy reveals a preoccupation with relativism, and practically all systems of classification are fundamentally derived from the culture-area concept. Basically, the culture area is characterized by a distinctive element content, which, on a tribal level at least, constitutes the shared behavior of all members of the society. Classification may give equal weight to all elements, as in Klimek's statistical handling of the culture-element lists which were compiled in the University of California survey of western tribes or as in the midwestern or McKern method of classifying archaeological complexes. The former yields culture areas and subareas; the latter gives categories of associated elements, which of themselves are placed neither in time nor in space. Following Wissler, culture area classifications have tended strongly to emphasize economic features, although not all postulate so close a relationship between culture and environment as Wissler, and noneconomic traits receive emphasis which varies with the individual scholar and which may lead to a diversity of classificatory schemes for the same data. Thus South America has been grouped into five areas by Wissler (1922), eleven by Stout (1938), three by Cooper (1942) and by Bennett and Bird (1949), four by the *Handbook of South American Indians* (Steward, 1946-48), and twenty-four by Murdock (1951). Each gives primacy to features of interest to the individual. All these classifications are particular to the data of South America. None endeavors to recognize in any of the three to twenty-four areas structural or developmental features which are common to areas outside South America.

Classifications of cultures in terms of value system or ethos has essentially the same basis as that of culture areas. Such classifications all presuppose a common core of shared culture traits which cause all members of the society to have the same outlook and psychological characteristics. Benedict's concept of pattern, Gorer's and Mead's concept of national character, and Morris Opler's concept of themes derive from a taxonomic approach that is basically like that of Wissler, Kroeber, Murdock, Herskovits, and others.

If a taxonomic system is to be devised for the purpose of determining cross-cultural parallels and regularities rather than of stressing contrasts and differences, there is needed a concept which may be designated "culture type."[3] The difficulty of empirical determination of significant types has constituted the principal obstacle to a systematic search for regularities and parallels. By the present definition, a culture type differs from a culture area in several respects. First, it is characterized by selected features rather than by its total element content. Since no two cultures are quite alike in their element totality, it is necessary to select special constellations of causally interrelated features which are found among two or more, but not necessarily among all, cultures. Second, the selection of diagnostic features must be determined by the problem and frame of reference. Conceivably, any aspect of culture may be attributed primary taxonomic importance. Third, the selected features are presumed to have the same functional interrelationship with one another in each case.

Illustrative of cultural types are Wittfogel's "oriental absolute society" (Wittfogel, 1938, 1939), which exemplifies cause-and-effect

---

[3] Ralph Linton uses the term "culture type" but clearly has in mind the culture-area concept rather than types which are found in different cultural traditions. See Ralph Linton, *The Study of Man* (New York: Appleton-Century-Crofts, 1936), p. 392.

regularities between a special kind of sociopolitical structure and an irrigation economy; the present author's "patrilineal band," which is characterized by certain inevitable relationships between a hunting economy, descent, marriage, and land tenure (Steward, 1936); Redfield's folk society (Redfield, 1941, 1947), which has certain general features common to many, if not most, societies at a simple development or integrational level and which reacts to urban influences — at least to influences of the modern industrial type of urbanism — according to postulated regularities; and a feudal society (Princeton Conference, 1951), which once characterized both Japan and Europe, where it exhibited similarities in social and political structure and economy.

These few, illustrative types make economic and sociological features primary because scientific interest is widely centered in such features and because socioeconomic structure has therefore been more broadly examined and more readily formulated than other aspects of culture. Economic patterns are generally ascribed considerable importance because they are inextricably related to social and political patterns. Certain aspects of religion, however, are also included in Redfield's types. In an elaboration of Wittfogel's irrigation societies, the author has tentatively formulated developmental types which include not only social and political patterns but also technological, intellectual, military, and religious features that mark successive areas in the history of these societies (Steward, 1949, and Chapter 11).

A taxonomic scheme designed to facilitate the determination of parallels and regularities in terms of concrete characteristics and developmental processes will have to distinguish innumerable culture types, many of which have not as yet been recognized. A methodology like that of White and of Childe which ignores local particulars and deals only with world stages will not serve the purpose we have in mind. A stage of hunting and gathering, for example — or of savagery, to use the evolutionists' term — is far too broad a category. The functional relations and cultural-ecological adaptations which led to a patrilineal band, consisting of a localized lineage, were very different from those which produced a nomadic, bilateral band composed of many unrelated families (Steward, 1936). But these are only two of many types of hunting and gathering societies which developed as the result of particular cultural-historical and cultural-ecological circumstances. There are also types characterized by dispersed family groups, such as the Shoshoni and Eskimo, and by cohesive tribelets, such as those of California. Moreover, it does not at all follow that all hunters and gatherers are classifiable into types which have cross-cultural significance. Many may be unique, except as some limited feature of their culture parallels a similar feature of another culture — for instance, the development of clans.

Since hunting and gathering tribes fall into an undetermined number of cultural types, any larger developmental scheme cannot with certainty take any type as representative of a universal early stage, except in characteristics that are so general as to signify nothing concretely about any particular culture. The absence among hunters and gatherers of dense and stable population, of large permanent towns, of social classes and other kinds of complex internal specialization, of priesthoods, group ceremonialism, money, investment, writing, mathematics, and other characteristics of "civilized" people is to be expected. The particular forms of marriage, family, social structure, economic co-operation, socioreligious patterns, and other features found among these primitive societies differ in each type. Consequently, the objective is to ascertain the detailed processes by which hunters and gatherers were converted into farmers or herdsmen and these latter into more "civilized" people, and it is necessary to deal with particular types.

Among the farming cultures there is also a large variety of cultural types which have not been systematically classified with reference to problems of cross-cultural parallels or formulations of causality. Irrigation civilizations have received considerable attention (Chapter 11). But the term "tropical forest agriculture" still refers merely to those who farm in the tropical rain forests rather than to specific crops, methods of farming, markets, and related cultural features. Possibly the culture areas of the rain forest in the Old and New World, including both the Mediterranean and the northern hardwood forests, developed indigenous unique culture types. It is more likely that significant parallels between such areas would be disclosed if they were compared with reference to environment, technology, and era of development.

At present, interest in parallels centers in the development of Old and New World civilizations. The parallels are striking and undeniable. They include the independent development — independent, that is, according to most but not all anthropologists — of an impressive list of basic features: domesticated plants and animals, irrigation, large towns and cities, metallurgy, social classes, states and empires, priesthoods, writing, calendars, and mathematics. Although there is still considerable tendency to stress the distinguishing features of each center or tradition and thus to view each as a culture area rather than as a culture type, interest in function and processes is gradually leading toward the use of comparable terminology. Instead of narrow technological terms like "Old Stone Age," "New Stone Age," and "Bronze Age," such potentially typological terms as "Formative," "Florescent" or "Classical," and "Empire" or "Fusion" are being used for the New World. For Old World development, Childe has introduced partially equivalent terms, such as "Urban Revolution."[4] I think it is safe to predict that as interest centers more and more upon the functional interrelationship of cultural features and upon the processes by which cultures are adapted to a variety of environments, a taxonomy suggesting significant parallels will appear.

The conceptual basis of multilinear evolutionary taxonomy is no less applicable to contemporary trends of cultural change than to pre-Columbian changes. Today, the many distinctive varieties of native culture areas of the world — and these include whole nations, subcontinents, and continents, such as China, India, Southeast Asia, Africa, and Latin America — are being strongly affected by industrialization which diffuses primarily from Europe and America and secondarily from subcenters created in all continents.

Whether the particular features of industrial developments — the mechanization of farm and factory production, the cost accounting methods, corporate and credit financing, and the national and international systems of distribution and marketing — are considered to be a single world development or a number of quasi-independent growths from a general industrial basis, there appear to be rather striking parallels in the consequences of the diffused features. These parallels are classifiable in terms of trends toward the production of cash commodities, purchase of manufactured articles, individualization of land tenure, appearance of a cash-based rationale in values and goals, reduction of the kinship group to the nuclear family, emergence of middle classes of business, service, and professional personnel, sharpening of interclass tensions, and rise of nationalistic ideologies. All these are features which also characterize the peoples of Euro-American

---

[4] These terms and their significance have been reviewed by Julian H. Steward and Wendell C. Bennett. See Julian H. Steward, "Cultural Causality and Law: A Trial Formulation of the Development of Early Civilization," *American Anthropologist*, LI (1949), 1-27; and Wendell C. Bennett (ed.), *A Reappraisal of Peruvian Archaeology*, Memoir, *Society for American Archaeology*, Vol. XIII, Part II (1948).

nations. But it would be too simple an explanation to say that these features were also merely diffused from Europe. Detailed study of native populations discloses processes which made the development of these features inevitable, even in the absence of sustained, face-to-face contacts between the native populations and Europeans which could introduce new practices and a new ethic. There is good reason to believe that the very fundamental changes now occurring in the most remote parts of the world are susceptible to formulation in terms of parallels or regularities, despite various local overtones which derive from the native cultural tradition. Although no very deliberate effort to formulate these regularities has yet been made, considerable contemporary research is directly concerned with modern trends, and the substantive results are probably sufficiently detailed to permit preliminary formulations.

Not all parallels need be based essentially upon a developmental sequence. Thus Redfield's postulated regularities in the changes of a folk society under urbanizing influence can hardly be called "evolution." However, it is our basic premise that the crucial methodological feature of evolution is the determination of recurrent causal relationships in independent cultural traditions. In each of the cultural types mentioned above, certain features are functionally related to others, and time depth or development is necessarily implied; for, regardless of which features are considered causes and which are considered effects, it is assumed that some must always be accompanied by others under stipulated conditions. Whether it requires ten, twenty, or several hundred years for the relationship to become established, development through time must always take place. Therefore, parallel developments which require only a few years and involve only a limited number of features are no less evolutionary from a scientific point of view than sequences involving whole cultures and covering millenia.

CONCLUSIONS

Cultural evolution may be regarded either as a special type of historical reconstruction or as a particular methodology or approach. The historical reconstructions of the nineteenth-century unilinear evolutionists are distinctive for the assumption that all cultures pass through parallel and genetically unrelated sequences. This assumption is in conflict with the twentieth-century cultural relativists or historical particularists, who regard cultural development as essentially divergent, except as diffusion tends to level differences. This disagreement concerning fundamental historical fact is reflected in cultural taxonomy. The major categories of the unilinear evolutionists are primarily developmental stages applicable to all cultures; those of the relativists and particularists are culture areas or traditions. The difference in point of view also involves the very logic of science. The evolutionists were deductive, a priori, schematic, and largely philosophical. The relativists are phenomenological and esthetic.

Twentieth-century research has accumulated a mass of evidence which overwhelmingly supports the contention that particular cultures diverge significantly from one another and do not pass through unilinear stages. Since this basic fact of cultural history is no longer a matter of major controversy, those who have sought to keep the tradition of nineteenth-century evolution alive have been forced to shift their frame of reference from the particular to the general, from a universal scheme into which all individual cultures may be fitted to a system of broad generalizations about the nature of any culture. They concede that particular cultures have distinguishing features caused by divergent development in different areas as well as by the stage of development, but they now profess to be interested in the evolution of culture generically considered and not of cultures. Their reconstruction of world culture history is, as a matter of fact, made in such general terms as to be quite acceptable to everyone. No one doubts that hunting and gathering preceded farming and herding and that the last two were preconditions of "civilization," which is broadly characterized by dense and stable populations, metallurgy, intellectual achievements, social heterogeneity and internal specialization, and other features.

Because the weight of evidence now seems to support divergent cultural development, the proposition that there are significant parallels in cultural history is regarded with suspicion. Nonetheless, probably most anthropologists recognize some similarities in form, function, and developmental processes in certain cultures of different traditions. If interest in these parallels can be divested of the all-or-none dogma that, because cultural development is now known not to be wholly unilinear, each tradition must be wholly unique, a basis may be laid for historical reconstruction which takes into account cross-cultural similarities as well as differences. The formulation of the similarities in terms of recurring relationships will require a taxonomy of significant features. Taxonomy, which is discussed at length in Chapter 5, may be based upon few or many features and upon a varying number of different cultures. The developmental formulation may involve long or short historical sequences.

For those who are interested in cultural laws, regularities, or formulations, the greatest promise lies in analysis and comparison of limited similarities and parallels, that is, in multilinear evolution rather than in unilinear evolution or universal evolution. Unilinear evolution is discredited, except as it provides limited insights concerning the particular cultures analyzed in detail by the nineteenth-century students of culture. Universal evolution has yet to provide any very new formulations that will explain any and all cultures. The most fruitful course of investigation would seem to be the search for laws which formulate the interrelationships of particular phenomena which may recur cross-culturally but are not necessarily universal.

2

The Concept and Method
of Cultural Ecology

OBJECTIVES IN ECOLOGICAL STUDIES

At the risk of adding further confusion to an already obscure term, this chapter undertakes to develop the concept of ecology in relation to human beings as an heuristic device for understanding the effect of environment upon culture. In order to distinguish the present purpose and method from those implied in the concepts of biological, human, and social ecology, the term *cultural ecology* is used. Since cultural ecology is not generally understood, it is necessary to begin by showing wherein it differs from the other concepts of ecology and then to demonstrate how it must supplement the usual historical approach of anthropology in order to determine the creative processes involved in the adaptation of culture to its environment.

The principal meaning of ecology is "adaptation to environment." Since the time of Darwin, environment has been conceived as the total web of life wherein all plant and animal species interact with one another and with physical features in a particular unit of territory. According to Webster,[1] the biological meaning of ecology is "the mutual relations between organisms and their environment." The

---

[1] *New International Dictionary* (2nd ed., unabridged, 1950).

concept of adaptive interaction is used to explain the origin of new genotypes in evolution; to explain phenotypical variations; and to describe the web of life itself in terms of competition, succession, climaxes, gradients, and other auxiliary concepts.

Although initially employed with reference to biotic assemblages, the concept of ecology has naturally been extended to include human beings since they are part of the web of life in most parts of the world. Man enters the ecological scene, however, not merely as another organism which is related to other organisms in terms of his physical characteristics. He introduces the super-organic factor of culture, which also affects and is affected by the total web of life. What to do about this cultural factor in ecological studies has raised many methodological difficulties, as most human and social ecologists have recognized (Alihan, 1938). The principal difficulty lies in the lack of clarity as to the purpose of using the concept of ecology. The interaction of physical, biological, and cultural features within a locale or unit of territory is usually the ultimate objective of study. Human or social ecology is regarded as a subdiscipline of its own right and not as means to some further scientific end. Essentially descriptive, the analysis lacks the clear objectives of biology, which has used ecology heuristically to explain several kinds of biological phenomena. If human or social ecology is considered an operational tool rather than an end in itself, two quite different objectives are suggested: first, an understanding of the organic functions and genetic variations of man as a purely biological species; second, a determination of how culture is affected by its adaptation to environment. Each requires its own concepts and methods.

The first, or biological objective, involves several somewhat different problems, all of which, however, must view man in the web of life. Since man is a domesticated animal, he is affected physically by all his cultural activities. The evolution of the Hominidae is closely related to the emergence of culture, while the appearance of *Homo sapiens* is probably more the result of cultural causes than of physical causes. The use of tools, fire, shelter, clothing, new foods, and other material adjuncts of existence were obviously important in evolution, but social customs should not be overlooked. Social groups as determined by marriage customs as well as by economic activities in particular environments have undoubtedly been crucial in the differentiations of local populations and may even have contributed to the emergence of varieties and subraces of men.

The problem of explaining man's cultural behavior is of a different order than that of explaining his biological evolution. Cultural patterns are not genetically derived and, therefore, cannot be analyzed in the same way as organic features. Although social ecologists are paying more and more attention to culture in their enquiries, an explanation of culture per se has not, so far as I can see, become their major objective. Culture has merely acquired greater emphasis as one of many features of the local web of life, and the tools of analysis are still predominantly borrowed from biology. Since one of the principal concepts of biological ecology is the community — the assemblage of plants and animals which interact within a locality — social or human ecology emphasizes the human community as the unit of study. But "community" is a very general and meaningless abstraction. If it is conceived in cultural terms, it may have many different characteristics depending upon the purpose for which it is defined. The tendency, however, has been to conceive of human and biological communities in terms of the biological concepts of competition, succession, territorial organization, migration, gradients, and the like. All of these derived fundamentally from the fact that underlying biological ecology is a relentless and raw struggle for existence both within and between species — a competition which is ultimately determined by the genetic potentials for adaptation and survival in particular biotic-environmental situations. Biological co-operation, such as in many forms of symbiosis, is strictly auxiliary to survival of the species.

Human beings do not react to the web of life solely through their genetically-derived organic equipment. Culture, rather than genetic potential for adaptation, accommodation, and survival, explains the nature of human societies. Moreover, the web of life of any local human society may extend far beyond the immediate physical environment and biotic assemblage. In states, nations, and empires, the nature of the local group is determined by these larger institutions no less than by its local adaptations. Competition of one sort or another may be present, but it is always culturally determined and as often as not co-operation rather than competition may be prescribed. If, therefore, the nature of human communities is the objective of analysis, explanations will be found through use of cultural historical concepts and methods rather than biological concepts, although, as we shall show, historical methods alone are insufficient.

Many writers on social or human ecology have sensed the need to distinguish between biological and cultural phenomena and methods, but they have not yet drawn clear distinctions. Thus, Hollingshead recognizes a difference between an "ecological order [which] is primarily rooted in competition" and "social organization [which] has evolved out of communication" (Hollingshead, 1940; Adams, 1935, 1940). This attempt to conceptualize competition as a category wholly distinct from other aspects of culturally determined behavior is, of course, artificial. Bates (1953), a human biologist, recognizes the importance of culture in determining the nature of communities, but he does not make clear whether he would use human ecology to explain the range of man's biological adaptation under environmental-cultural situations or whether he is interested in man's culture. The so-called Chicago school of Park, Burgess, and their followers were also primarily interested in communities of human beings, especially urban communities. Their methodology as applied to Chicago and other cities treat the components of each as if they were genetically determined species. In analyzing the zoning of a modern city, such categories as retail businesses, wholesale houses, manufacturing firms, and residences of various kinds, and even such additional features as rate of delinquency, are considered as if each were a biological species in competition with one another for zones within the urban area. Such studies are extremely enlightening as descriptive analysis of spacial distributions of kinds of activities within a modern Euro-American city. They do not, however, necessarily throw any light on world-wide ecological urban adaptations, for in other cultures and periods city zoning followed very different culturally prescribed principles. For example, most of the cities of ancient civilizations were rather carefully planned by a central authority for defensive, administrative, and religious functions. Free enterprise, which might have allowed competition for zones between the institutions and subsocieties arising from these functions, was precluded by the culture.

A fundamental scientific problem is involved in these different meanings attached to ecology. Is the objective to find universal laws or processes, or is it to explain special phenomena? In biology, the law of evolution and the auxiliary principles of ecology are applicable to all webs of life regardless of the species and physical environments involved. In social science studies, there is a similar effort to discover universal processes of cultural change. But such processes cannot be conceptualized in biological terms. The social science problem of explaining the origin of unlike behavior patterns found among different societies of the human species is very different from the problems of biological evolution. Analyzing environmental adaptations to show how new cultural patterns arise is a very different matter than seeking universal similarities in such adaptation. Until the processes of cultural ecology are understood in the many particulars exemplified by different cultures in different parts of the world a formulation of universal processes will be impossible.

Hawley, who has given the most recent and comprehensive statement of social ecology (Hawley, 1950), takes cultural phenomena into account far more than his predecessors. He states that man reacts to the web of life as a cultural animal rather than as a biological species. "Each acquisition of a new technique or a new use for an old technique, regardless of the source of its origin, alters man's relations with the organisms about him and changes his position in the biotic community." But, preoccupied with the totality of phenomena within the locale and apparently with a search for universal relationships, Hawley makes the local community the focus of interest (Hawley, 1950:68). The kinds of generalizations which might be found are indicated by the statement: "If we had sufficient knowledge of a preliterate peoples to enable us to compare the structure of residence groups arranged in order of size from smallest to largest, we should undoubtedly observe the same phenomena — each increment in size is accompanied by an advance in the complexity of organization" (Hawley, 1950:197). This is the kind of self-evident generalization made by the unilinear evolutionists: cultural progress is manifest in increasing populations, internal specialization, over-all state controls, and other general features.

Hawley is uncertain in his position regarding the effect of environmental adaptations on culture. He states: "The weight of evidence forces the conclusion that the physical environment exerts but a permissive and limiting effect" (Hawley, 1950:90), but he also says that "each habitat not only permits but to a certain extent necessitates a distinctive mode of life" (Hawley, 1950:190). The first statement closely conforms with the widely accepted anthropological position that historical factors are more important than environmental factors, which may be permissive or prohibitive of culture change but are never causative. The second is nearer to the thesis of this paper that cultural ecological adaptations constitute creative processes.

CULTURE, HISTORY AND ENVIRONMENT

While the human and social ecologists have seemingly sought universal ecological principles and relegated culture in its local varieties to a secondary place, anthropologists have been so preoccupied with culture and its history that they have accorded environment only a negligible role. Owing in part to reaction against the "environmental determinists," such as Huntington and Semple, and in part to cumulative evidence that any culture increases in complexity to a large extent because of diffused practices, the orthodox view now holds that history, rather than adaptive processes, explains culture. Since historical "explanations" of culture employ the culture area concept, there is an apparent contradiction. The culture area is a construct of behavioral uniformities which occur within an area of environmental uniformities. It is assumed that cultural and natural areas are generally coterminous because the culture represents an adjustment to the particular environment. It is assumed further, however, that various different patterns may exist in any natural area and that unlike cultures may exist in similar environments.

The cultural-historical approach is, however, also one of relativism. Since cultural differences are not directly attributable to environmental differences and most certainly not to organic or racial differences, they are merely said to represent divergences in cultural history, to reflect tendencies of societies to develop in unlike ways. Such tendencies are not explained. A distinctive pattern develops, it is said, and henceforth is the primary determinant of whether innovations are accepted. Environment is relegated to a purely secondary and passive role. It is considered prohibitive or permissive, but not creative. It allows man to carry on some kinds of activities and it prevents others. The origins of these activities are pushed back to a remote point in time or space, but they are not explained. This view has been best expressed by Forde, who writes:

Neither the world distributions of the various economies, nor their development and relative importance among the particular peoples, can be regarded as simple functions of physical conditions and natural resources. Between the physical environment and human activity there is always a middle term, a collection of specific objectives and values, a body of knowledge and belief: in other words, a cultural pattern. That the culture itself is not static, that it is adaptable and modifiable in relation to physical conditions, must not be allowed to obscure the fact that adaptation proceeds by discoveries and inventions which are themselves in no sense inevitable and which are, in any individual community, nearly all of them acquisitions

✸ or impositions from 'without. The peoples of whole continents have failed to make discoveries that might at first blush seem obvious. Equally important are the restrictions placed by social patterns and religious concepts on the utilization of certain resources or on adaptations to physical conditions. [Forde, 1949:463.]

The habitat at one and the same time circumscribes and affords scope for cultural development in relation to the pre-existing equipment and tendency of a particular society, and to any new concepts and equipment that may reach it from without. [Forde, 1949:464.]

But if geographical determinism fails to account for the existence and distribution of economies, economic determinism is equally inadequate in accounting for the social and political organizations, the religious beliefs and the psychological attitudes which may be found in the cultures based on those economies. Indeed, the economy may owe as much to the social and ritual pattern as does the character of society to the economy. The possession of particular methods of hunting or cultivating, of certain cultivated plants or domestic animals, in no wise defines the pattern of society. Again, there is interaction and on a new plane. As physical conditions may limit the possibilities of the economy, so the economy may in turn be a limiting or stimulating factor in relation to the size, density and stability of human settlement, and to the scale of the social and political unit. But it is only one such factor, and advantage may not be taken of the opportunities it affords. The tenure and transmission of land and other property, the development and relations of social classes, the nature of government, the religious and ceremonial life — all these are parts of a social superstructure, the development of which is conditioned not only by the foundations of habitat and economy, but by complex interactions within its own fabric and by external contacts, often largely indifferent to both the physical background and to the basic economy alike. [Forde, 1949:465.]

CULTURAL ECOLOGY

Cultural ecology differs from human and social ecology in seeking to explain the origin of particular cultural features and patterns which characterize different areas rather than to derive general principles applicable to any cultural-environmental situation. It differs from the relativistic and neo-evolutionist conceptions of culture history in that it introduces the local environment as the extracultural factor in the fruitless assumption that culture comes from culture. Thus, cultural ecology presents both a problem and a method. The problem is to ascertain whether the adjustments of human societies to their environments require particular modes of behavior or whether they permit latitude for a certain range of possible behavior patterns. Phrased in this way, the problem also distinguishes cultural ecology from "environmental determinism" and its related theory "economic

determinism" which are generally understood to contain their conclusions within the problem.

The problem of cultural ecology must be further qualified, however, through use of a supplementary conception of culture. According to the holistic view, all aspects of culture are functionally interdependent upon one another. The degree and kind of interdependency,
however, are not the same with all features. Elsewhere, I have offered
the concept of *cultural core* — the constellation of features which are
most closely related to subsistence activities and economic arrangements. The core includes such social, political, and religious patterns
as are empirically determined to be closely connected with these
arrangements. Innumerable other features may have great potential
variability because they are less strongly tied to the core. These latter,
or secondary features, are determined to a greater extent by purely
cultural-historical factors — by random innovations or by diffusion —
and they give the appearance of outward distinctiveness to cultures
with similar cores. Cultural ecology pays primary attention to those
features which empirical analysis shows to be most closely involved in
the utilization of environment in culturally prescribed ways.

The expression "culturally prescribed ways" must be taken with
caution, for its anthropological usage is frequently "loaded." The
normative concept, which views culture as a system of mutually
reinforcing practices backed by a set of attitudes and values, seems
to regard all human behavior as so completely determined by culture
that environmental adaptations have no effect. It considers that the
entire pattern of technology, land use, land tenure, and social features
derive entirely from culture. Classical illustrations of the primacy of
cultural attitudes over common sense are that the Chinese do not
drink milk nor the Eskimo eat seals in summer.

Cultures do, of course, tend to perpetuate themselves, and change
may be slow for such reasons as those cited. But over the millenia
cultures in different environments have changed tremendously, and
these changes are basically traceable to new adaptations required by
changing technology and productive arrangements. Despite occasional cultural barriers, the useful arts have spread extremely widely,
and the instances in which they have not been accepted because of
pre-existing cultural patterns are insignificant. In pre-agricultural
times, which comprised perhaps 99 per cent of cultural history, technical devices for hunting, gathering, and fishing seem to have diffused
largely to the limits of their usefulness. Clubs, spears, traps, bows,
fire, containers, nets, and many other cultural features spread across

many areas, and some of them throughout the world. Later, domesticated plants and animals also spread very rapidly within their
environmental limits, being stopped only by formidable ocean barriers.

Whether or not new technologies are valuable is, however, a function of the society's cultural level as well as of environmental potentials. All pre-agricultural societies found hunting and gathering
techniques useful. Within the geographical limits of herding and
farming, these techniques were adopted. More advanced techniques,
such as metallurgy, were acceptable only if certain pre-conditions,
such as stable population, leisure time, and internal specialization were
present. These conditions could develop only from the cultural ecological adaptations of an agricultural society.

The concept of cultural ecology, however, is less concerned with
the origin and diffusion of technologies than with the fact that they
may be used differently and entail different social arrangements in
each environment. The environment is not only permissive or prohibitive with respect to these technologies, but special local features
may require social adaptations which have far-reaching consequences.
Thus, societies equipped with bows, spears, surrounds, chutes, brush-
burning, deadfalls, pitfalls, and other hunting devices may differ
among themselves because of the nature of the terrain and fauna. If
the principal game exists in large herds, such as herds of bison or
caribou, there is advantage in co-operative hunting, and considerable
numbers of peoples may remain together throughout the year, as
described in Chapter 8. If, however, the game is nonmigratory,
occurring in small and scattered groups, it is better hunted by small
groups of men who know their territory well (Chapter 7). In each
case, the cultural repertory of hunting devices may be about the same,
but in the first case the society will consist of multifamily or multilineage groups, as among the Athabaskans and Algonkians of Canada
and probably the pre-horse Plains bison hunters, and in the second
case it will probably consist of localized patrilineal lineages or bands,
as among the Bushmen, Congo Negritoes, Australians, Tasmanians,
Fuegians, and others. These latter groups consisting of patrilineal
bands are similar, as a matter of fact, not because their total environments are similar — the Bushmen, Australians, and southern
Californians live in deserts, the Negritoes in rain forests, and the
Fuegians in a cold, rainy area — but because the nature of the game
and therefore of their subsistence problem is the same in each case.

Other societies having about the same technological equipment
may exhibit other social patterns because the environments differ to

the extent that the cultural adaptations must be different. For example, the Eskimo use bows, spears, traps, containers and other widespread technological devices, but, owing to the limited occurrence of fish and sea mammals, their population is so sparse and co-operative hunting is so relatively unrewarding that they are usually dispersed in family groups. For a different but equally compelling reason the Nevada Shoshoni (Chapter 6) were also fragmented into family groups. In the latter case, the scarcity of game and the predominance of seeds as the subsistence basis greatly restricted economic co-operation and required dispersal of the society into fairly independent family groups.

In the examples of the primitive hunting, gathering, and fishing societies, it is easy to show that if the local environment is to be exploited by means of the culturally-derived techniques, there are limitations upon the size and social composition of the groups involved. When agricultural techniques are introduced, man is partially freed from the exigencies of hunting and gathering, and it becomes possible for considerable aggregates of people to live together. Larger aggregates, made possible by increased population and settled communities, provide a higher level of sociocultural integration, the nature of which is determined by the local type of sociocultural integration. Chapters 9 to 12 illustrate certain of these types.

The adaptative processes we have described are properly designated ecological. But attention is directed not simply to the human community as part of the total web of life but to such cultural features as are affected by the adaptations. This in turn requires that primary attention be paid only to relevant environmental features rather than to the web of life for its own sake. Only those features to which the local culture ascribes importance need be considered.

THE METHOD OF CULTURAL ECOLOGY

Although the concept of environmental adaptation underlies all cultural ecology, the procedures must take into account the complexity and level of the culture. It makes a great deal of difference whether a community consists of hunters and gatherers who subsist independently by their own efforts or whether it is an outpost of a wealthy nation, which exploits local mineral wealth and is sustained by railroads, ships, or airplanes. In advanced societies, the nature of the culture core will be determined by a complex technology and by productive arrangements which themselves have a long cultural history.

Three fundamental procedures of cultural ecology are as follows:

First, the interrelationship of exploitative or productive technology and environment must be analyzed. This technology includes a considerable part of what is often called "material culture," but all features may not be of equal importance. In primitive societies, subsistence devices are basic: weapons and instruments for hunting and fishing; containers for gathering and storing food; transportational devices used on land and water; sources of water and fuel; and, in some environments, means of counteracting excessive cold (clothing and housing) or heat. In more developed societies, agriculture and herding techniques and manufacturing of crucial implements must be considered. In an industrial world, capital and credit arrangements, trade systems and the like are crucial. Socially-derived needs — special tastes in foods, more ample housing and clothing, and a great variety of appurtenances to living — become increasingly important in the productive arrangement as culture develops; and yet these originally were probably more often effects of basic adaptations than causes.

Relevant environmental features depend upon the culture. The simpler cultures are more directly conditioned by the environment than advanced ones. In general, climate, topography, soils, hydrography, vegetational cover, and fauna are crucial, but some features may be more important than others. The spacing of water holes in the desert may be vital to a nomadic seed-gathering people, the habits of game will affect the way hunting is done, and the kinds and seasons of fish runs will determine the habits of riverine and coastal tribes.

Second, the behavior patterns involved in the exploitation of a particular area by means of a particular technology must be analyzed. Some subsistence patterns impose very narrow limits on the general mode of life of the people, while others allow considerable latitude. The gathering of wild vegetable products is usually done by women who work alone or in small groups. Nothing is gained by co-operation and in fact women come into competition with one another. Seed-gatherers, therefore, tend to fragment into small groups unless their resources are very abundant. Hunting, on the other hand, may be either an individual or a collective project, and the nature of hunting societies is determined by culturally prescribed devices for collective hunting as well as by the species. When surrounds, grass-firing, corrals, chutes, and other co-operative methods are employed, the take per man may be much greater than what a lone hunter could bag.

Similarly, if circumstances permit, fishing may be done by groups of men using dams, weirs, traps, and nets as well as by individuals.

The use of these more complex and frequently co-operative techniques, however, depends not only upon cultural history — i.e., invention and diffusion — which makes the methods available but upon the environment and its flora and fauna. Deer cannot be hunted advantageously by surrounds, whereas antelope and bison may best be hunted in this way. Slash-and-burn farming in tropical rain forests requires comparatively little co-operation in that a few men clear the land after which their wives plant and cultivate the crops. Dry farming may or may not be co-operative; and irrigation farming may run the gamut of enterprises of ever-increasing size based on collective construction of waterworks.

The exploitative patterns not only depend upon the habits concerned in the direct production of food and of goods but upon facilities for transporting the people to the source of supply or the goods to the people. Watercraft have been a major factor in permitting the growth of settlements beyond what would have been possible for a foot people. Among all nomads, the horse has had an almost revolutionary effect in promoting the growth of large bands.

The third procedure is to ascertain the extent to which the behavior patterns entailed in exploiting the environment affect other aspects of culture. Although technology and environment prescribe that certain things must be done in certain ways if they are to be done at all, the extent to which these activities are functionally tied to other aspects of culture is a purely empirical problem. I have shown elsewhere (Chapters 6, 7, 10) that the occurrence of patrilineal bands among certain hunting peoples and of fragmented families among the Western Shoshoni is closely determined by their subsistence activities, whereas the Carrier Indians are known to have changed from a composite hunting band to a society based upon moieties and inherited statuses without any change in the nature of subsistence. In the irrigation areas of early civilizations (Chapter 11) the sequence of sociopolitical forms or cultural cores seems to have been very similar despite variation in many outward details or secondary features of these cultures. If it can be established that the productive arrangements permit great latitude in the sociocultural type, then historical influences may explain the particular type found. The problem is the same in considering modern industrial civilizations. The question is whether industrialization allows such latitude that political democracy, communism, state socialism, and perhaps other forms are equally pos-

sible, so that strong historical influences, such as diffused ideology —
e.g., propaganda — may supplant one type with another, or whether
each type represents an adaptation which is specific to the area.

The third procedure requires a genuinely holistic approach, for if
such factors as demography, settlement pattern, kinship structures,
land tenure, land use, and other key cultural features are considered
separately, their interrelationships to one another and to the environment cannot be grasped. Land use by means of a given technology
permits a certain population density. The clustering of this population
will depend partly upon where resources occur and upon transportational devices. The composition of these clusters will be a function of
their size, of the nature of subsistence activities, and of cultural-
historical factors. The ownership of land or resources will reflect subsistence activities on the one hand and the composition of the group
on the other. Warfare may be related to the complex of factors just
mentioned. In some cases, it may arise out of competition for resources and have a national character. Even when fought for
individual honors or religious purposes, it may serve to nucleate
settlements in a way that must be related to subsistence activities.

THE METHODOLOGICAL PLACE OF CULTURAL ECOLOGY

Cultural ecology has been described as a methodological tool for
ascertaining how the adaptation of a culture to its environment may
entail certain changes. In a larger sense, the problem is to determine
whether similar adjustments occur in similar environments. Since in
any given environment, culture may develop through a succession of
very unlike periods, it is sometimes pointed out that environment, the
constant, obviously has no relationship to cultural type. This difficulty disappears, however, if the level of sociocultural integration
represented by each period is taken into account. Cultural types
therefore, must be conceived as constellations of core features which
arise out of environmental adaptations and which represent similar
levels of integration.

Cultural diffusion, of course, always operates, but in view of the
seeming importance of ecological adaptations its role in explaining
culture has been greatly overestimated. The extent to which the large
variety of world cultures can be systematized in categories of types
and explained through cross-cultural regularities of developmental
process is purely an empirical matter. Hunches arising out of comparative studies suggest that there are many regularities which can
be formulated in terms of similar levels and similar adaptations.

3

Levels of Sociocultural Integration:
An Operational Concept[1]

[1] This chapter is a revision of my article "Levels of Sociocultural Integration: An Operational Concept," *Southwest Journal of Anthropology*, VII (1951), 374-90.

THE THEORY OF LEVELS OF INTEGRATION

Many anthropologists who began their careers in research on tribal societies now find themselves involved in the analysis of such complicated contemporary sociocultural systems as China, Russia, India, or the United States. It is not surprising that they bring to these newer tasks methodological tools that were devised primarily for the study of tribal society. Valuable as these tools are for many purposes, they are not adequate to deal with all the phenomena encountered either in the study of modern nations or in the analysis of the acculturation of native populations under the influence of these nations. There is some tendency to meet the difficulty by borrowing concepts and methods from the other social sciences which have had long experience in dealing with contemporary societies. Where this leads to new interdisciplinary approaches it is healthy scientific development, but often it appears that anthropologists are ready to abandon the unique methods of their own science and to imitate the other social sciences. While there is no objection to cross-disciplinary

43

fertilization, it should be possible to revise basic anthropological concepts and methods to meet the needs of the new and enlarged subject matter so long as the problem is cultural.

The greatest need is an adequate conceptualization of the phenomena of sociocultural systems above the tribal level.[2] Because anthropology is distinctive in its primary concern with culture — a concept which perhaps represents its greatest contribution to the social sciences — it seems to be widely held that a general definition of culture is sufficient to dictate problem and method in the study of *any* culture. There would probably be no great disagreement with the bare statement that culture consists of learned modes of behavior that are socially transmitted from one generation to the next and from one society or individual to another. To have operational utility, however, this definition would have to be modified in the case of each particular kind of culture. Anthropology's present working definition of culture was devised largely for the study of preliterate, primitive societies, and it does not at all meet certain needs in the analysis of more complicated contemporary cultures.

The concept of primitive or "tribal" culture is based on three fundamental aspects of the behavior of members of tribal societies.[3] First, it is a construct that represents the ideal, norm, average, or expectable behavior of all members of a fairly small, simple, independent, self-contained, and homogeneous society. It is a norm derived from the somewhat varied or deviant modes of individual behavior. It represents essential uniformities which are shared by all persons, despite some special modes of behavior associated with age, sex, occupation, and other roles; for there are definite and fairly narrow limits to deviant behavior in most tribal cultural activities. Tribal society is not divisible into genuine subcultural groups which have a quasi-

[2] A. L. Kroeber and Clyde Kluckhohn in "Culture: A Critical Review of Concepts and Definitions," published since the present chapter was written in *Papers of the Peabody Museum of American Archaeology and Ethnology*, Harvard University, Vol. XLVII, No. 1 (1952), do not include a single reference to the concept of levels of sociocultural integration.

[3] Legal considerations in the recent Indian land claims before the United States Indian Claims Commission have shown that there are no attributes of a "tribe" that are found among all preliterate, primitive people. This is one of many terminological deficiencies of our science. "Tribal society" herein really has negative connotations. "Tribes" lack state organization, class structure, literacy, and other features commonly ascribed to "civilized" societies — that is, features representing a higher level of sociocultural integration — but there are *no* features shared by tribes that are common to all mankind.

independent existence and distinctive way of life. The concept of tribal culture emphasizes shared behavior.

Second, tribal culture is usually said to have a pattern or configuration. Pattern has a considerable variety of meanings but it seems generally intended to express some underlying consistency and unity, some over-all integration. Pattern should perhaps connote structuring; but it is difficult to express structure concretely except in terms of some special component of culture, such as social organization. Benedict met this difficulty by conceiving pattern as synonymous with basic attitudes, life view, or value system shared by all tribal members and thereby giving uniformity to behavior. It is a natural step from this definition of pattern to the concept of cultural personality; for attitudes are an expression of a personality type which has been produced by cultural uniformities. Emphasis is again upon shared characteristics, although the auxiliary concept of status- and role-personality is introduced to explain certain special deviants.

Third, the concept of tribal culture is essentially relativistic. The culture of any particular tradition — the norm and the pattern manifest in the tradition — is seen in contrast to cultures of other traditions. It is viewed as unique. The tendency to emphasize the persistence of patterns — and usually also of content — within a tradition plays down the qualitative differences between developmental levels or stages. This point is discussed further in Chapter 5 in connection with "culture area," "co-tradition," and "culture type."

Conceptualization of tribal culture in terms of its normative, patterned, and relativistic aspects has been a useful tool for analysis and comparison, especially when contrasts are sought. But as a tool for dealing with culture change it has found little utility, even on the primitive level. Archaeology has continued to deal primarily with element lists, and even ethnology has relied extensively upon element distributions in attempting to reconstruct cultural history by means of the age-area hypothesis. It is significant that the more functional and genuinely holistic ethnological approaches have either stressed the normative and persistent quality of primitive cultures — and in many cases been forthrightly antihistorical or unhistorical — or, if dealing with a culture that has been greatly altered under the influence of modern nations, have paid primary attention to the disruption, imbalance, and internal conflicts of the culture. In cases where the native culture has been substantially changed but has not broken down, the concept of pattern is usually abandoned and acculturation is treated in terms of categories of elements, that is, subpatterns, such as religion, economics, social organization, and the like.

In the analysis of cultural change and acculturation of more complicated sociocultural systems, there are phenomena which cannot be handled by the normative and relativistic concept of culture. The culture of a modern nation is not simply a behavioral norm, which may be ascertained by the observation of all or of a significant sample of individuals. Different groups of individuals are substantially dissimilar in many respects. They have subcultures, which is a concept that has long been understood but surprisingly disregarded in social science. Moreover, certain aspects of a modern culture can best be studied quite apart from individual behavior. The structure and function of a system of money, banking, and credit, for example, represents supra-individual aspects of culture. To say that in the final analysis a banking system, like all culture, exists in the minds of men is not to say that its operation can best be ascertained by using an ethnographic or psychological method to study the behavior of bankers. The system not only has complicated rules, regulations, and principles of its own, but it cannot be understood without reference to world trade, industrial development, marketing, legal systems, and many other factors. The national aspects of banking can be ascertained from economists who have made them their specialty. It would certainly be approaching the problem in the most difficult way to use the ethnographic method.

Not only is the concept that culture consists only of the common denominator of traits shared by all individuals an inadequate characterization of contemporary sociocultural systems, but the nature of culture patterns found among primitive peoples is by no means applicable to contemporary societies. Nations are not patterned in terms of uniformities of individual behavior. They are extremely heterogeneous entities whose total "pattern" consists of intricately interrelated parts of different kinds. It is only subcultural groups — these might be called subsocieties — whose individual members share a substantial core of behavior.

When tribal acculturation under the influence of a modern nation is being examined, it is wholly inappropriate to view the process simply as replacement of individual tribal behavior (the tribal pattern) by a national core of traits of individual behavior (the so-called national pattern). No individuals or groups of individuals carry an entire national pattern. They participate only in very special portions of the entire culture. They are members of a subculture which has a special relation to the national whole. The "assimilation" of any ethnic minority, therefore, means first that certain traits have been adopted from the particular subcultural group with which the minority had contact and second that certain aspects of the national culture have affected the minority culture to the extent of integrating it as a new subculture, that is, a specialized dependent part of the whole. The process of assimilation is by no means a simple replacement of native features by an entire national pattern. Just what traits are adopted to constitute the new subculture and how this is integrated into the larger sociocultural whole differ in individual cases.

The following pages will examine some of the different characteristics or aspects of sociocultural systems that are important both in structural-functional analysis of modern societies and in the historical analysis of the developmental succession of qualitatively different kinds of societies.

In order to delineate some of the significant components of contemporary sociocultural systems and thereby to indicate the features that are susceptible to analysis by the ethnographic method, I have previously suggested that these systems can be viewed in terms of levels of sociocultural integration (Steward, 1950). According to this concept a total national culture is divisible into two general kinds of features: first, those that function and must be studied on a national level; second, those that pertain to sociocultural segments or subgroups of the population. The former include the suprapersonal and more or less structured — and often formally institutionalized — features, such as the form of government, legal system, economic institutions, religious organizations, educational system, law enforcement, military organization, and others. These institutions have aspects which are national and sometimes international in scope and which must be understood apart from the behavior of the individuals connected with them.

The sociocultural segments or subcultural groups of individuals are amenable to the methods of direct observation used by ethnology. There are several categories of such groups in modern states and nations. First there are localized groups, which may result from differentiation that has occurred during national development — for example, subcultures arising from local specialization in production or cultural ecological adaptations — or which may consist of ethnic minorities. The latter may be native inhabitants who have survived from a prenational period or immigrants who brought a distinctive culture into the nation. Second, there are "horizontal" groups, such as castes, classes, occupational divisions, and other segments, which hold status positions in an hierarchical arrangement and usually crosscut localities to some extent. These, too, may represent segments which either have been differentiated during national development or have been incorporated from the outside.

The ethnographic method is applicable to sociocultural segments but not to national institutions. Much recent anthropology has dealt with "nations," "national culture," and "national characteristics." "National" cannot have the same meaning as "tribal," for many aspects of modern cultures do not represent shared behavior which lends itself to the direct observation of individuals. "National culture" has in fact several special meanings apart from the totality of culture, and it is necessary to distinguish these.

First, "national culture" may signify "cultural products" or national achievements in the fields of science, literature, philosophy, religion, and the like, which presuppose a national level of sociocultural integration. In some societies, these may be limited largely to the upper classes. Thus, national religion, art, writing, and learning in the early irrigation states was produced for and consumed by the upper class far more than for the basic population.

In Latin America, the cultural stereotype is one which emphasizes gracious living, spiritual over material values, political acumen, and other features which of necessity can only be held by an upper class. The subculture of this comparatively small and privileged group has in the past been conditional upon their ownership of wealth, control of most state institutions, and generally superordinate position. While conditions have changed radically in recent decades under industrial influence which has brought business and professional middle and upper class persons into prominence, the national cultural products — philosophy, art, literature, etc. — were largely produced for and consumed by the upper class. (See Chapter 4.)

Second, "national culture" may be understood to mean governmental, economic, religious, and other institutions which function on a national scale. Although all members of the society will be affected by these institutions, the effect may be quite different among the various sociocultural segments.

Third, "national culture" may mean the common denominator of behavior that is shared by all members of the nation and that can be ascertained by direct observation of individuals. The method of study requires techniques for sampling large populations, although some use has been made of indirect evidence, such as "cultural content analysis" of novels, motion pictures, and the like. It is not my purpose at present to review the methods for ascertaining the common denominator of national characteristics.[4] I would stress, however, that current research seems to be more concerned with how to ascertain these characteristics than with what they signify. So far as significance is concerned, they are widely supposed, especially by the more psychoanalytically-minded social scientists, to evidence a basic personality or national character which constitutes the mainspring of all national behavior. The national common denominator of shared behavior, however, actually consists of behavior traits of different kinds and origins. For this reason some traits change fairly readily while others, more deeply rooted, are extremely persistent.

If national character is analyzed from the point of view of levels of sociocultural integration, the common denominator will be seen to be affected by the following factors. First, certain behavior and personality traits result from practices of child-rearing. They are acquired by the individual as a member of the family under influences that continue from infancy for many years. In a large heterogeneous society, however, the families of all sociocultural subgroups will not be essentially similar in child-rearing. The nature of differences is a purely empirical question. Moreover, socialization with respect to the local in-group or community — at least the social community — starts in early childhood, and, unless the individual shifts residence, it continues throughout life. Community patterns of behavior, however, do not affect so deep a level of the personality because they do not involve food, physical comfort and well-being, and security to the extent involved in family behavior. At the same time, these community patterns will be distinctive of the subcultures. It is extremely important, therefore, that nationally shared features of socialization be distinguished from subcultural features which may differ on both the local and family levels.

Second, there is common behavior of all persons within a nation to the extent that they participate in the same national institutions. All individuals presumably obey the same laws, and they may share in

---

[4] Otto Klineberg has presented an excellent review of the subject in "Tensions Affecting International Understanding," *Social Science Research Council Bulletin*, No. 62 (New York, 1950).

some measure national religious, military, social, and other institutions. Nonetheless, these national institutions may have very unlike effects upon members of subcultural groups.

Third, there may be a common denominator that derives from the influence of mass means of communication. In industrialized nations which have state education, general literacy, newspapers, magazines, radio and television which reach nearly everyone, and nationally standardized and syndicated ideals of behavior, certain uniformities of behavior are introduced to all individuals to an extent unimaginable in pre-industrial societies. As yet, however, there is no way to measure the cultural effects of mass communications on a national scale. Indices of use of mass media are suggestive of the extent of their effects — a qualitative estimate — but since the quality or nature of the effects may well depend upon the subcultural context of their consumption, it must be ascertained through detailed ethnographic analysis of the subcultures. While mass media are therefore undoubtedly potent in helping to level subcultural differences, empirical research must also be alert to the probability that their meaning is somewhat repatterned according to the total point of view of the consumer.

These three kinds of traits are not wholly comparable, and each may change somewhat independently of the others. International relations, we know, have changed recently at a vertiginous rate, and the attitudes of individuals toward other nations have changed correspondingly. Attitudes toward internal political ideologies, however, have not undergone similar abrupt transformations. Nevertheless, the latter may change significantly under the pressure of economic factors and the influence of mass communications. Commensurate alteration of family types and ideals does not occur.

The effects of nationally shared practices of child-training and family patterns, of common participation in national institutions, and of mass communications all serve to develop national uniformities of individual behavior. But, since there remain important regional occupational, ethnic, class, and other differences it cannot be assumed a priori that the national common denominator so outweighs the subcultural differences in importance that individual behavior can be adequately understood with reference solely to the former. A modern society is extremely heterogeneous, and even the common denominator of shared behavior is a composite, a machine of wheels within wheels, some turning faster than others and each geared to some different aspect of national institutions. A broad definition of national culture, therefore, must include many different kinds of features.

The distinctions between the different aspects of national culture clearly imply that a great many different methods must be used to study any national culture in its totality. The problem of how to study a national culture does not ordinarily arise in most of the social sciences. Except anthropology and sociology, the social science disciplines and humanities usually deal with special categories of data representing state or national-level aspects of culture, e.g., economics, political science, philosophy, science, and others. While these disciplines at times relate their state- or national-level institutions to local behavior or the "grass roots," their emphasis is upon the former, and local differences are of interest as they affect specific institutions and not as they manifest total subcultures. These categories of data represent only portions of a national culture. Each category has manifestations on the national level and on the level of the subcultural groups. Religion, for example, may have a state or even international organization and a formal doctrine — viz. Catholicism — but it also has a great variety of local meanings and manifestations. The utility of distinguishing levels of sociocultural integration as well as categories of phenomena can be strikingly illustrated in studies of culture change and acculturation.

In the growth continuum of any culture, there is a succession of organizational types which are not only increasingly complex but which represent new emergent forms (Steward, 1950:106-14). The concept is fairly similar to that of organizational levels in biology. In culture, simple forms, such as those represented by the family or band, do not wholly disappear when a more complex stage of development is reached, nor do they merely survive fossil-like, as the concepts of folkways and mores formerly assumed. They gradually become modified as specialized, dependent parts of new kinds of total configurations. The many-faceted national culture previously delineated represents a very high developmental level.

The application of the concept of developmental levels, or emergent evolution, to cultural phenomena is not new. The idea that "advanced" cultures are differently integrated than "simple" cultures is implicit in most studies; but its methodological utility has been pretty much ignored. A reason for this may be that it suggests the now widely discredited schemes of cultural evolution. The concept of levels of integration does not presuppose any particular evolutionary sequence. In biology, the concept that higher levels of life have different organizing principles than lower ones is in no way concerned with the evolution of particular life forms, such as birds, mammals, or reptiles. Similarly, this concept applied to culture is essentially heuristic and does not purport to explain the developmental sequences of particular cultural types. The cultural evolution of Morgan, Tylor, and others is a developmental taxonomy based on concrete characteristics of cultures. The concept of levels of sociocultural integration, on the other hand, is simply a methodological tool for dealing with cultures of different degrees of complexity. It is not a conclusion about evolution.

Another obstacle to acceptance of the concept of levels of sociocultural integration is the very strong hold of the concept of relativity. So long as the differences between cultural traditions are regarded as the most important qualitative differences, that is, so long as each culture area is seen primarily in terms of a fixed pattern which endures throughout its history, developmental stages will be thought of in terms only of quantitative differences, as matters of mere complexity. The concept of levels of sociocultural integration provides a new frame of reference and a new meaning to pattern; and it facilitates cross-cultural comparison.

THE FOLK SOCIETY AS A LEVEL OF INTEGRATION

The research value of the concept of levels of sociocultural integration is largely unexplored. The historical approach to cultural studies has been divided mainly between a relativistic emphasis upon the continuity of traditional patterns of local areas without regard to succession of qualitatively different levels and upon postulation of universal evolutionary stages without regard to local differences.

An outstanding contribution which bears directly upon the problem of integrational levels, even though it approaches it somewhat tangentially, is Redfield's concept of the folk society and the folk culture (Redfield, 1947). The characteristics which Redfield ascribes to folk society and culture and which are presumably attributes of a large number of tribal societies and cultures are more descriptive of a level of integration than of any particular culture type. I judge that Redfield's characterization of the folk society is intended to be applicable to the culture of societies at a certain level of sociocultural integration in wholly different cultural traditions. Further comparative analysis will no doubt require redefinition of the concept, but for the present purposes we can assume that most of the diagnostic features are significant. Folk societies are small, isolated, close-knit, homogeneous, patterned around kinship relations, oriented toward implicit goals and values, and pervaded by general supernaturalism.

Redfield did not attempt to conceptualize suprafolk levels of sociocultural integration, but in his studies of Yucatan (Redfield, 1941), he uses the urban society as a contrasting type. Subjected to urbanization, the folk society is secularized, individualized, and disorganized. Urbanization, however, is but one of the processes through which a folk society may be integrated into a larger sociocultural system; for cities are but specialized parts of such systems. Some folk societies are incorporated into states and nations as regionally specialized subcultures which do not undergo urbanization at all and which are readapted rather than transformed. Even when the folk society is transformed, the individual is not only secularized, individualized, and disorganized but he adopts scientific or naturalistic explanations in place of supernatural ones, he participates in occupational, class, ethnic, or other sociocultural segments of the city, and in general he is reintegrated in a new kind of system.

Redfield's concepts of the folk society and the folk culture are based largely on his studies of the Maya Indians of Yucatan. Historically, the Maya villages were once parts of city states and federations, sometimes called "empires," and they became relatively independent after the Spaniards destroyed the state or national superstructure. The evident stability of their society and culture through the upheavals of the Spanish conquest and later events suggest a fairly high degree of integration. Whether the nature of this integration is essentially similar to that of tribal societies and to what is broadly called "folk societies" in other cultural traditions is a question to be answered by comparative, cross-cultural analysis. It is significant that the term "tribal society" remains an exceedingly ill-defined catchall. Once a typology of integrational levels is established empirically, it will be possible to examine the reintegration of simpler societies into larger sociocultural systems and to make generalizations about processes which go beyond what Redfield derived from the process of urbanization.

It is certain that further discriminations will require recognition of integrational levels that are lower than the folk level. The biological or nuclear family represents a level that is lower in a structural sense, and in some cases it appears to have been historically antecedent to higher forms. Among the aboriginal Western Shoshoni and probably most of the Great Basin Shoshoneans (Chapter 6), practically all features of the relatively simple culture were integrated and functioned on a family level. The family was the reproductive, economic, educational, political, and religious unit. It reared its children in comparative isolation, obtained its own food, and cared for its members at birth, sickness, death, and other crises. It made its own decisions on virtually all matters. Family dependence upon outsiders was rare and its patterns restricted. The family sometimes called a shaman to treat the sick, co-operated with other families in communal hunts and dances, and visited relatives and friends when the opportunity permitted. But it could and did exist during most of the year without these extrafamilial relations. Extrafamilial dependency represented only a slight tendency toward a higher level of organization; patterns of multifamily unity had not become fixed.

The nuclear family, despite its many varieties, is basic in every modern society, and it seems safe to suppose that it has always been basic. In many cases, it was probably antecedent to the extended family, band, community, and other multifamily forms. In any event, there are probably several levels of sociocultural integration between the family and the folk society which should be distinguished. And above the folk society there are many significantly different levels of integration. For the purpose of the present exposition, however, it is sufficient to discuss only three levels — the nuclear family, the folk society, and the state. These are qualitatively distinctive organizational systems, which represent successive stages in any developmental continuum and constitute special kinds of cultural components within higher sociocultural systems.

Folk societies or multifamily sociocultural systems develop when activities requiring a suprafamily organization appear. Productive processes may become patterned around collective hunting, fishing, herding, or farming. Property rights requiring interfamilial understandings are established. Unity achieved in economic behavior may be reinforced through group ceremonialism, through patterned forms of extended kinship and friendship, and through recreational activities. Society acquires a structure appropriate to the particular kinds of interfamilial relations that develop in the cultural tradition, and patterns of social control and leadership emerge.

One of the most common forms of multifamily integration is an extended kin group of some kind. Not all peoples, however, have a suprafamily organization based on extended kinship. The nuclear family may be integrated directly into a larger, multikin structure.

What may be called roughly a state level of integration is marked by the appearance of new patterns that bring several multifamily aggregates, or folk societies, into functional dependence upon one another within a still larger system. Communities or other sociocultural segments of a folk type may participate in state projects, such as the construction of irrigation works, roads, religious edifices, and so on; they may produce special foods or manufactured objects for exchange with other communities and for state purposes; they may join other communities in offensive and defensive warfare; they may accept state rules, regulations, and standards concerning property, credit, commerce, and other matters of mutual concern. They frequently accept a state religion. The system of controls arising from economic, military, and religious needs creates a political hierarchy and a social system of classes and statuses. Qualitatively new institutions appear on the state or national level: governmental structure and control of those aspects of life which are of state concern; social stratification; and national cultural achievements. All of these have national aspects that are distinguishable from their varied folk manifestations.

There are many kinds of state sociocultural systems, each having characteristics determined by factors which are peculiar to the area and to the cultural tradition. But all states can be said to represent a broad level of sociocultural organization which is more than the sum-total of the families and communities of which it consists.

There is nothing new in the idea that each stage of sociocultural development entails new forms of co-operation and interaction, and that societies may be arranged in general developmental series, such as family, village, and state, *Gemeinschaft* and *Gesellschaft,* and others. But these are primarily taxonomic concepts. The point I wish to stress is that the concept of levels may be used as an analytic tool in the study of changes within any particular sociocultural system, for each system consists of parts which developed at different stages and through different processes and which, though functionally specialized in their dependency upon the whole, continue to integrate certain portions of the culture. The problem of acculturation may be rephrased so that the phenomena can be handled not merely in terms of categories of elements and total patterns but also of functional levels. This is necessary in any acculturational situation involving a modern state or nation, for the different categories of cultural features — religion, economics, government, and the like — cut across the nation, community, class, and family levels and function differently at each. National religions, for example, involve a formal organization and dogma, but their community or class manifestations may be quite varied, while a considerable amount of supernaturalism functions on the individual or family level.

SOCIOCULTURAL LEVELS IN ACCULTURATION STUDIES

Three brief examples will suffice in the present chapter to illustrate the utility of the concept of sociocultural levels in acculturational studies, although application of the concept will be evident in all the remaining chapters of this volume. The present examples are offered to show how the concept can be used as a research tool and not to present definitive, substantive results, for little detailed research has been done. Western Shoshoni acculturation exemplifies the influence of a modern nation upon a family level of sociocultural integration. Changes in the Inca Empire under the Spanish conquest illustrate how the culture of a native state may be more radically affected at the national level than at lower levels. Post-conquest changes in the Circum-Caribbean culture show loss of state functions and deculturation to a folk level.

Western Shoshoni Acculturation

The distinctive features of Western Shoshoni acculturation are best understood if contrasted to the acculturation of other Indians who had a tribal culture. American Indians since post-white times have been potentially subject to influences from both the national and folk levels of European culture. National institutions affecting the Indian include trade relations, such as markets for furs, farm produce, and craft objects and a source of manufactured goods; governmental services, such as schools, hospitals, work projects, grants of money and goods, and farm extension aid; laws; reservations; and many restrictive measures. In some cases there was armed intervention in tribal affairs. National influences likewise have been introduced through special groups, such as churches. All of these influences were mediated through agents of one kind or another. But the contacts with the agents of the national institutions were rarely so continuous and powerful that the personal behavior patterns of the individual agents were adopted to any appreciable degree by the Indians.

In many cases, however, the Indians came into daily contact with white settlers — miners, farmers, and ranchers — which presented the opportunity for acculturation of each group toward the folk culture of the other. In early times, the white trappers were often strongly acculturated toward the Indian way of life. Later, the white farmers introduced rural American patterns which began to influence the Indians.

The reaction of the Indians to these national and folk or community patterns depended upon their own native level of cultural development. Most Indians had some kind of multifamily organization, some fairly cohesive in-group, from which an individual detached himself to enter the context of the neighboring rural white culture only with difficulty. The reservation is therefore a result as well as a cause of group cohesion. Only the extremely acculturated individuals have been able to break from tribal life and, race prejudice permitting, behave like rural whites.

But native patterns do not necessarily remain intact because individual Indians do not participate in white society. All "tribes" have been brought into a relationship of dependency upon American national culture through economic, governmental, and often religious institutions. In most cases, the influence of the institutions of the larger sociocultural system has been sufficient to destroy the native pattern, often with traumatic effects. It was the most serious weakness of the New Deal policy for the Indians to suppose that an uncontaminated native core of attitudes and values could be preserved while the tribe became increasingly dependent upon national institutions. One of the most tragic cases of present cultural conflict is the Navaho. Their very dependence upon livestock as cash produce for a national market puts them into competition with one another and threatens to destroy the native culture. The situation is aggravated by the limited grazing resources.

The Western Shoshoni were spared the more crucial difficulties experienced by Indians who had a fairly tightly-woven fabric of community culture. When white miners and ranchers entered their country a century ago, individual families readily attached themselves to white communities. When their native hunting and gathering resources were depleted, they worked for wages sufficient to maintain their very low standard of living. Later, they were given reservations, but these consisted of little more than small residence sites. A few who obtained arable land undertook farming in a small way, very like their white neighbors. Most Western Shoshoni, however, were only loosely tied to any definable locality or cohesive social group, for there were no community bonds beyond kinship and friendship. Persons commonly wandered from place to place, covering distances of several hundred miles if they could manage transportation.

On the whole, Western Shoshoni acculturation has come about more through face-to-face association with whites than through governmental services. The influence of schools, health services, work projects, and other federal benefits has been sporadic. Facilities have been poor, and the Indians have been too mobile. Association with rural whites has not been very sustained, but it has been sufficient to acculturate the Shoshoni toward the Great Basin American ranching and mining subculture, especially where economic needs have forced them into the role of nomadic wage laborers. But it has not wiped out all Indian practices. Acculturation has consisted primarily of modification of those patterns necessary to adjust to the rural white culture. It has brought wage labor, white styles of dress, housing, transportation, food, and other material items, use of English and some literacy, and considerable adaptability in dealing with whites, though race prejudice has prevented full participation in white social relations. The Shoshoni retain, however, many practices and beliefs pertaining to kinship relations, child-rearing, shamanism, supernatural powers and magic, and recreation, especially gambling games.

Many other American Indian groups retain features of this kind after other portions of their native culture have been lost. These features, however, are those that functioned on a family level and may survive apart from group patterns. The difference between the Western Shoshoni and most other Indians is that the former did not have to experience the break-up of suprafamily-level institutions. The individual families were quite free to adjust to changed circumstances in the most expedient way without facing conflict. Perhaps this is why they are generally quite amiable toward the whites, exhibiting no deep-seated hostility.

Changes in the Inca Empire

At the time of the Spanish conquest, the Inca of the South American Andes had a fairly elaborate empire. The conquest produced radical changes in the national institutions, but the lower levels of the native sociocultural system were affected far less.

The native Inca Empire was controlled through highly centralized political, military, economic, and religious institutions. These had developed in the course of empire growth, national or imperial institutions being imposed upon the local states just as local state institutions had evidently been imposed upon the earlier communities. The Inca institutions affected the states and communities to the extent that it was necessary to make the empire function, but this did not mean that everything at the lower levels had to be changed. Much was left alone. The imperial political structure consisted of a hierarchy of positions, the more important being held by members of the royal family while the lesser were left to native rulers. Community affairs that did not conflict with the state were evidently handled much as in pre-Inca times. Economic production was reorganized under the empire in order to channel a portion of goods and services to the ruling bureaucracy and to the Inca Sun Temple, but the kinds and quantities of goods produced and consumed in the home and village were not greatly changed, except perhaps through the introduction of methods of quantity production. The Inca Sun God was forced upon all communities as the supreme deity, but local gods, cults, and rites and household fetishes, shrines and beliefs were not disturbed.

Under the conquest, Spanish national institutions replaced those of the Inca, but the lower levels of native culture were not so drastically altered. Spaniards took over the key positions in the political hierarchy and Spanish law was imposed to the extent necessary to maintain the Spanish institutions. But many native rulers were retained in lower positions and a large portion of village activities went on as in native times. Spanish economic patterns introduced a system of cash produce, money, credit, and commerce, but Spanish policy was designed at first primarily to drain off wealth, especially gold, for the Spanish Crown and the upper classes. Instead of contributing goods and services to the Inca ruling classes, the common people were drafted into the mines to produce gold for export and were forced to pay tribute in various forms to their conquerors. Once these obligations were discharged, however, village and family affairs seem to have been carried on in traditional ways.

Spanish religion likewise affected the Inca culture differently at different levels. The Catholic Church, which in feudal Spain had sanctioned and implemented state policies, completely replaced the Inca sun cult, for it could not tolerate a rival national religion. All Peruvians became nominal Catholics, accepting the Christian God and saints and contributing to Church support, but they did not abandon local shrines, ancestor worship, household gods, shamanism, and other lower level forms of religion. And the Catholic fathers were content to regard these community and family practices as mere "paganism," which was innocuous provided it did not threaten the state religion.

Modern, republican Peru is very different from sixteenth-century colonial Peru, but a great deal of native community and family culture has survived in the areas least touched by commercialism. Over the centuries, however, national economic patterns have struck deeply at the heart of community culture. The production of cash crops, both by independent small farmers and by plantation wage laborers, has linked the people to the national society. Wage labor in pottery, textile, and other factories, service in the army, work on roads and other government projects, and adoption of many cash-oriented occupations, together with loss of lands, is destroying the basis of the native communities and converting the mass of the Indians into a national laboring class. The local sociocultural segments are being replaced by class subcultural groups which extend horizontally across communities. This trend is occurring in all parts of the world as native populations are drawn into the orbit of an industrial world through specialized production of cash commodities.

Post-Conquest Changes in the Circum-Caribbean Culture

Among certain of the Circum-Caribbean Indians, the Spanish conquest destroyed native state institutions without effectively substituting Hispanic national patterns. These people were consequently deculturated to a community level of sociocultural organization.

This deculturative process may be illustrated by the Cuna-Cueva Indians of the Isthmus of Panama (Lothrop, 1948 a, b; and Stout, 1948). Archaeological evidence and historical documents show that at the time of the conquest these Indians had a rather elaborate state organization. There was a ruling class consisting of chiefs and nobles whose status is evidenced by rich burials. These rulers were interred with several wives or retainers and a wealth of luxury goods, including gold objects, carved stone, pearls, precious stones, and ceramics. The priests were also members of the upper class, and they presided over a cult which depended in part upon human sacrifice. Since prisoners of war were used as sacrificial victims, warriors could achieve some upward mobility of status through taking captives. The common people were the farmers and the artisans who produced luxury goods for the state. At the bottom of the scale were some kind of so-called slaves, apparently female captives and perhaps those males who were not sacrificed.

The Spanish conquest struck the Cuna with sufficient force to wipe out the national or state institutions. Military expeditions eliminated the upper classes and confiscated their wealth. Human sacrifice and the state religion based on it were suppressed. But Spanish rule and the Catholic Church were not very effectively substituted for the native institutions, for the people moved into regions where the Spaniards did not care to follow. Left comparatively unmolested and yet unable to maintain state functions, the Cuna resumed life on a community basis. The content and organization of the Cuna community in recent times is strikingly like that of the Tropical Forest Indians of South America, and it must be assumed that this type of culture was always part of the more elaborate Circum-Caribbean state organization. Today, the Cuna farm for home consumption and make their own fairly simple household goods and utensils. The luxury objects were no longer made after the upper classes for which they were intended were wiped out. The manufactures now include pole-and-thatched houses, dugout canoes, baskets, simple pottery, and bark cloth. The village is the largest political unit, and it is controlled by a headman assisted by one or more shamans. These shamans do not have the priestly functions of the native Cuna, for loss of state religion has left little more than a simple village religion which centers around girls' puberty ceremonies and death rites.

CONCLUSIONS

In the three cases just described, much of the significance of the acculturation would have been lost if changes in the native society had been viewed solely in terms of a monolithic concept of total cultural pattern or configuration. Whether the substantive conclusions suggested are correct or not, it is clear that cultural and social interaction take place on different levels. National, community, and family levels were selected for illustration, but there are no doubt other levels which will have greater significance for certain problems.

The concept of levels of sociocultural integration is a conclusion about culture change only in the sense that there do appear to be phenomena which cannot be explained by any other frame of reference. Any aspect of culture — economic, social, political, or religious

— has different meanings when viewed in terms of its national functions and its special manifestations in different subcultures. Stated differently, the individual's participation in culture is of a somewhat different order at the family, community, and national levels. As a member of the family, he is concerned with the most basic human needs — procreation, subsistence, child-rearing, sickness, and death. Even where community or state institutions intervene to assist the family, these functions still remain the primary reason for the existence of the family. Because they are directly concerned with biological survival, they are charged with emotions — emotions involving sex, hunger, fear of sickness and death, and social anxieties. In the development of the individual, they are among the earliest learned and the most deeply ingrained attitudes. This presumably is why behavior which functions on a family level is the most difficult to change in a changing culture.

The individual, of course, reacts as a total person in his functions as a member of the family, community, and nation. Nevertheless, community functions may develop without completely altering the family. New patterns of co-operation and social interaction lift certain responsibilities from the family and make it a specialized dependency of a larger sociocultural unit. But they by no means supersede all of its functions.

State functions, too, may be mediated to the individual through the community or they may reach him directly. But he does not surrender his role in the family and community by virtue of becoming a member of a nation. His relationship to the nation is specialized according to the subculture of his local group or class.

The inference of these observations for studies of national characteristics and national character is clear. Personal behavior is not something that can be understood simply by studying random samples of the total national population. The several aspects of national culture previously defined — national institutions, national cultural achievements, subcultural patterns, family patterns, behavior in situations involving different subcultural groups, and the common denominator — should be distinguished and the role of each appraised. The significance of each of these aspects will depend upon the particular culture, and for this reason proper conceptualization of the culture studied is essential.

These comments on the usefulness of the concept of levels of sociocultural organization to studies of national characteristics and national character are offered because such studies have wide current interest. The concept, however, will have value to another problem or objective of anthropology which will surely become of major importance in the future. The search for cross-culturally valid laws or regularities has suffered as much for want of adequate methodological tools as for lack of interest. So long as developmental stages within any cultural tradition are regarded primarily as quantitative differences and the traditions are assumed to be qualitatively unique, formulation of cross-culturally significant regularities is foredoomed. If, however, stages are recognized as qualitatively distinctive, the way is clear to establish developmental typologies that are valid for more than one cultural tradition. Even if this typology were based solely on general forms of the kind I have discussed, it would facilitate the analysis of the processes of change from one form to another. Distinction of levels of internal organization within sociocultural systems would also facilitate the discovery of regularities. Instead of dealing with total configurations, which are made virtually unique by definition, it would be possible to isolate special components, which, having been analyzed in their relation to the whole, could safely be compared with similar components in other cultural traditions.

4

National Sociocultural Systems[1]

The concept of levels of integration is applicable to the internal structure of modern nations no less than to the emergence of new kinds of organization in a developmental sequence. The most important internal differentiation is that between *national* (and international) *patterns* on the one hand and *subcultures* or sociocultural segments on the other. Once this distinction is clarified, other aspects of national culture, such as *national characteristics, national character, national cultural achievements,* and *institutional behavior,* may be related to the different levels.

NATIONAL PATTERNS AND SUBCULTURES

National patterns are here considered to be those portions or aspects of culture that function on a national level, for example, the legislative system and legal code, the governmental structure, the educational system, the military, organized religion, money, banking, commerce, and public services. These different national patterns have traditionally been the subject matter of various special disciplines, each of which uses its own distinctive method. Although all of them are part of

[1] The concepts described in this chapter were developed largely during field study of four different kinds of rural communities and the upper class in Puerto Rico.

culture in a broad sense, the ethnographic method is not at all adapted to the analysis of their principal characteristics.

An ethnographic approach to national institutions or patterns could deal only with what we may call culturally prescribed *institutional behavior,* that is, with the formalized and stereotyped behavior expected of an individual in his capacity as a participant in the institution. This behavior, however, would represent a very incomplete portion of the subculture of the individual or of the larger functions of the institution itself. The laborers, clerks, agents, managers, owners, and the like who meet in the context of a factory conform to certain behavioral expectations of the job situation. While their varied roles and statuses give some clues to their off-the-job life, their total subcultures — their religion, family life, and other features — are not directly manifest in the factory. Similarly, the meaning of the factory in relation to a larger system of technology, credit, distribution, and the like cannot well be grasped by merely observing the behavior of factory personnel. There are many other institutionalized situations, such as the church, school, moving picture theater, baseball park, and the like, which draw persons from various subcultures but which have their own standards of behavior. Even where these situations permit class distinctions, for example, where there is segregation on an economic or racial basis which might be manifest through deference shown by lower class individuals to their superiors, they do not reveal the nature of the subcultural differences associated with the classes.

It is only in a country with well-developed mass communications, a high standard of living, and a relatively high degree of socioeconomic mobility, such as the United States, that the number of institutional situations in which individuals of different subcultures can intermingle increases to the point where shared behavior seems to predominate and subcultural differences are correspondingly reduced. Even in the United States subcultures are by no means completely leveled, but the leveling process has gone so far, especially in the urban centers, which provide a larger number of situations for interclass contact, that it would be easy to underestimate the importance of subcultural differences and to overestimate the nationally-shared behavior.

The national institutions have functional and structural aspects which are distinguishable from the cultural behavior of the people connected with them. The processes of manufacturing, marketing and trade, like the principles of money and banking, are studied by the specialized methods of economics, which need not be concerned with how people connected with a factory or bank live. Analysis of governmental structure and a system of legislation deals with phenomena of a different order than the subculture of lawmakers. For certain purposes, it may be very important to know the individual behavior patterns of people involved in economic or legislative activities, but there are some aspects of these activities which can best be understood by the specialized methods of economics and political science.

The individual lives within the framework of a set of national institutions, but his noneconomic daily activities are normally carried out within the context of a fairly small segment of society that consists of people substantially like himself and who therefore may be said to have a subculture. There are two principal types of sociocultural segments. First there are locally distinctive segments, such as communities, rural neighborhoods, and ethnic minorities, which may be considered *vertical cleavages* within the larger society. Second, there are *horizontal cleavages,* which separate segments following occupational or class lines and, in some cultures, caste lines. These may crosscut local cleavages.

Society at a tribal level has only local or vertical segments, each band, village, or other segment constituting a comparatively independent functional unit which is not internally class-structured. (There are of course many so-called "tribes," such as those of West Africa and elsewhere, which are internally differentiated into segments that extend across local groups.) More developed sociocultural systems, however, have both kinds of segments. The European feudal estate, for instance, was a fairly well integrated society which functioned in comparative independence of the larger society and consisted of two distinct but interdependent sociocultural classes. Modern industrialization and its concomitants have brought new kinds of national patterns or institutions which, though producing nation-wide institutions, have caused extreme sociocultural differentiation on a horizontal basis. Occupational specialization has not only divided the laboring class into many special groups but it has created a large number of new middle classes. It has also tended to establish bonds between equivalent segments of different communities. In some cases, there may be greater cultural similarities and stronger loyalties between the widely scattered members of the same segments than between members of different segments within the local community.

Virtually all modern communities consist of several distinctive sociocultural segments which have differing positions in a system of social statuses. This suggests a cultural definition of classes: *classes are sociocultural groups, subcultures, or segments arranged in an hierarchical order.* But the hierarchy functions principally in the locality. It does not always follow that segments having the same relative status in different localities will be equivalent if the local or regional subcultures are unlike.

During the sixteenth and seventeenth centuries Puerto Rico had a few towns and plantations which were internally divided into a number of sociocultural segments, but the predominant type of rural society was the simple, undifferentiated subsistence farm. In the eighteenth century, plantations which grew cash crops and rural communities which functioned as commercial and administrative centers began to develop on an important scale. Since that time, the community or municipio, which includes the town center and the dependent farm area, has constituted the structural and functional context within which the majority of the people live. Communities are not culturally homogeneous units, like primitive, preliterate societies, for there are important subcultural differences between town and country, between merchants, artisans, laborers, and the like within the town and between landlords and laborers, large and small landowners, and owners and sharecroppers in the country. But the community has a high degree of sociocultural integration. It is the center of primary marketing of produce and ultimate distribution of commodities; it is the locale in which churches, schools, public health, law enforcement, and other services directly reach the people; and it is the place where the people are reared and educated, marry, work, visit, worship, and amuse themselves. It is in the community that the different rural subcultural groups interact with one another in a set of reciprocal, face-to-face relationships.[2]

Although the national patterns or institutions and the subcultural segments are distinguishable and must be treated separately, the two are so interdependent functionally that neither can be understood properly unless it is related to the other. In analysis of contemporary Puerto Rican culture, for example, it was found necessary to distinguish two aspects of the national patterns: first, the more formal, insular-wide, and institutionalized aspects, such as the governmental and legal system, political parties, labor unions, educational systems,

[2] There are of course many kinds of communities each having different characteristics and functions. A preliminary typology and terminology of communities is badly needed.

export and import trade, money, banking, and credit organizations, churches and official church doctrines, the military, certain organized sports, and others; and, second, the community manifestations of the national patterns.

In Puerto Rico, governmental agencies, for example, are organized and controlled on an insular or federal basis, but the government agent in a local community has to adapt his work to the "realities" of the situation. Health, education, farm extension work and other services have meaning particular to the community and to the classes within it. One kind of community stresses the value of education while another is indifferent; people utilize the health clinic in some areas but rely on folk medicine in others; and so forth. Similarly, there are great local differences in the manifestations of Catholicism, in political attitudes, and in obedience to the law. Despite the Church's international organization and standardized procedures and doctrines, orthodoxy is greatest among the upper class. In certain communities, "Catholicism" consists of a cult of the saints and in others it is mixed with witchcraft, spiritualism, and even Protestantism. The local manifestation of any national pattern can be comprehended only with reference to the distinctive context of the subcultural segment and the community.

Not all community culture, however, consists of local aspects of formal national institutions. The family, for example, is an entirely local matter. It is true that a type of family may prevail over much or even most of an area and that marriage laws may be established on a national level, but the family is not a functional part of any kind of national organization. It is, therefore, a very different kind of institution than a chain of banks or a political party. The same is true of certain other features of local culture, such as settlement pattern. Both the family and settlement pattern, however, are profoundly influenced by national institutions.

These two aspects of insular institutions, the formal and informal, the national and the local, reflect the traditional division of labor among the social science disciplines and suggest the terms of collaboration. The former are the subject matter of various specialists; the latter, in their community or class manifestations — that is, as characteristics of the different sociocultural segments—lend themselves to a cultural or social anthropological approach. The following two lists, though very incomplete, illustrate how these two aspects are distinct yet complementary.

Local aspects	Formal insular or extra-insular aspects
Subsistence farming	Government regulations and aid
Cash crop production and trade	Insular economy, world markets, sources of credit, etc.
Land tenure	Basic economy, land laws, inheritance system
Settlement pattern	None
Marriage and family	Marriage and inheritance laws
Social classes	Insular social structure
Occupational groups	Economic system and insular specialization
Labor union locals	Labor unions
Local government	National government
Political affiliations and ideologies	National parties and ideologies
Local associations	National clubs and societies
Church and supernaturalism	Organized churches
Schools and learning	Educational system and mass media of communication
Recreation	Organized sports, e.g., baseball
Hospitals, doctors, curers	Government health measures

A fairly static society which had developed slowly would presumably achieve a comparatively well integrated total culture in which the national institutions and the sociocultural segments had acquired a fairly stable and fixed interrelationship to one another. In the European feudal pattern, communities based on the ownership of large tracts by landlords were functional parts of a state whose governmental, religious, and social system sanctioned and supported the rural land use and tenure system. But where any parts of the total configuration are radically altered, the whole is thrown out of adjustment. An understanding of the processes of readjustment requires interdisciplinary collaboration, that is, analysis on both the community and national levels. Rural Puerto Rican communities have changed very radically during the four and a half centuries since the Spanish conquest. An understanding of these changes required analysis at the community level of cultural adaptations to land-use potentials and at the national level of insular changes which occurred during the Spanish colonial period and during the American period. Detailed analysis of the national institutions for their own sake was beyond the scope of anthropological research. Nonetheless, these institutions have to be taken into account in order to understand the national or insular institutional framework within which the communities developed.

NATIONAL PATTERNS AND NATIONAL CULTURAL ACHIEVEMENTS

There are certain aspects of any culture, such as art, literature, music, philosophy, science, and ideologies, which are often subsumed under the humanities rather than under the social sciences. Because these commonly represent the highest intellectual and esthetic attainments of a nation, they are sometimes designated *national cultural achievements.*

In any sociocultural system above the tribal level, however, it is necessary to distinguish the national achievements from the folk achievements. Throughout much of human history, the finest art, music, and literature has been produced for the state or government, or for the classes representing them; and intellectual and scientific discoveries have been made by members of the priestly or ruling classes. Although national achievements tend to filter outward and downward to the general population, they are consumed by all segments of the society only in proportion to the availability of general education and other means of mass communication and consumption. Otherwise, folk music, literature, art, dance, religious thought, and ideologies may survive, and these may or may not vary locally.

It is necessary to bear this distinction in mind, for national culture is too often conceived solely in terms of those esthetic and intellectual achievements which in many societies are understood only by the upper classes and which may be little known to the illiterate, isolated folk communities. The latter may participate in only limited manifestations of these achievements, as when they take part in religious ceremonialism.

NATIONAL PATTERNS AND THE UPPER CLASS

The subculture of the Puerto Rican upper class has differed historically from that of the other sociocultural segments in several important respects. It is distinguished not only by its considerably greater wealth and its superordinate social position with respect to the other classes but by its special relationship to the national patterns or institutions and by its role in the power structure.

During most human history, when sociocultural systems have developed to a state level, the national or state institutions have given rise to special ruling classes, whose subcultures might consist in large measure of functions pertaining to the national institutions. This may be illustrated in a somewhat simplified manner by the ancient irrigation civilizations, such as those of the Maya of Yucatan or the Bronze Age Egyptians. The political, religious, and military institutions of these societies produced an upper class of rulers who not only controlled such matters as state irrigation works and distribution of goods, military affairs, government, and religion, but whose subcultural behavior was in large measure determined by their participation in national or state affairs. Management of public affairs was part of their daily life. They were the creators of complex calendars, mathematics, writing, literature, and systematized ideologies pertaining to the national institutions, and they alone fully understood these matters. Thus, they were also consumers as well as producers of the national esthetic and intellectual achievements to a degree and in ways that were foreign to the lower classes.

In contemporary societies, the national institutions have created a much greater range of occupational specializations and statuses than were found in the basically two-class societies of antiquity. Nevertheless, it is normally the upper class far more than any other social segment which understands and controls the national institutions, which makes use of higher education, technological inventions, advanced medicine, and the like, and which incorporates the best achievements of national literature, art, music, and the theater into its daily living. The upper class is least integrated in terms of locality, and it is the most cosmopolitan. In many respects its way of life represents an *international upper class culture*. As technology develops, as the standard of living is raised, and as mass communication is advanced, these national achievements become available to the middle classes and finally to the lower classes. Meanwhile, new national and international features develop and these too become available first to the upper classes.

This is not to say that all culture change originates in the upper class. Changes in national institutions, as we have seen, may penetrate to the community and family. Moreover, an imbalance may be created in the total pattern by overpopulation, concentration of wealth, realignment of social and economic structure, and the creation of unsatisfied desires in lower and middle classes. These lead to movements of varying magnitudes ranging from individual bargaining through collective bargaining and political action to revolution, all producing a change in the power structure and an overhauling of the total socioeconomic system. In Puerto Rico, the mass of the people have definitely achieved greater power than they had under the

Spanish regime, and many national changes which were initiated when power shifted to the lower and middle classes have reacted upon the total culture.

Meanwhile, the upper class of Puerto Rico retains a prominent, although very unclear, place in the power structure; and it participates to a greater degree than any other class in the national institutions. Moreover, it is in a better position than other classes to borrow foreign cultural traits. This class is culturally distinctive largely because of its participation in the national features and its adoption of behavior patterns from outside the island. Whatever role it plays in the power structure, its wealth, opportunity, mobility, and contacts have permitted it to become cosmopolitan in the sense that any upper class is cosmopolitan. It is upper class in terms of the United States social structure as well as the Puerto Rican, and many of its members reside for extended periods on the continent. It has acquired many of the political attitudes, economic practices, forms of social behavior, intellectual interests, recreational outlets, and other cultural characteristics of wealthy continentals. As improved standards of living, education, and other opportunities spread throughout Puerto Rico, much culture characteristic of the upper class begins to appear among other classes. To understand the process of acculturation of the masses of the population, however, it is important to recognize that they do not mechanically imitate American behavior or Puerto Rican upper class behavior. Any borrowing presupposes a basis of opportunity and needs, and, as these factors show marked local variation in the different major regions, borrowed culture becomes readapted to fit the community patterns.

NATIONAL CHARACTERISTICS

I have stressed the importance of viewing the culture of a modern nation as a composite of various subcultures as well as of nationally shared traits which distinguish all members of one nation from the members of any other nation. At this point it is necessary to consider the nature of the shared traits or national characteristics.

In the tribal society, the common denominator of shared traits is more or less co-extensive or synonymous with the total culture. It represents family and "tribal" (usually band, lineage, or community) levels of function and integration, there being no larger integrational units. The individual acquires these shared traits by learning from members of his subcultural group. The national characteristics of a contemporary society, on the other hand, consist of features of various kinds and origins.

There are three kinds of features or traits which make up the national cultural common denominator: first, those which arise from more or less compulsory conformity with the basic national institutions that affect all individuals; second, traits of the common cultural heritage, for example, the Hispanic heritage of Puerto Rico; and third, uniformities produced by mass media of communications. None of these, however, necessarily produces uniformities in total behavior.

All members of a nation participate in the same general economy, are subject to a uniform set of laws, receive somewhat similar public education and other benefits, and are subject to taxation, military service, and the like. But the national institutions themselves actually may not always bring about a similarity among all subcultural groups and may produce internal heterogeneity rather than uniformity. An economy of free enterprise and industrialization introduces cash-orientation and competitive striving in all segments of the society it affects, but it also sharpens differences between factory owner and worker, landlord and peasant, merchant and consumer, and other groups. In addition, economic development entails local specialization and sharp differences in patterns of farm production as well as in economic status. Participation in education, government, and other national institutions is in turn partly a function of economic role and status. In Puerto Rico, the far-reaching effects of national institutions under American sovereignty as compared with those under Spanish sovereignty have increased rather than lessened the island's internal heterogeneity. Moreover, many of the subcultural groups that have developed in response to new national trends are not distinctive of Puerto Rico but are very similar to groups in other parts of the world where comparable economic and political factors have been introduced. Basic national institutions, therefore, cannot at all be considered synonymous with cultural uniformities of individual behavior nor as necessary causes of uniformities.

The second category of national uniformities consists of features derived from the basic cultural heritage. Puerto Rico shares a substantial Hispanic heritage with all other Latin American nations. Certain features of this heritage are commonly cited as evidence of its vitality and importance: the Spanish language; a double standard and male dominance in the family; ritual kinship; the paseo; the town plaza; Catholicism; the lottery; cockfighting; Spanish styles in music, literature, art, and architecture; emphasis upon spiritual and human rather than commercial values; interest in poetry, literature, and philosophy rather than in science and industry; and emphasis upon hospitality and interpersonal relations rather than upon competitive individualism. These components of the Hispanic heritage, however, are of different orders, and not all of them are equally represented among the different sociocultural classes.

The older Hispanic sociocultural system was internally differentiated into two sociocultural classes: the upper class of wealthy landlords and public and church officials; and the lower class of farm workers and artisans. Many of the characteristics commonly considered typical of Latin America are essentially upper class characteristics which depend upon wealth, leisure, and status and which could not function among the lower classes. The cultivation of philosophical values and of art, literature, and music, for example, presuppose considerable education and financial security. The lower classes, especially those in the tradition of the feudal estate, are too poor, too illiterate, and too preoccupied with sheer physical existence to indulge in philosophical and esthetic matters on other than the simple folk level where "philosophy" is about the same as implicit values and esthetic interests are not clearly separable, as on a more sophisticated level, from both religion and economics. Catholic orthodoxy is largely an upper class religion, whereas various forms of folk Catholicism are found among the lower classes. Even the patriarchal family and the double standard imply status, property, and regulated forms of marriage. They are therefore most characteristic of the upper class. Among the lower class, male dominance may be greatly weakened and, under certain conditions, the woman may be the focal point of the family, while a "double standard" signifying extramarital relations means little under common law marriage. That is to say, in families of extremely low income, without property, and with uncertain employment, sexual unions last only as long as both parties so desire. In the absence of property and private or state reasons for registered and/or church marriage, the pair is free to separate at any time. Since children remain with the mother, who may have a succession of consorts, the woman and her children in effect constitute the family. If the man has relations with other women, it is more likely to mean a dissolution of the union than what, according to the conception of the double standard, would be an extramarital affair.

What the two sociocultural classes once shared in countries having the Hispanic culture were: first, common submission to national laws and other national patterns, which, however, supported and sanctioned the superordinate position and special privileges of the upper class; second, a set of implicit understandings and habitual behavior and attitudes which regulated the superordinate-subordinate relationship controlling the interaction of the two classes; and third, some forms of customary institutional behavior of a secondary nature, such as cockfighting, the lottery, the paseo, and others, which are not strongly connected functionally with the national institutions. Class discrimination, however, carried over even into the standardized behavior of situations where the two sociocultural groups mingled. Lower class members were subordinated to the upper classes in such matters as segregation, even when walking on the streets, while there was often actual physical segregation in public conveyances, churches, theaters, cockfight pits, and the paseo. These features may be found today in certain areas of Latin America.

The Spanish heritage, therefore, consists more of traits characterizing subcultures than of a national common denominator. Where the older social arrangements survive, as in the Puerto Rican coffee area, the upper class continues to exhibit some of the so-called "typical" Spanish patterns while the lower class preserves folk patterns. Where the upper classes are being weakened and middle classes have arisen under the influence of industrialization, the principal survival of the Hispanic heritage is in language, art, music, and recreational activities which were not strongly integrated with the older national patterns or the subcultures. The attitudes which once regulated interclass relations are breaking down under modern trends.

The situation in Puerto Rico is comparable to that in Japan. Benedict's analysis of Japan stressed the importance of universally accepted attitudes and behavior traits which governed an individual's behavior toward persons above and below himself in the hierarchy of statuses (Benedict, 1946). In both countries, however, modern influences are undermining these authoritarian and personalized relationships and substituting more impersonal and commercial standards (Embree, 1939).

In large measure, then, a list of national characteristics of the Spanish heritage consists of a limited number of secondary features. The national patterns produce differences rather than similarities between the subcultures. Under United States influence many new features have been introduced, such as paved roads, transportation by motor vehicles, sanitation systems, general education, and others. But these, as previously mentioned, have become a common denominator only to the extent that wealth, opportunity, a new cash-orientation, and all that these imply have penetrated to all classes. Actually, there is great variation in the use made of these features. Under United States influence, too, secondary features that are not dependent upon either national patterns or subcultures have been introduced and become uniformities. Baseball, for example, has become the major sport of virtually all classes and regions.

The third major source of the national common denominator is mass means of communications. In contrast to national patterns or institutions, which have a differential effect on subcultures, education, radio, newspapers, moving pictures, and other means tend strongly to level subcultural differences to the extent that economic status will permit change toward uniform national patterns. Constant propaganda and indoctrination affects attitudes toward practices of child-rearing, recreation, national political and economic institutions, and even international relations. Mass communications also make national cultural achievements in art, literature, music, and science available to all segments of the population.

Finally, I must mention practices of child-rearing and family types, which, according to certain contemporary anthropologists, constitute national uniformities and are the primary factors in the formation of national character. The concept of *national character* is discussed subsequently. I wish only to point out here that whether all members of any nation are really substantially similar in their practices of child feeding, weaning, care, toilet training, swaddling, and the like is purely an empirical question. These practices function on a family level, and they are not directly subject to national institutions. In fact, it is expectable that subcultural groups should differ in child-rearing just as they differ in family structure. There are strong class differences in the time the mother can spend with the child, in use of relatives or hired nurses to care for the child, in diet, in number and relationship of siblings and other relatives to the child, in the familial role of the father, and in other crucial factors. In addition, any nation that consists of several ethnic minority groups — for example, Russia, Poland, China, or Mexico, whose political expansion incorporated diverse cultures within a large area, or the United States, which has acquired many ethnic minorities through immigration — will certainly not be uniform in familial patterns. It is only where economic opportunity permits developed communications to affect the family level that uniformities emerge.

This analysis indicates that the problem of national characteristics is a very complicated one. In Puerto Rico, the regional and class sub-cultures are so distinctive that no single community can be considered to represent the entire island in microcosm. To ascertain the common core of shared behavior would require a carefully devised sampling of the whole island. This common core, however, would not be very illuminating, for most shared traits have a special meaning in each subculture. The lottery is principally a form of recreation to some groups, while to others, where socioeconomic mobility is impossible, it presents the only opportunity to win a stake with which to start an independent business. The paseo is a form of courtship in some towns, while in others it is no more than an evening stroll. Ritual kinship, though common to all Puerto Ricans, has several very different functions which reflect local social and economic patterns. All people in the island are striving to better themselves, but specific methods for achieving socioeconomic mobility depend upon the availability of jobs, education, and other factors.

Most features of the common denominator have different local meanings because they are functional parts of the total patterns of the different subcultures. These local differences could not be adequately revealed merely by sampling the entire island population with a questionnaire covering all aspects of culture. Such a procedure would encounter almost insurmountable difficulties. It would be impossible to frame appropriate questions before the subcultures were known; it would be a forbidding task to sample all aspects of culture in an entire nation; and it would be very difficult to obtain accurate answers during brief interviews. More importantly, questionnaire results could not reveal the functional relationships between phenomena within the different subcultural patterns. A statistical correlation of variables would show that certain distinctive features were associated with one another, but it would not show why. Results of this type are no substitute for an ethnographic approach — for prolonged, intensive, firsthand observation and analysis of each subculture as a whole. At best, a questionnaire could provide only a preliminary indication of variables that might warrant more intensive investigation.

5

Culture Area and Cultural Type

in Aboriginal America:

Methodological Considerations[1]

THE HEURISTIC ROLE OF TAXONOMY

While the question of classification is inherent in all methodological considerations, cultural typology warrants separate consideration. The present chapter will discuss problems of cultural taxonomy with special reference to the theory and substance of Americanist studies. It is necessary to pay particular attention to the concept of the *culture area* because this concept has played so important a role in the thinking of American anthropologists who have generally classified data on aboriginal cultures in area categories. Alternative taxonomic systems, such as the Kulturkreis, which has been used by many German and Austrian anthropologists, have had comparatively little effect upon American methodology. Similarly, British functional approaches such

[1] This paper was first prepared as part of a symposium on native American cultures for the 1952 meeting of the American Anthropological Association. In February, 1953, a meeting of Midwestern anthropologists held at Chicago under the auspices of the Wenner-Gren Foundation touched upon certain basic points made in the 1952 paper. Instead of writing additional comments and communications to the editor of the *American Anthropologist,* this paper has been revised. The revisions give special emphasis to the conceptual and terminological implications of culture area types and the complementary concept of uniformities, cross-cultural types, and cross-cultural regularities.

as those represented by Malinowski and Radcliffe-Brown, though pro-
vocative of new ideas in Americanist studies, have not led to any
systematic classification. A cultural taxonomy which uses unilinear
evolutionary categories, though widely accepted in the last century
and now wholeheartedly embraced by Russian anthropologists, is not
widely employed by contemporary western anthropologists. The concept of multilinear evolution (Chapter 1), however, suggests a basis
for cultural typology.

It would seem hardly necessary to reiterate that any scientific
method, such as taxonomy, has validity and usefulness as an operational tool only with reference to the problems it is designed to solve
and that cultural "facts" are simply conceptualizations of human behavior which acquire significance from their relevance to a particular
problem or theoretical frame of reference. In practice, however, it is
all too easy to accept methods — for instance, the holistic, the comparative, the historical, the stratigraphic, or a taxonomic method — as
ends in themselves; to regard them as distinctive features of anthropology, deriving from the inherent nature of the subject matter.

The *culture area* concept has become so crucial a tool in the operations of anthropologists that to question it might seem to throw doubt
on anthropology itself. The great value of this concept in descriptive
ethnology and in teaching has almost led to its reification as an objective and inherent feature of nature. It has led to the assumption —
which most anthropologists would probably deny on theoretical
grounds yet accept in practice — that cultural "facts" have an existence independent of problem and that it is therefore possible to write
an "ideal" ethnology which records *all* cultural data for the permanent record. Consideration of modern problems and of facts relevant
to these problems, however, should suffice to discredit this proposition.
Studies of culture and personality, for example, require "facts" of
child-training which did not exist a half century ago because the conceptual schemes which then prevailed had no place for them. Even
today the definition of "fact" in studies of socialization depends upon
phrasing of the problem and upon psychological assumptions.

The development of the *culture area* concept was not entirely without theoretical significance. As we shall see, *culture area* implies a
certain kind of history. In Americanist studies, however, it became
important principally as a means of classifying rapidly accumulating
ethnographic data, and thus it achieved the dignity of an end in itself.
So long as description and analysis of cultural data in terms of *culture*

area predominates, anthropology may be said to remain in what Northrop (1947) has called a "natural history" stage of science — a stage in which the phenomena of nature are grouped in common sense categories based on the daily experience of people. In the biological sciences, the "natural history" stage was exemplified by the taxonomy of Linnaeus and his successors, a taxonomy based upon fairly obvious morphological similarities between living organisms. This taxonomy was a necessary precondition of the theory of evolution. The theory of evolution, however, brought about explicitly formulated scientific problems which in turn required new conceptualizations and new categories of facts. For example, modern genetics deal with innumerable "facts" which previously did not exist in a scientific sense.

The history of anthropological taxonomy represents a somewhat inverted sequence because the "natural history" stage was the successor of the idealistic evolutionary taxonomy. The evolutionary categories which postulated a succession of developmental cultural types were derived from an a priori and somewhat philosophical construct, being based more upon the concept of progress than upon empirical data. These categories were not the logical sequitur of a phenomenological taxonomy, as in the case of biological evolution. Anthropological classification of cultural data, particularly of New World data, entered a stage comparable to the "natural history" stage of the biological sciences only after the evolutionary preconceptions had been tested and rejected.

Twentieth-century Americanist studies began with a strong interest in cultural phenomena and a compelling drive to collect "facts," a drive which became increasingly urgent when the native cultures were disappearing under the influence of Euro-American civilization. From this phenomenological approach, several taxonomic problems of a "natural history" order arose.

First, it was felt that all data of every culture should be recorded, and that it was necessary to devise standard headings to ensure completeness of the record. Wissler's "universal pattern" or "culture scheme" (Wissler, 1923:73-97) offered nine subdivisions or headings which were to serve as descriptive categories for recording the culture of any society in the world. A far more comprehensive set of categories was developed some years later by the Yale University "Human Relations File," which set up 55 principal headings and 557 secondary headings. The construction of categories which subsume the data of all cultures might seem to imply that all groups of mankind have fundamental similarities.[2] Actually, these categories of the Wissler and Yale schemes were designed primarily to record culture content and to present features which distinguish *culture areas* from one another.

The second task in factual reporting was to fill in the categories with concrete material. Since it was considered that a complete ethnographic record should include all culture elements, the question was how far cultural phenomena could be split into irreducible elements. Such items as pottery, the wheel, the bow, shamanism or polyandry might be entered as single elements or they might be split into innumerable details. The effort to record all facts was carried to the logical extreme in the University of California element list surveys which reduced the cultures of various groups of Indians west of the Rocky Mountains to between 3,000 and 6,000 elements. The tribal lists grew out of one another, and the absence as well as presence of elements was recorded on each list. The practical limitations of this procedure in dealing with more complex cultures may readily be seen from the fact that when the United States military forces landed at Casa Blanca during World War II they were reported to have been equipped with more than 500,000 different kinds of material items. Many of these items, moreover, were not truly elements such as those recorded among native American Indians, for such things as tanks, automobiles, and the like obviously consisted of innumerable lesser elements.

The growing interest in social structure, in configurations, and in function has recently led to analytic studies which of necessity interrelate features in different descriptive categories. Such analyses, however, still tend to attach primary importance to the areal distinctiveness of the phenomena involved. In other words, the *culture area* set the pattern for anthropological thinking and it led naturally to cultural relativism.

ETHNOGRAPHY AND CULTURE AREA

The culture areas of America were first set forth systematically by Wissler in terms of ethnographic data (Wissler, 1922). Subsequent

---

[2] The implication of "universal categories" for studies of cultural similarities and differences has been considered by Kluckhohn in "Universal Categories of Culture," in *Anthropology Today*, ed. A. L. Kroeber (Chicago, 1953). On theoretical grounds, I should say that all these categories represent conceptualizations of cultural data drawn from Euro-American societies. Cross-culturally valid categories will apply only to similar cultural types. That is, types that recur in a multi-evolutionary scheme will be distinguished by unique categories.

writers, though employing essentially the same taxonomic principles, have disagreed with Wissler and with one another. Disagreement is inevitable because the *culture area* is essentially a geographical delimitation of peoples sharing certain features and because there is no objective means for weighing the importance of local differences and for deciding which categories of elements shall be ascribed greatest importance. Wissler divided North America into nine culture areas; Kroeber (1939) lists six "grand areas," twenty-one "areas," and innumerable "sub-areas" for North America; and other scholars have divided it in still different ways. South America has been divided into twenty-four areas by Murdock (1951), eleven by Stout (1938), five by Wissler (1922), four by the Handbook (Steward, 1946-48) and by Kroeber (1948), and three by Cooper (1942) and by Bennett and Bird (1949).

In all these culture area divisions, the principal criterion has generally been the number or percentage of elements or features shared by adjoining tribes or societies. Since the degree of similarity necessary to assign two or more tribes to the same culture area has usually been based upon impressions rather than upon definable quantitative standards, any amount of splitting or lumping has been equally justified.[3] Another somewhat heuristic consideration, however, has been involved in the delineation of culture areas. Since these areas are presumed to have acquired their shared traits through diffusion — Wissler postulated primary centers of inventiveness and Kroeber speaks of "culture climaxes" — their limits are defined by the similarity of societies to one center rather than to another and different center. This implies that diffusion had been going on for a long time, which brings us to the problem of historical depth in relation to taxonomy.

HISTORIC CHANGE AND CULTURE AREA

When historic depth is taken into account, the utility of the *culture area* concept is complicated by three facts: first, the culture centers or climax points and the boundaries may shift from period to period; second, the nature of the culture may change so profoundly in successive periods that the culture in a given period may have greater

---

[3] James Ford has made it clear in "On the Concept of Types," *American Anthropologist,* LVI (1954), 42-54, that culture variation and culture area are dependent variables of each other and that neither can therefore define the other. See my comments on Ford in "Types of Types," *American Anthropologist,* LVI (1954), 54-57.

resemblance to cultures in other areas than to its predecessor or successor in the same area; and third, portions or subdivisions of the area, although representing a basic tradition in terms of diffused culture elements, may have very unlike structural patterns. In practice, the second and third facts have received comparatively little attention.[4] So far as the *culture area* is conceived in terms of content, it is generally assumed that the center of creativeness remains within the area, that it is rooted in antiquity, and that it has contributed features to societies within the area at all periods. Thus, differences between periods and localities are based more upon quantitative than upon qualitative criteria.

To illustrate these difficulties, the Greater Southwest can be considered as an enduring "cultural sphere" or "greater area" — to use Kroeber's terms — which is characterized by a considerable list of traits found in its climax areas, the Anasazi and Hohokam, and by a diminishing list of traits in its peripheral areas of southern California, northern Mexico, and elsewhere. Included in this sphere would be the Navaho, Apache, Pima, Papago, the Yuman-speaking people, and the Great Basin and southern California Shoshonean-speaking people, all of whom differed rather profoundly from the Pueblo and from the Hohokam and yet were demonstrably influenced by these climaxes in terms of culture elements. The sphere also is known to have at least two principal developmental sequences, the first running from the hunting and gathering Cochise through several periods of the Hohokam continuum and the second, the Anasazi, running from Basket Maker through the Pueblo periods.

One effort to resolve the contradictions between ethnological and archaeological classifications is Bennett's (1948) concept of the co-tradition, which he has illustrated in the case of the Central Andes and which Martin and Rinaldo (1951) have applied to the Southwest. The co-tradition is a regional delimitation in which "only the territory is considered within which the component cultures formed a culture area at every time period, and not the territory of maximum expansion during a particular time period" (Bennett, 1948:1). On the basis of a stipulated list of features, the Central Andes is a co-tradition. Bennett's suggestion that a large part of the Southwest constitutes a co-tradition, however, faces the difficulty that of the principal tradi-

---

[4] Benedict's concept of pattern is based on ethos or values, not upon structure and function. See Benedict, *Patterns of Culture* (Boston: Houghton Mifflin Company, 1934).

tions — Anasazi, Hohokam, and Mogollon-Mimbres — only the first endured through all time periods and even its territory shrank so greatly toward the end of its history that very dissimilar cultural configurations invaded its previous area; for example, the Great Basin Shoshonean cultures supplanted it in the northern periphery of the Southwest. In applying the concept of co-tradition to the Southwest, Martin and Rinaldo seem less concerned with enduring boundaries than with the idea that "the principal elements or characteristics should be found in each subdivision [cultural or areal?] and in each time period" (Martin and Rinaldo, 1951:216).

The search for the lasting common denominator of the Southwestern co-tradition, however, also encounters the serious difficulty not only that boundaries changed but that the nature of the culture changed period by period. Although the Cochise culture had continuity with that of the subsequent Hohokam farmers in its use of seeds and of metates for grinding them,[5] the sociocultural units of the nonfarming Cochise were surely more like those of many hunting and gathering tribes than their sedentary farming successors. Similarly, the culture type of the first Basket Makers might be better compared with such people as the historic Southern Paiute than with their modern Pueblo descendants.

The taxonomic difficulty of assigning such early Southwestern peoples as the Cochise or Basket Makers and such later peoples as the Shoshonean-speaking people in a single classificatory niche has been met in part by the category of "Marginal cultures." This category has been used to include not only the Great Basin and California tribes, but also those of northern and western North America and southern and eastern South America. This category is, however, much too broad because it is based so largely upon the absence of certain features found among more developed societies. The criterion of absences is a universal and negative characteristic and has limited heuristic value. The "Marginal" tribes have little uniformity of culture content and no demonstrable linkage through diffusion from a culture center or climax. Moreover, the very term "Marginal" is relative; any culture is marginal to some other culture, but it may fail to share the more important features of the general area. "Hunters and gatherers" and other similar terms are equally unsatisfactory, for they lump all non-farmers of the world together without regard to the particulars of their cultures. A comparison of hunting and gathering tribes would show

---

[5] To judge by the evidence of Bat Cave, some Cochise may have grown maize.

enormous difference of cultural content and thus afford grounds for subdividing them into innumerable areas, as Murdock and Stout have done with the South American Marginal tribes.

If the so-called "Marginal" tribes are to be reclassified, however, the crucial question is whether the basis shall be element content or morphological features. To illustrate the difficulty, the Great Basin Shoshoneans, though linked to the Anasazi through many borrowed elements, also borrowed from the neighboring California, Plateau, and Plains areas, so that the shared elements of groups on the eastern and western sides of the area had only a .5 correlation. Despite this element variation, the basic sociopolitical features were very similar.

Cooper, like Nordenskiöld and others, classed the prehorticultural peoples at the northern and southern peripheries of the Western Hemisphere in an area of Marginals on the assumption that they represented the survival of an early stratum of native culture, sharing such features as primacy of hunting and gathering, temporary houses, earth ovens, skin garments, and others. They implied that early America comprised a single, simple culture area. This implication is not supportable. Even if the shared cultural inventory of prehorticultural America was large, there is little doubt that the socioeconomic patterns were quite varied because of local forms of cultural ecological adaptations.

The culture area position of the recent Marginal tribes is also complicated by the fact that many of them have borrowed a considerable number of traits from near-by agricultural climaxes or subclimaxes.

The Southwest thus presents problems which cannot be answered by any culture area criteria. Whether the hunting and gathering Shoshonean groups of southern California be classified in the Greater Southwest because their cultural inventory was largely borrowed from that of the Anasazi or with other American Marginals because they shared certain features with prefarming tribes depends entirely upon whether they are viewed in local or continental perspective. But there is a third taxonomic possibility. I have suggested in an earlier paper (Steward, 1936. See Chapter 6) that the southern California Shoshoneans could be classed with Fuegians, Australians, Bushmen, and others because all share a patrilineal, patrilocal, land-owning, exogamous type of hunting band; that is, because they share similar structural patterns rather than cultural content. The taxonomic position of the Great Basin Shoshoneans similarly cannot be fixed in culture area terms. Their inventory of cultural traits has closest relationship to that of the Anasazi but their culture was integrated on a family level and lacked the social, religious, economic, and political elaborations of the Anasazi. Are they part of the Anasazi sphere because of an element list correlation, or do they merit a separate category? What of the Basket Maker II peoples whose culture content and structure seem to have corresponded rather closely to that of the modern Southern Paiute yet represent a stage of Anasazi development?

Similar difficulties arise in the application of the culture area concept to other parts of America. East of the Rocky Mountains in Kroeber's eastern "Grand Area," the Folsom, Yuman, and other early cultures were followed by a Hopewell-Woodland tradition which affected much of the area and by a later Temple Mound tradition (Phillips, Ford, and Griffin, 1951). The Pleistocene and palaeo-Indian hunters shared little with the later cultures, although their areas of distribution overlap. The Temple Mound culture appears to have been more similar to that of early Meso-America than to other cultures of the eastern United States. But it influenced neighboring areas, such as certain Caddoan tribes of the Plains and the southeastern tribes whose local patterns became distinctive. Thus, there are two difficulties in classifying the eastern United States as a culture area. First, the early hunters had little in common with the developed farmers who themselves may represent two separate traditions. Second, apart from the question of shared traits, the people influenced by the Mississippi "pattern" or tradition differed among themselves so greatly that some might best be classed with Meso-America and others, such as the southeastern tribes, might be grouped with the South American Circum-Caribbean type.

The classification into areas of the high civilizations from Mexico to Bolivia also presents difficulties. First, despite the continuity of local traditions and climaxes in such areas as the Valley of Mexico, Yucatan, and the Central Andes, the early and latest periods of each sequence were very dissimilar. There would be as much justification for classifying the early Cuicuilco culture of Mexico with Huaca Prieta in Peru and Aztec with Inca as for grouping Cuicuilco with Aztec and Huaca Prieta with Inca. The areas which have borrowed heavily from Meso-America and the Andes are even more confused taxonomically. Central America has clearly drawn elements from both of these climaxes, while much of its material culture and many community features — house type, village organization, shamanism and others — are strikingly similar to those of the Tropical Forest area of South America.

But the religious, military, and political patterns of many Central American states warrant the inclusion of these groups with most peoples of Colombia, Venezuela, the Greater Antilles, and pre-Inca Ecuador in a Circum-Caribbean area.

The culture area concept obviously suffers severe strain in the face of the early post-Columbian loss of these state institutions and the necessity of reclassifying most of the deculturated Circum-Caribbean people in the Tropical Forest area. Because of these many difficulties, no two authors have classified Central America, the Antilles, and South America in quite the same way. There is greatest agreement concerning the nature and extent of the Tropical Forest area, and perhaps this is explainable by almost complete ignorance of its archaeology, which has obviated the need to take historic change into account. Moreover, the culture is rather highly adapted to the tropical rain forest environment.

The *culture area* is used with least difficulty when it is conceived in terms of elements which have diffused from certain centers. Its boundaries are drawn more or less where features from one center begin to outnumber those from another. Its heuristic value, therefore, consists of determining areas of diffusion. Its practical value lies in subsuming the innumerable data of areas in such a way that attention is readily drawn to cultural differences, especially to differences in content.

THE THEORETICAL BASIS OF THE CULTURE TYPE

In the analysis of form, function, and developmental process, the culture area has serious limitations. We have already seen that no matter how the culture area boundaries are drawn, they include societies whose structures and functional interrelations of elements are more similar to those of societies in wholly different areas than to those of their immediate neighbors. An area, sphere, or co-tradition is a historic unit defined in terms of shared elements, but it may be very diversified in terms of sociocultural integration, for a number of qualitatively distinctive configurations may result both from local adaptations and from historical development through different periods. The occurrence of such configurations among a number of contiguous societies is generally taken to imply historical influence. Their occurrence among widely separated societies suggests that similar processes or causal factors have been operating independently in each.

It is necessary, therefore, to make certain conceptual and terminological distinctions. First, since the term "culture type" has been used in many ways, it is proposed that *culture area type* be used to designate a sociocultural system which is locally and relativistically distinctive and that *cross-cultural type* be used to designate one that is found in several historically unrelated areas or traditions. Second, it is proposed that the term *uniformities* be understood to refer to the similarities of form and content which characterize a single area or co-tradition and that *regularities* be understood to mean similarities which recur cross-culturally in historically separate areas or traditions.

Area type and *cross-cultural type* are complementary rather than opposing concepts, and the same is true of *uniformities* and *regularities*. An *area type* is defined in terms of *uniformities* which represent concrete phenomena classified and described under categories based on the observer's experience. It is difficult to derive causal relations from the *area type* because the *uniformities* are presumably brought about through diffusion and not through recurrent and independent operation of similar causal processes. "Cause" is conceived as historical events which are described rather than analyzed. It is only when one compares two historically independent areas that it is possible to stipulate that a particular set of phenomena are causally interrelated; that is, to state that certain conditions presuppose or depend upon certain other conditions. Causally interrelated phenomena are *regularities*.

Regularities are discovered through use of the comparative method, but in the present stage of anthropology there can be no cut-and-dried procedure for their formulation. Most often, they probably first appear as hunches in the minds of investigators familiar with diversified cultures. Once these hunches are tentatively and explicitly formulated as hypotheses, however, it is possible to make systematic analysis through cross-cultural comparisons of the phenomena which are and are not necessarily interrelated. *Regularities* will probably never involve total cultures, if by the latter is meant the entire element content as well as structure. Most regularities investigated to date pertain to limited portions of culture, such as kinship, social structure, religion, government and the like. These might be called *cross-cultural kinship types, cross-cultural social types,* etc.

But it is also possible to discover *regularities* in the interrelationships of the major features of culture. These justify the term *cross-cultural type*. Since such a type requires some degree of abstraction of general features from the hundreds of potentially variable elements, we shall call it the *cultural core,* a concept which contrasts with *total culture.* *Cross-cultural types* consist of the *cultural cores* of those area types which recur two or more times in historical independence of one another and which represent similar levels of sociocultural integration.

It must be emphasized that the concept of *culture core* and certain subsidiary concepts to be mentioned subsequently are heuristic devices and not postulations of universal characteristics of culture. This point is stressed because certain constantly used concepts in anthropology have tended to become ends in themselves.[6] A *cultural core* that has cross-cultural significance cannot have concrete features which are universal. To the contrary, it will have particular and distinguishing characteristics, and these must be abstracted in each case from the empirical data.

A *cultural type* consists of core features that, first, are determined by cross-cultural regularities of cultural ecological adaptation and second represent a similar level of sociocultural integration. Ecological adaptations can be considered causative in the sense that a degree of inevitability in cultural adjustments is directly observable. Patrilineal bands of the Bushmen, Australians, Tasmanians, Fuegians, and others (Chapter 7) represent a type in that the ecological adaptation and the level of integration are the same in all of these cultures. In these and other cases, factors producing similar types such as environment, food resources, means of obtaining food, the social co-operation required, population density, the nature of population aggregates, sociopolitical controls, the functional role of religion, warfare, and other features, will have an understandable relationship to one another.

It is purely an empirical question whether ecological adaptations set broad or narrow limits in the possible range of these various features of culture and whether social structures are fixed by limited possibilities or have potential variations which may be affected by diffusion. Where, however, similarities in the culture of several societies are brought about by diffusion, as in the case of culture areas, these

---

[6] It is pertinent to remark in passing that the very concept of culture, which many anthropologists have considered their distinctive domain, has been subject to redefinition for many years. Kroeber and Kluckhohn, in "Culture," *Papers of the Peabody Museum of American Archaeology and Ethnology,* Harvard University, Vol. XLVII, No. 1 (1952), a recent survey and appraisal of scores of definitions of culture, seemingly feel the need for a universally valid concept, for they class these definitions under logical rather than heuristic categories. It should be clear that what is meant by culture depends upon the aspects of human behavior one seeks to explain and how one proceeds. Any number of different concepts may be appropriate for certain purposes.

represent uniformities rather than regularities and I would not subsume them under my definition of type.

There are two other kinds of classifications of culture which do not employ the concept of type as described herein. First, the hypothetical universal developmental stages of the unilineal evolutionists, though implicitly integrational levels, do not distinguish local varieties of cultural ecological adaptations. As I have explained in Chapter 1, these stages are characterizations of culture as a general category of natural phenomena but they are not types of particular cultures. This evolutionary taxonomy permits only such general and self-evident statements about process as "state organization succeeds nonstate organization" or "culture develops from the simple to the complex."

Coon attempted to devise a more precise quantitative definition of cultural types. He conceives six levels of complexity which are determined "quantitatively" by their degree of development along four axes: specialization of individuals, amount of trade, number of institutions to which an individual belongs, and complexity of institutions (Coon, 1948: vi-vii, 611-14. See also Chapple and Coon, 1942). The cultures illustrating these levels are chosen from throughout the world without reference to local cultural tradition or ecological adaptation. For example, the fifth level, which is characterized by "hierarchies and compound institutions," includes the Vikings, Tenochtitlan in Mexico, early India, and a modern Indian village. These cultures are comparable to one another in Coon's quantitative sense, but each is very distinctive in the qualities of its institutions and in the specific developmental and ecological processes which produced them.

If cultural studies have a scientific rather than descriptive purpose, cross-cultural comparisons should lead to causal formulae which state that certain synchronic or diachronic conditions or factors presuppose certain other conditions or factors. If features A, B, and C occur only when features D, E, and F occur, some fundamental relationship between all six features may be postulated. In their cross-cultural recurrence, these features may have identity or near-identity of both form and function, as in the case of the early irrigation civilizations of Egypt, the Near East, China, Meso-America and Peru (Chapter 11) where the formal structure consisted of an absolute state ruled by a theocratic-militaristic class whose principal function was control of water works and other state projects. Differences between these states were secondary; and even should further analysis require modification of my provisional hypotheses, the theoretical proposition remains that when similar form and function develop independently they may be classed in a single cultural type.

A cross-culturally significant type need not however consist only of core features that are similar in both form and function. Since identical forms may serve many different functions while quite unlike forms may fill similar needs, the key concept can be adequately designated only by the compound term *form-function*. The inseparability of the two concepts, form and function, is illustrated in Chapter 7, which analyzes the patrilineal hunting band. This kind of band, found among the Congo Negritos, Bushmen, Australians, Tasmanians, southern California Shoshonean groups, Fuegians, and others, is a cultural type because in all cases there is a similar functional relationship between the exploitation of food resources, territorial control, social and kinship structure, and marriage patterns. In a formal sense, the environments and their resources differed greatly. The Congo is a humid, tropical rain forest; South Africa, Australia, and southern California are steppes and deserts; and Tierra del Fuego is cold, rainy plains. The species of fauna were different in each case, but, since the animals were sparse and dispersed in all cases their functional relationship to human beings was similar. The human population was sparse, and owing to the practical requirements of the hunting techniques it was grouped in localized, landowning, patrilocal, exogamous bands. In structure and in social function the bands were virtually identical, but in adaptation to environment they were similar in function rather than in concrete features.

A simpler but more cogent illustration of the need for the form-function concept is provided by several kinds of extended kinship relations. In most societies a person has need for solidarity with individuals beyond those of his immediate biological or nuclear family. This need may be met by various patterns such as extended kinship bonds, ritual kinship, and blood brotherhood, which are quite unlike one another in a formal sense. When the Latin American peasant enters into a *compadre* or co-parent relationship with innumerable persons, he acquires a broad basis of social and economic security comparable to that afforded the Chinese peasant through extended patrilineal family and clan relationships. At the same time, similar kinship relations may serve quite unlike functions. The Puerto Rican worker on the corporation sugar plantation becomes *compadre* to many fellow workers in order to create solidarity within a group of co-equal individuals, whereas the laborer on the coffee plantation seeks the *patrón* as his *compadre* in a system of reciprocal and unequal duties and services between members of two sharply differing classes.

If cultural typology is to expedite the recognition of cross-cultural regularities, it must take into account both form and function. A comparative approach that emphasizes only formal features leads to cultural relativism. The early irrigation civilizations had very unlike concepts of gods, ritual detail, religious architecture, and other specific features. The function of these features in sanctioning a ruling theocratic class, however, constituted such near-identity that this class was structurally similar in broad features in each case.

The concept of the *cross-cultural type* combines the concept of ecological adaptation, which implies that different, although not necessarily unique cultures, will be found in different areas, with the concept of levels of sociocultural integration, which implies that the developmental periods in any area tradition or co-tradition are qualitatively different and therefore are taxonomically as distinguishable from one another as are culture areas (Steward, 1951). In this frame of reference, there are two sets of variable factors: the environmental adaptation and the level of development. Consequently, a taxonomy which classifies kinds of human behavior in order to explain them must take into account both dimensions.

CULTURAL TYPOLOGY IN NATIVE AMERICA

Despite the prevalence of the culture area approach in dealing with native America there is a significant trend toward a problem-oriented rather than a natural history–oriented taxonomy. This trend is evidenced, for example, by the increasing attention paid to developmental factors and configurations in Meso-America and the Andes. Considerable thought is being given to the interrelationship of subsistence; demographic change; growth of communities and cities; amalgamation of communities into states; internal divisions of societies into specialized groups of farmers, artisans, rulers, social classes, and other specialists; and extrasocietal relations, such as warfare and trade. Moreover, *cross-cultural types* are being classified through comparison of New World and Old World data. Such students of the Near East as V. Gordon Childe (1951), Robert Braidwood (1952), and others have rejected the older technological criteria of developmental periods, such as Old Stone Age, New Stone Age, and Bronze Age, and begun to use such terms as Hunters, Food Producers, Urban Revolution, and the like. Meanwhile, American students of New World high civilizations have begun to group the smaller periods, which are defined by ceramic and other technological traits, into developmental eras of processual and functional significance. Bennett and Bird, Willey, Strong, and Steward (1949) reached substantial agreement on principal, if not on terminology, that the Andean cultural tradition began when Incipient Farmers living in small villages and having an undeveloped technology succeeded the Hunters and Gatherers; that the next significant stage was the Formative Era, which was characterized by the growth of villages, the establishment of the principal technologies, and the development of intervillage alliances based upon cooperation in irrigation, probably under religious leadership; that this era was followed by a Florescent Era, when cultures became regionally distinctive largely in esthetic terms, which apparently was related to the growth of localized states, and reached a peak of technical and artistic production; and that finally, during an era of "Fusion and Conquest," "Empire," or "Cyclical Conquests," these states were incorporated into empires, which brought unprecedented political organization and leveled many of the local cultural differences (Steward, 1949).

This interest in form, function, and developmental process had implications for cross-cultural comparison in that Meso-American sequences have been grouped in somewhat comparable terms. Armillas, working in the Mexican Highland, and Thompson, working in Yucatan, recognized rather similar developmental eras. Indeed irrigation civilizations of the Old World reveal many of the same processes, forms, and sequences as shown in Chapter 11.

It is not my contention that the developmental eras of Meso-America or the Andes have yet been placed on any final basis of functional and processual relationships. Obviously, the diagnostic features of any given era — *the cultural core* — will depend in part upon particular research interest, upon what is considered important; and there is still a healthy if somewhat confusing disagreement regarding these matters. It should be noted, however, that functionally interrelated economic, social, political, religious, and military patterns as well as technological and esthetic features have become the basis for developmental taxonomies. These features do not constitute total cultures. They form *culture cores,* which are defined according to the empirical facts of *cross-cultural type* and level.

A substantive distinction between the *culture area* concept and the *culture type* concept is illustrated by Murdock's and my classifications of South America. Murdock's twenty-four areas are based primarily upon language, land-use, technology, house type, and social organization. He does not interrelate demography, the size, stability and structure of communities, intercommunity relationship, and the functional significance of social classes, militarism, a priesthood, state religion, and political controls, although these phenomena have little meaning if they are merely listed as independent features. One of Murdock's nine criteria of culture areas lumps "relative degree of trade, social classes and political institutions," but kinds of trade, specialization, social structure, and political institutions are not distinguished, while warfare and religious patterns are nowhere mentioned either as cultural features or as functional adjuncts of total structures (Murdock, 1951). In terms of the traditional concept of culture area, Murdock's classification is as justifiable as any. My own fourfold classification, on the other hand, accords more attention to *cultural core,* that is, to functional interdependency of features in a structural relationship. The Circum-Caribbean area is distinguishable from the Andean area less because of element content than because of the kind of integration of elements. In the Central Andes, there was an absolute ruler, an empire, frozen and caste-like social classes, a priestly caste, and a conscript army which fought wars of territorial and political conquest. In the Circum-Caribbean area, the states were small and fluctuating, upward social mobility was possible through military achievements and probably through religious activity, and warfare was essential to religion and thus to social status through supplying sacrificial victims. These and other related features were integrated in a Circum-Caribbean *cultural core* whose structure differed profoundly from that of the Central Andes.

If particular cross-cultural typlogical terms are to serve the purposes suggested here, it is important that they be used only with full awareness of their heuristic import. Thus, *Incipient Farmers, Formative, Regional Florescent,* and *Empire and Conquest* constitute a tentative developmental typology not only for the irrigation areas of the Central Andes but for Meso-America and for similar Old World areas. For descriptive purposes, these terms have been applied to many other parts of the world, but indiscriminant application may rob them of value in constructing regularities. For example, while any society in the initial stages of farming may properly be called *Incipient Farmers,* the term has no cross-cultural typological significance unless it is precisely defined. To the extent that early farm communities were small, independent of one another, internally unspecialized, and based upon kinship and other informal controls, they were similar despite differences in element content. But in this sense, *Incipient Farmers* has little more utility than *Marginal Peoples*. It may be a world-wide characterization of a level in Coon's quantitative sense, but it does not necessarily represent a cross-cultural type, for local adaptations almost certainly produced fundamentally different kinds of cultural cores.

The term *Formative* also has been widely used in archaeological literature. In a semantic sense it is entirely legitimate to designate an early stage of any culture as *Formative* since it obviously refers to the time when the characteristic features were taking form. From a relativistic point of view, it is perhaps implicitly understood that the features in question are those unique to the tradition. Similarly, *Florescent* has been applied to many different traditions. If, however, the purpose is to designate developmental types of cross-cultural significance, it is necessary to modify the terms so that the *regularities* implied are beyond question. Thus, if *Formative* is a cross-cultural developmental type of the Andes and Meso-America, a more definitive term is *State Formative,*[7] for the cultures of the era in both traditions or areas were characterized by theocratic states, dispersed settlements, temple mounds, a class structure, and some skill in weaving, ceramics, and other technologies. It may or may not be appropriate to designate this widespread culture as *Formative*. Possibly it was less specifically tied to local environments and subsistence technologies than subsequent periods in the Andes and Meso-America, and there may be reason for including the Mississippi "pattern" or tradition in this category. As a cross-cultural type of considerable breadth, it might also include the Colonial and Sedentary periods of the Hohokam culture of southern Arizona; for, although the Hohokam lacks temple mounds, a priesthood, and some of the technological achievements of the *State Formative*, it clearly had large-scale irrigation works which suggest intervillage organization and which possibly imply that a state was taking form. Still, it is doubtful whether the Hohokam had a full-fledged *Formative* culture of the type in question.

If the term *Florescent* means not merely that any culture floresced but that special kinds of local states achieved a high degree of esthetic

---

[7] I cannot be sure that other Americanists attach precisely this meaning to the *Formative Era* of Meso-America and the Andes, for terminological usage has not yet been based on a general understanding of the distinction between *culture area type* and *cross-cultural type*.

and material production because they possessed certain basic technologies, had a subsistence which supported specialists, and an organization which channeled production to the state, there is clearly nothing in the Southwest comparable to the Andean and Meso-American *Regional Florescent* states. There is still less to suggest that the Anasazi or Hohokam had an era comparable to the Meso-American and Andean *Empire* or *Fusion and Conquest* culture. The Hohokam may or may not have achieved what might be defined as a state. The Anasazi almost certainly remained throughout its history on a village level of sociocultural integration.

This consideration of the applicability of Meso-American and Andean developmental categories to the Southwest has been stimulated by Daifuku's very interesting classification of the latter in terms of the former (Daifuku, 1952). If these terms are relative and have descriptive meaning, they may be used for any and all areas. If they have cross-cultural typological meaning, they must be defined very precisely in terms of cultural ecological adaptations within a particular kind of area and in terms of developmental levels which distinguish a succession of qualitatively different cultural types or cores. The Southwest shares many cultural elements with Meso-America, but its cross-cultural typological position cannot be stated in Meso-American terms. Unless it represents a unique type of cultural ecological adaptation, it might be suggested that it could be compared with the similar desert-adapted cultures of northeast Argentina, which acquired elements from the Andean civilization but readapted them in local patterns.

These substantive suggestions concerning native American cultural types are limited and tentative. There are undoubtedly many recurrent types other than those mentioned here. For example, there are certain interesting parallels between the combination of kinship and status groups found on the Northwest Coast and among the Natchez. There are many societies based on localized, exogamous lineages which might warrant analysis and comparison. There are several societies in which virtually all culture functions on a family level, as among the Western Shoshoni, Eskimo, Mura, and Guato. There are many groups of undeveloped farmers which no doubt will some day be grouped in types. There are probably several types of bands which have developed as a result of horse nomadism, for example, the predatory bands described in Chapter 6. And there are probably also many cultures which are typologically unique so far as native America is concerned but which have Old World parallels, for example, some of the Tropical Forest peoples. In the final analysis, a cultural typology is more meaningful if based upon world data, for extensive comparison serves to clarify structural-functional relationships that recur cross-culturally.

In conclusion, it should be emphasized that since the concept of *cross-cultural type* discussed in this paper is a methodological tool for analyzing functional relationships and processes of change rather than an end in itself, it will need considerable refinement. The particular problem is to ascertain what kinds of phenomena and what kinds of interrelationships between them have diagnostic and typological importance. Perhaps there will be many kinds of typologies, each related to a particular interest.

III. substantive applications

6

The Great Basin Shoshonean Indians:
An Example of a Family Level of
Sociocultural Integration[1]

The types of cultures and processes of development illustrated in this and following chapters are arranged in a sequence of successively higher levels of sociocultural integration. This does not imply a unilinear evolutionary sequence of cultural development. Since particular cultures have unlike configurations and element content resulting from their distinctive origins, histories, and ecological adaptations, many different local or areal types of culture may represent the same level of sociocultural integration. Thus, the Shoshonean Indians of the Great Basin and the Eskimo illustrate an essentially family level of integration, although their respective ways of life and cultural types differed quite profoundly. Every level could be exemplified by several different cultures, some representing cross-culturally recurrent types and other unique developments.

The Shoshonean-speaking Indians — the Ute, Western Shoshoni, and Northern Paiute of western Colorado, Utah, Nevada, and eastern Oregon and California — acquired most of their hunting and gathering techniques from other peoples, but their general adaptation to the intermontane steppes and deserts was so distinctive that they con-

---

[1] This chapter is essentially a condensation of "Basin-Plateau Sociopolitical Groups," *Bureau of American Ethnology Bulletin 120,* 1938.

stitute a special culture area usually called the Great Basin or Basin-Plateau area. In a quantitative sense, this culture was extremely simple. An "element list," which breaks the culture down into details such as basket weaves and shapes, religious beliefs, social practices, and other details, includes a total of about 3,000 items. By comparison, the U. S. forces landing at Casa Blanca during World War II unloaded 500,000 items of material equipment alone. The total "elements" of modern American culture would probably run to several million.

Shoshonean culture, however, is of interest for the nature of its organization as much as for its quantitative simplicity. Virtually all cultural activities were carried out by the family in comparative isolation from other families. A contrast with modern America helps clarify this point. In the United States today, people are highly specialized workers in an economic system geared to national and international patterns; education is increasingly standardized and the community or state takes over this function from the family when the child is six years old or younger; health practices are dictated largely by research carried out on an international scale and in part administered by the state and community; recreation more and more involves the consumption of products made by national organizations; religious worship is carried on in national or international churches. These growing functions of the community, state, and nation increasingly relieve the family of functions it performed in earlier historical periods. It is perhaps difficult to imagine that a family, alone and unaided, could obtain virtually all the food it consumed; manufacture all its clothing, household goods, and other articles; rear and train its children without assistance; take care of its sick except in time of crisis; be self-sufficient in its religious activities; and, except on special occasions, manage its own recreation. Why this was so in the case of the Shoshoneans is explainable largely in terms of their cultural ecological adaptations.

Owing to the nature of the natural environment of the Great Basin area and to the simple hunting and gathering techniques for exploiting it, it was inevitable that the individual family or at the most two or three related families should live in isolation during most of the year. "Family" in this case signifies the nuclear, biological or bilateral family, consisting of mother, father, and children. Unlike many primitive peoples, the Shoshoneans were not organized in extended family or lineage groups and, although, as we shall see subsequently, the imme-

diate family was frequently enlarged through plural spouses and
different families were closely allied by marriage, the functioning unit
was the nuclear family, augmented only by a grandparent, aunt, or
uncle who otherwise would be homeless.

ENVIRONMENT AND RESOURCES

The natural resources which were exploitable by Shoshonean culture were so limited that the population was extremely sparse. In the
more fertile portions of this area there was perhaps one person to five
square miles, while in the vast stretches of nearly waterless terrain the
ratio was one to fifty or even one hundred square miles. The mean
for the whole area was between one person to twenty or thirty square
miles.

The territory once inhabited by the Shoshonean Indians is extremely
arid, but technically most of it is classified as "steppe" rather than true
"desert" although there are large areas devoid of vegetation. The
country consists of large arid valleys lying between mountain ranges
which run north and south. These valleys are from five to twenty miles
wide and twenty to eighty miles long. The greater portion of the
Shoshonean habitat lies within the Great Basin, a vast area of interior
drainage between the Wasatch Mountains of Utah and the Sierra
Nevada Range of California and Oregon, but it also includes portions
of the Columbia River Plateau of Idaho and eastern Oregon and
the Colorado River Plateau of eastern Utah and western Colorado.

The flora and fauna of all these areas are very similar. There are
several biotic zones, which set the basic conditions for a society
equipped only with very simple hunting and gathering techniques. In
the valleys, which lie between 4,000 and 6,000 feet elevation, the low
rainfall — five to twenty inches a year — together with high evapora-
tion supports a predominantly xerophytic vegetation, that is, such
drought-resisting plants as sagebrush and greasewood. This vegetation
has very limited value to human beings or animals. Plants bearing
edible seeds and roots occur in some abundance immediately along
the stream banks, but, except in favored areas, such as the piedmont
of the Wasatch Mountains and the Sierra Nevada Mountains, the
streams are small and widely-spaced. In the Great Basin, the streams
end in saline marshes or lakes. In the vast sandy areas between the
streams, the quantity of edible plants depends directly upon rainfall,
which varies from year to year and from place to place. These plants
only afforded small quantities of food for the Indians, and they could

not support game in herds comparable to the bison of the Great Plains or the caribou of the far north. The two species of greatest importance to the Indians were antelope and rabbits. These not only supplied meat and skins, but the communal hunts in which they were sometimes taken were among the few collective cultural activities. The numbers of both species, however, were limited, and the hunts were infrequent.

It is impossible to estimate the quantitative importance of different animal foods in the valley zone, but the Shoshoneans probably ate more rats, mice, gophers, locusts, ants, ant eggs, larvae of flies which breed in the salt lakes, snakes, and lizards than large game. In the rivers, such as the Owyhee, John Day, Crooked, Snake, Truckee, Carson, Walker, and Humboldt rivers, fish were an important supplement to other foods, but the runs were seasonal, the quantity did not compare with that of fish in coastal rivers, and the fish were evidently not suited for preservation and storage.

The zone of piñon and juniper trees lies between about 6,000 and 8,000 or 9,000 feet. This zone is largely restricted to the flanks of the mountain ranges since most valleys lie below this altitude. The juniper had little value to the Indians except for its wood, but the piñon (*Pinus monophylla* in the north, *Pinus edulis* in the south), which occurred throughout the Shoshonean area to a little north of the Humboldt River in Nevada, yielded pine nuts which were the most important of all food species. North of the piñon area, the seeds of certain other species of pines were eaten, but they were a relatively minor item in the diet. Since there was greater rainfall in the piñon-juniper belt than in the valleys, this zone afforded more seeds, roots, and grasses, and it had more game, especially deer. But it constitutes only a small portion of the total area, and the growing season is short. A few mountain ranges rise above 8,000 or 9,000 feet into the zone of the ponderosa pine, where vegetation is lush and where mountain sheep as well as deer were hunted.

The Shoshonean tribes were of necessity gatherers of vegetable foods and lower forms of animal life rather than hunters. They utilized nearly a hundred species of wild plants. The more important of these yielded small, hard-shelled seeds, which were collected in conical basketry containers, roasted with live coals in shallow baskets, ground on flat stones or metates, and eaten from basketry bowls. In the higher altitudes and latitudes where rainfall is greater, roots were relatively more important as food. When seeds and roots could not be had, especially in early spring, leafy vegetables or greens from many plants were eaten.

SOCIALLY FRAGMENTING EFFECT OF THE CULTURAL ECOLOGY

All of the plant and animal foods had in common the extremely important characteristic that the place and quantity of their occurrence from year to year were unpredictable, owing largely to variations in rainfall. A locality might be very fertile one year and attract large numbers of families, but offer little food for several years thereafter. Few localities had foods in sufficient quantity and reliability to permit permanent settlements. Throughout most of the area, the families were concerned predominantly with warding off potential starvation by moving from place to place. These movements were determined by reports from friends or relatives about the probable quantities of foods to be had. Families from different localities would assemble at places where food was temporarily plentiful, but, owing to the impossibility of storing large quantities of food for the future, they soon dispersed to seek elsewhere.

The typical Shoshoni family living in the piñon area of Nevada traveled alone or with one or two related families during the spring and summer, seeking seeds, roots, various small mammals, rodents, insects, larvae, and other edible items. In the late summer when a family heard reports that the pine nuts seemed very promising in a certain portion of a mountain range, it arranged its travels so as to arrive in that locality in late October or early November, when the first frosts would have opened the cones and made the nuts ready to harvest. Other families who had also been foraging for food within a radius of perhaps twenty to thirty miles of that locality came there for the same reason.

In gathering the pine nuts, each family restricted itself by common understanding to a limited area, because there were so many pine nuts in the locality as a whole that no one could gather them all before they dropped and because each family could harvest more if it worked alone. The different families remained from several hundred yards to a mile or more apart. Each gathered pine nuts as rapidly as it could and stored them in earth caches. If the harvest was good, it might support the family throughout most of the winter.

The winter encampment consisted of perhaps twenty or thirty families within easy visiting distance of one another. Early spring generally found the people suffering more or less acutely from hunger.

The families then had to go their separate ways to forage for greens, game, and any other foods they could find. Throughout spring and summer, the migrations of a particular family, although limited in general to the terrain it knew well, were determined almost week to week by its knowledge of available foods. It might learn that sand grass seeds were promising in one place, rabbits numerous elsewhere, fly larvae abundant in a certain lake, and antelope ready for a communal hunt under a shaman or medicine man over in the next valley.

Although the pine nut was perhaps the most important factor in determining the whereabouts of the winter encampment and which families would be associated in it, most other foods had a very similar effect in causing seasonal variations in interfamilial contacts. Owing to yearly and local variations in rainfall, the whereabouts of other wild seed and root crops and animal resources was unpredictable. Rabbits might be so numerous in a portion of a valley in a given year that people would assemble from considerable distances to hold a communal hunt. Several years might then follow before it was worth while to hold another such hunt in the same place, whereas rabbits were ready for a hunt in an adjoining valley the next year. The same was true of antelope. A co-operative hunt would so reduce the antelope that it required eight or ten years for their number to be restored. Even such foods as grasshoppers and locusts, or "Mormon crickets," were unpredictable. In certain years locusts occurred in such numbers as to be a major source of food to the Indians — and a plague to the modern farmers — and then during several years they were of no importance.

A limitation of the value of animal products was the absence of preservation and storing techniques. Rabbits, antelope, and fish might afford more meat than the people who assembled to take them could eat, but after a few days or weeks, they spoiled. Fish, unlike other animal species, occurred with some annual regularity in fixed places. During runs, a considerable number of families came from far and wide to fish for a few weeks, after which they had to disperse in search of other foods. Had the Shoshoneans been able to dry and smoke fish, like the Northwest Coast Indians, it is possible that fairly large permanent populations might have developed along certain of the better fishing streams and lakes. In the absence of this possibility, the winter inhabitants of these areas were limited to the few families who used fish as a supplement to other foods. Consequently, the effect of fishing resources on social groups was like that of other foods: it permitted large aggregates of people to assemble for short periods and it helped tide a small number of local families over the winter.

Shoshonean society was affected not only by the erratic and unpredictable occurrence of practically all principal foods and by the limited technical skills for harvesting and storing most of them, but it was also shaped by the predominant importance of wild vegetable products, which put a premium upon family separatism rather than upon co-operation. Anyone who has gathered wild berries in a party knows that he can pick far more if he finds a patch of his own. Unlike certain forms of hunting — for example, collective rabbit drives or antelope hunts — participation of many persons in seed and root gathering not only failed to increase the per capita harvest, but it generally decreased it so greatly that individual families preferred to forage alone so as not to compete with other families.

The competitive aspect of seed and root gathering together with the erratic annual occurrence of practically all principal foods and the inability of the people to store foods in any locality in sufficient amount to permit considerable numbers of families to remain there for a major portion of the year, all contributed to the fragmentation of Shoshonean society into nuclear family units, which moved about the country seasonally and annually in a unpredictable itinerary.

PROPERTY

The concept of property rights among the Shoshoneans was directly related to their mode of life. These Indians assumed that rights to exclusive use of anything resulted from work expended by particular individuals or groups and from habitual use. This is a rather obvious, simple, and practical concept, and it seems to have entailed a minimum of conflict.

In most parts of the area, natural resources were available to anyone. The seeds gathered by a woman, however, belonged to her because she had done the work of converting a natural resource into something that could be directly consumed. If a man made a bow or built a house, these were his, although prior to making objects of them, the trees he utilized belonged to no one. Any family might fish in a certain river or stream, but if a group of families built a fish weir, it alone had the right to use that weir.

When a number of families came into potential conflict in the utilization of natural resources, the same principle held. In seed gathering, it was "first come, first served." The families which entered a seed plot or piñon grove selected the best portion and, by virtue of having started to work on it, had prior rights. Other families gathered pine nuts elsewhere, which was reasonable and necessary because if they gathered in competition with the first family, all would have harvested less. In rabbit drives, the person who clubbed or shot a rabbit or who owned the net which caught it had first claim. In deer or mountain sheep hunting, the man whose arrow first entered the game was entitled to the skin and the choice portions of the meat.

This principle of property rights was essential to survival in the Shoshonean area. Owing to the erratic annual and local occurrence of foods, the arbitrary exclusion of territorially delimited groups of families from utilization of other territories would have caused starvation and death. With few exceptions, the habitat of most families always provided such uncertain subsistence that the territorial interpenetration of families living in different localities was necessary to the survival of all. The absence of property claims of local groups to delimitable areas of natural resources upon which work had not been expended was the corollary of the fragmented nature of Shoshonean society.

In a few portions of the Great Basin, such as Owens Valley in eastern California, which was occupied by Northern Paiute, the many streams flowing from the high Sierra Nevada Range afforded food resources which were comparatively so abundant and reliable that each family could be reasonably certain of finding enough to eat within one or two days' travel from a permanent village. Instead of wandering an unpredictable course determined by the vicissitudes of nature, these families were able to make forays from permanent headquarters. Habitual use of resources within readily accessible portions of the terrain led to the concept that each local village or group of villages had exclusive rights to resources within bounded areas. This economic stability and permanent residence of a particular group of families provided a basis for association, leadership, and organization in band groups.

CO-OPERATION AND LEADERSHIP AS INTEGRATING FACTORS

The typical Shoshonean family was independent and self-sufficient during the greater part of the year, perhaps during 80 or 90 percent of the time. It subsisted and fulfilled most cultural functions with little assistance from other families. It probably could have survived in complete isolation.

But human history provides no instances in which nuclear families had progeny and perpetuated their culture without associating with and intermarrying with other families. Moreover, nuclear families have always co-operated with other families in various ways. Since this is so, the Shoshoneans, like other fragmented family groups, represent a family level of sociocultural integration only in a relative sense. It is relative in that most societies having a higher level of intergration possess patterns of co-operation and leadership among a permanent membership. I classify the Shoshoneans as an exemplification of a family level of sociocultural integration because in the few forms of collective activity the same group of families did not not co-operate with one another or accept the same leader on successive occasions. By another definition, however, it might be entirely permissible to view this ever-changing membership and leadership as a special form of suprafamilial integration. While the Shoshoneans represent a family level of sociocultural integration in a relative sense, their suprafamilial patterns of integration involved no permanent social groups of fixed membership despite several kinds of interfamilial co-operation.

Collective Hunting

The most important co-operation consisted of collective hunts. In these hunts, rabbits, antelope, deer, and mud hens were the principal species taken. Communal hunts could be held, however, only when there was sufficient game, when a considerable number of families could assemble, and when an appropriate leader was available. Under these circumstances, co-operation yielded many times the quantity of game that individuals, expending the same effort, could take alone.

The principal collective hunt was the rabbit drive. It could be held fairly often, and it yielded not only meat which could be consumed during a short period but furs which, cut into long strips and twisted, were woven into robes and blankets. The only distinctive technical feature of these drives was a net of about the height and mesh of a modern tennis net but often several hundred feet long. A number of these nets were placed end to end to form a huge semicircle. Men, women, children, and dogs beat the brush over a wide area, gradually closing in so that rabbits which were not clubbed or shot by the drivers became entangled in the nets, where they were killed.

Custom determined the several crucial aspects of the drive and the division of game. Experienced men — in recent years called rather appropriately "rabbit bosses" — were given supreme authority to coordinate all activities in this fairly complex operation. They chose the locality of the drive, directed disposition of nets, regulated the drivers, and divided the game according to customary understandings. Anyone who killed a rabbit with a bow or throwing stick in the course of the drive could claim it. Since, however, only a few families owned rabbit nets, net owners received a somewhat greater portion of the rabbits caught in the nets.

In spite of the rather rigid direction of these drives, there were several reasons why they did not bring about permanent integration or cohesion of territorial or social groups of fixed membership. First, drives were held only when rabbits were sufficiently numerous in a particular locality. Second, participants in the drive consisted of families who, because of the rather fortuitous annual occurrence of seeds and other foods in one place or another, happened to be in the locality where the drive was worth holding. Third, the drive was held only if an experienced leader and families owning nets happened to be present. Since the occurrence of these factors was rather haphazard, since the place, the participants, and the leaders were never quite the same in successive years, the drives provided only temporary bonds between independent families. A given family was under no obligation whatever to participate in a drive with a fixed group of families under a permanent leader. And, since, the "rabbit boss" held authority only during the drive, the family paid little heed to him in other times, places, and contexts.

The communal antelope hunt had a social function like that of the rabbit drive. It was held in any given locality at intervals of several years and the participants consisted of those families which happened to be in the vicinity. It was held less frequently than the rabbit drive because it took much longer for the antelope herds to recover their number. A major difference in form rather than function between the rabbit drive and the antelope hunt is that whereas the former were led by men of experience and prestige — qualifications which anyone might develop — the latter were led by "antelope shamans." According to Shoshonean belief, these men were qualified less by their practical ability — though no doubt they were far from incompetent — than by their possession of supernatural power which enabled them to charm the antelope into a state of helplessness.

The practical procedures in the antelope drives were as appropriate to the situation as those in the rabbit hunts. The people built a brush corral from which wings, consisting of piles of brush or stones, extended outward a half mile or so. Drivers spread out several miles from the corral, formed a line across the valley, and slowly closed in, urging the antelope between the wings and into the corral. Antelope differ from rabbits in that they not only flee from something threatening but they are drawn by curiosity toward strange objects. The antelope shaman evidently became one of the chief functionaries in native Shoshonean culture because his role combined this peculiarity of antelope with a basic belief about sickness. It was thought by many primitive peoples, including the Shoshoneans, that sickness might be caused by loss of one's soul. While the antelope shaman was not a curer of human ills, he was thought to possess the power to capture the souls of antelope before the hunt began and thus irresistably to draw them into the corral, where he stood during the drive.

The shaman's authority was very great during these drives, but he had no voice in other activities. Moreover, even this socioreligious leadership like the lay authority found in rabbit drives failed to integrate social groups of fixed membership.

The other hunting activities involved much less co-operation than rabbit and antelope drives. Mud hen hunts were held only by small groups in the lake areas, while deer drives, held in the mountains, were infrequent and involved few persons.

Dancing, Gambling, and Visiting

The interfamilial associations of the Shoshonean Indians had to be adapted, as previously shown, to the exigencies of obtaining food by means of the techniques known to them. Although these families foraged throughout most of the year in isolation, their contacts with other families over many generations had contributed certain social patterns which strengthened bonds between them.

Whenever groups of Shoshonean families were together, they carried out certain recreational activities, such as dancing and gambling. Dancing, although popular, was originally limited to the circle dance, a performance in which men and women formed a circle and side-stepped to the accompaniment of singing. Gambling games were extremely numerous and included several forms of dice, the hand-game, sports such as racing and hockey, and games of skill such as the hoop-and-pole game and archery. Both dancing and games, however, could be held only when local abundance of food, such as rabbits, locusts, antelope, or pine nuts, made large gatherings possible. After a rabbit or antelope drive, for instance, people might dance and gamble for several days until the meat supply was exhausted, when each family had to go its separate way in the unending food quest.

Interfamilial contacts were not limited to such formalized activities as hunting, dancing, and gambling. Visiting was an important integrating fact since people were always eager to associate with one another whether or not they danced and gambled. They preferred to visit with relatives, but when food was plentiful, a large number of unrelated families could assemble.

Hostilities and Warfare

In aboriginal times most of the Shoshonean people had no national or tribal warfare. There were no territorial rights to be defended, no military honors to be gained, and no means of organizing groups of individuals for concerted action. When war parties of neighboring peoples invaded their country, the Shoshoneans ran away more often than they fought.

Hostilities generally consisted of feuds, not organized military action, and they resulted largely from the suspicion of witchcraft and from woman-stealing. They were therefore as often intratribal as intertribal. Death was generally ascribed to supernatural causes, especially to shamans, whose normally beneficent power had turned bad, perhaps even without the shaman's knowledge, and it was avenged by slaying the suspect. Usually, the malignant shaman was identified either as the person who had treated the deceased or as a member of a somewhat distant group. Accusations of witchcraft were rarely directed against relatives because kinship relations were too important to be endangered. It was, in fact, one of the most important kinship obligations to avenge the death of a relative. Once revenge had been taken, a series of reprisals and counter-reprisals might follow. These were purely personal and could not involve definable suprafamilial groups, for such groups did not exist.

The Rise of Predatory Bands

After the Shoshonean tribes acquired horses and the territory was occupied by white settlers, warfare of a collective nature developed. Under aboriginal conditions, horses had little value because they consumed the very plants upon which the Indians depended while contributing little to the hunting of rabbits, antelope, or deer. The few horses acquired in early times were eaten. When immigrant trains crossed the area and when white settlers introduced irrigation, crops, and livestock into the country, horses enabled the previously dispersed families to amalgamate and remain fairly constantly together in *predatory bands,* which lived somewhat parasitically by raiding the whites. Warfare involved in raiding and in defense against white reprisals was the principal if not sole function of these bands, and the chiefs had authority over little other than raiding activities. It was only among the Northern Shoshoni of Wind River, Wyoming, and of eastern Idaho and the Bannock, who probably acquired horses by 1800, that bison hunting and native warfare of the Plains type were also functions of the native bands. The Ute received horses sometime after 1820, and their bands were essentially predatory, first in raiding people outside their territory and later in raiding the Mormons and other white settlers inside it. The Western Shoshoni and Northern Paiute continued to be dispersed in family units until about 1845, after which mounted bands rapidly developed. Mounted bands were dissolved among the Shoshonean peoples by 1870 or soon thereafter when the United States Army defeated them.

In understanding the quite specialized nature of these predatory bands and the restricted authority of the chiefs, it is important to note that the bands probably never involved all the people of any region. During the early phases of band operations, there were many families which had no horses and continued to live according to the older pattern of family separatism while some of their friends and relatives engaged in raiding. Later, when the United States Army opposed the raiders, the Indians had to decide whether to continue to fight or whether to accept peace, relinquish certain territory, and live on reservations. At this stage, there were two kinds of chiefs. The first were leaders of predatory bands which were now on the defensive. The second were spokesmen for those who advocated peace and the signing of treaties.

After the Indians were defeated, the division between peaceful and warring factions soon faded and the functions of war leaders were eliminated. Thenceforth, the principal need for leaders was to deal with the white men, especially with the officials of the United States government.

Religion

Religion integrated families with one another only to a minor degree. Shoshonean culture lacked collective social and economic activities and common interests, except the communal hunts, dancing, and gaming previously mentioned. There was no functional need for ceremonialism dedicated to group purposes and led by priests holding a definite office. The communal antelope hunt was directed by a special shaman, but this leader did not serve any permanent group.

The relationship between human beings and supernatural powers was conceived largely as a matter of individual concern. Every person hoped to acquire a supernatural power or guardian spirit. This power, manifest in the form of animals, plants, clouds, mountains, and other natural phenomena, came to him in dreams and gave him special abilities, such as gambling luck, hunting skill, endurance, and others of benefit to himself alone. Shamans' powers differed from those of ordinary persons mainly in the ability to cure sickness in other people. The shaman did not lead group ceremonies. His curing performances might attract large numbers of families which happened to be in the vicinity because they liked not only to watch his singing, dancing, trance, laying-on-of-hands, and other rites but to visit other families. Shamans were influential because their curing abilities gave them prestige while their presumed capacity for practicing black magic made them feared, but they carried no specific authority.

A minor collective religious activity designed for the common good was the circle dance, which, according to the belief of some of the Western Shoshoni, promoted general fertility and benefited everyone. Harris (1940) reported that the Tosavits or White Knife Shoshoni of northern Nevada held group ceremonies for general welfare. It is more likely, however, that the principal feature of such ceremonies was the circle dance, which was held by whatever families came together at various stages of their food quest, and that the religious aspect was secondary and incidental to the recreational purpose. The "dance boss" was certainly not a religious leader. Similarly, the bear dance of the Ute was primarily recreational and only secondarily religious in heralding the spring season and providing protection against bears. Its leader, like that of the circle dance, was a layman.

Winter Encampments

The only prolonged accessibility of families to one another occurred in the winter encampments. These winter quarters have sometimes been called villages, but they were not tightly nucleated settlements which constituted organized communities. Instead, family houses were widely scattered within productive portions of the piñon zone. The location of each household was determined primarily by its pine nut caches and secondarily by accessibility to wood and water. The scattered families were able to visit one another to dance, gamble, and exchange gossip, and the men occasionally co-operated in a deer or mountain sheep hunt. Although dances and collective hunts required co-ordination, the leaders had no authority outside the particular activity.

Other interfamilial and interpersonal relationships were determined by customary usage. Disputes and hostilities arising from such matters as murder, theft, wife-stealing, and other violations of custom were settled between families. None of these was a "crime" against the community, for the community did not exist in any corporate or legal sense. Violations of custom threatened families, not larger socially integrated units. Thus, the very concept of crime presupposes some kind of suprafamily level of integration, some collectivity, which has a common purpose that must be protected against antisocial behavior by its members.

In addition to the leaders of special activities, each village or local area of scattered winter houses usually had a man of some importance whom modern Shoshonean informants frequently call the "village chief." So far as "chief" implies permanent authority over an identifiable group, this term is a complete misnomer, for this man had no authority and he served only one function. This function, however, was extremely important. It was to act as a clearing-house of information about where foods could be found. Since the Shoshoneans were constantly on the verge of starvation, especially at the end of winter, knowledge of where greens, seeds, rabbits, insects, and other foods were to be had made the repository of such information the most important person in the village.

The winter village cannot be considered a genuine suprafamilial form of social integration because it lacked permanent membership and even permanent location. Each year, families came from a general area to a locality of abundant pine nuts. Leaders were accepted by common consent to control such collective activities as required co-ordination. It was only in the few regions of uncommonly abundant and reliable food that a group of fixed membership occupied one or more permanent villages throughout most of the year and had a true village chief and permanent leaders of other activities.

Food-Named Groups

Considerable confusion concerning the nature of groups named according to special foods is found in the literature starting with the early accounts of the Shoshoneans and perpetuated in modern ethnographic studies.[2] It was the native custom throughout practically all of the area to name the people occupying different localities by some important or striking food found in them. Thus, several different and widely-separated groups were called Rabbit, Eaters and Fish Eaters. Other names were Pine Nut Eaters, Ground Hog Eaters, Grass Seed Eaters, and the like. These names, however, did not designate definable groups but were merely applied to whoever happened to be in the locality. Since there were no bands and no territorial limitations on movements in search of food, families frequently traveled from one food area to another and were known by the local name in each. Just as a Washingtonian today becomes a New Yorker upon living in New York, so a Ground Hog Eater of western Idaho became a Salmon Eater if he moved to the Snake River.

Most of the early accounts of the Shoshoneans were written after wars with the whites began and predatory bands developed. Sometimes these bands were named after their leaders and sometimes after the food area from which the leader and many of his followers came. Writers therefore assumed that the inhabitants of these food-named localities constituted aboriginal, territorial bands under over-all chieftainship. Data previously cited show clearly that this could not have been the case. The food-named areas were far too large for a foot people to associate in collective activities, even had the nature of Shoshonean subsistence not precluded integration in bands. After the whites entered the country, the "chiefs" of predatory bands not only failed to enlist the support of the peace faction in their own place of origin but their followers included persons from many other food-named areas.

Throughout the greater part of the area, therefore, food-names were a designation of people in a certain large region and nothing more. They implied no economic, recreational, religious, social, or political co-operation that would require collective action and lead to suprafamilial forms of integration.

KINSHIP RELATIONS

The economic and social relations of Shoshonean families previously described may be likened to a net in that each family had occasional

[2] O. C. Stewart, *Northern Paiute Bands* (Berkeley: University of California Press, 1939), p. 19, has mistaken food-named groups for aboriginal bands and leaders of post-white predatory bands for aboriginal chiefs.

associations with families on all sides of it and these latter with families farther away and these with still others so that there were no social, economic or political frontiers. The entire area consisted of interlocking associations of family with family. So far as subsistence, recreational, and religious activities are concerned, however, the analogy of a net is not entirely apt because no family was necessarily and consistently associated with certain other families. The net lacked knots; each family was at liberty to associate with whom it pleased. Kinship relations, however, supplied the knots and made a fabric of what otherwise would have been a skein of loose threads, each of which shifted about somewhat randomly. This is not to say that Shoshonean society was based on extended ties of kinship which gave cohesion to any definable group. The activities of a given family month by month were dictated primarily by the food quest, which took precedence over every other consideration. But marriage bonds were fairly enduring, and they created a strong fabric of close relationships, which extended from one locality to the next. They also made interfamilial economic and recreational associations somewhat less random, for kin preferred to co-operate with one another when possible. Moreover, the very absence of socioeconomic unity among inhabitants of local areas made the kinship ties seem relatively more important.

The irreducible minimum of Shoshonean society was the nuclear or biological family. Isolated individuals could not well survive in this cultural-environmental or ecological situation, and unmarried or widowed persons generally attached themselves to a nuclear family. This family was able to carry out most activities necessary to existence, for husband and wife complemented each other in food-getting and together they procreated, reared, and socialized their children. Women gathered vegetable foods, made the baskets needed for this purpose, and prepared all food. Men devoted most of their time to hunting, which, though not very rewarding, was extremely important and time consuming. It was important not only because meat was a desired dietary item, but because hides and furs were needed for clothing. The scarcity of game and the difficulty of hunting is evidenced by the fact that few men were able to kill enough deer or antelope to clothe their families in skin garments or even to make moccasins. Many persons were naked and barefoot during the summer, and in winter had only a rabbit skin blanket which served both as a robe and as bedding.

In the household, women maintained the home and took care of the children. Men also played an important part in child-rearing. In the absence of toys and games designed expressly for children, boys played with small bows and arrows and other objects used by men, while girls imitated their mothers. In this way, children quickly learned the rudiments of adult functions and absorbed the attitudes, values, and beliefs of their parents. This learning was accomplished largely within the context of the family, for association with other families was limited.

In the course of the very uncertain wanderings and activities of Shoshonean life, the most frequent associates of the members of a nuclear family were members of families with which they had inter-married. These families were companions on seed and root gathering trips, when there was enough food for several families to travel together, and they co-operated in hunting. Relatives were the favored visitors, and often a few families would camp together and spend evenings gossiping and telling legends. Relatives were to be counted on for support if suspicion of witchcraft led to a feud. And they, more than others, were willing to share food in times of shortage.

These close interfamilial bonds were expressed in the marriage system. Marriage was more a contract between families than between individuals. The preferred arrangement was several marriages between the children of two families. When a young man married, it was desired that his wife's brother marry his sister. Several brothers and sisters might marry several sisters and brothers. Shoshonean culture permitted plural spouses, wherein the same principle prevailed. If a man took several wives, custom prescribed that they be sisters, and penalties were imposed for failure to follow this custom. If a man's wife died, he was obligated to take her sister as his next wife. In a parallel way, a certain amount of polyandry, or plural husbands, was permitted. A woman might take a younger brother of her husband as a temporary spouse until he found a wife. If the husband died, his family was obligated to furnish a brother of the first husband if possible.

It was, of course, biologically impossible that the number and sex of siblings in two intermarrying families should be such that this cultural ideal could be met. Moreover, marriages of the parental and grandparental generation extended marital ties to many families. While marital ties often linked the younger generation of two families to one another somewhat more closely than either was linked to other families, the general pattern was one of innumerable interfamilial linkages extending over a wide area. It meant that a family in a given locality could probably find consanguinal or marital kin of one kind or another among a large proportion of the families which ranged its own territory and among many families farther afield.

These interfamilial marital and kinship bonds were not unbreakable, for, despite the contractual nature of marriage, separations or divorces were common. Individual temperament, incompatibility, and other factors were not to be discounted. Nonetheless, the cultural ideal ascribed these arrangements considerable importance. And this importance derived largely from the fact that these kinship bonds were the principal integrating factors in a cultural-environmental situation where the subsistence pattern prevented the development of bands, villages, or other social units consisting of permanent members having prescribed relationships to one another.

These marital and kinship ties were the knots of the social fabric of the various peoples in the Shoshonean area, but they did not constitute sociocultural frontiers. Marriage was contracted most often between families in contact with one another, but it was not governed by territorial or political units. While it united strands in the netlike fabric of Shoshonean society, it could not consolidate or integrate local groups in a political, social, or economic sense. To the contrary, it cut across local boundaries, making interfamilial ties diffuse and thus actually militating against band or community development.

THE THEORETICAL SIGNIFICANCE OF THE SHOSHONEANS

In a classification of cultures based on the concept of area, the Shoshoneans should probably be included in the Greater Southwest; for more of their culture elements, especially their material culture or technology, seem to have been derived from the Southwest than from any other area. Their economic, political, social, religious, and hostility patterns — general configurations which are not reducible to culture elements — were, however, wholly unlike those of the Southwest. Owing to the cultural ecological processes — to the exploitation of their particular environment by means of the techniques available to them — families functioned independently in most cultural activities, and the few collective interfamilial pursuits did not serve to give permanent cohesion to extended families, bands, communities, or other higher levels of sociocultural integration as in the Southwest.

The Shoshonean peoples were not unique in having a family level of integration. This level is also represented in North America by the Eskimo and in South America by the Nambicuara, Guató, Mura, and perhaps other groups. But this similarity of level does not mean that these tribes belonged to the same cultural type. In all cases, the food quest was of overwhelming importance, but, owing to the differences in environment and exploitative techniques, it entailed very unlike activities and associations between families. Perhaps there have been people similar to the Shoshoneans in other parts of the world; for the present, however, the Shoshoneans must be regarded as typologically unique.

This typological distinctiveness makes the Shoshoneans unique in cultural evolution. If the predecessors of any people who later developed to a community or state level were like the Shoshoneans, we have no way of knowing it. Even if all groups of mankind had begun their cultural evolution with sociocultural units integrated only on a family level, which is doubtful and certainly unprovable, it would not follow that they all had the same cultural configuration, that is, the same cultural type, as the Shoshoneans. Paleolithic data suggest that there were several major areas which differed in lithic technology, and within these areas many distinctive local cultural ecological adaptations must have taken place. So far as present evidence is concerned, therefore, the Shoshoneans represent a distinctive and nonrecurrent line of development in a scheme of multilinear evolution.

The family type of organization found among the Shoshoneans should not be confused with that which developed after white contacts among several peoples in various parts of the world. For example, many Indians in the northeastern United States and Canada, who previously had some form of band organization (see Chapter 8), broke up into family groups after the fur trade had become virtually essential to their existence, and each family came to own a clearly delimited trapping territory. Social, economic, and religious patterns which had given cohesion to the bands were seriously disrupted or disappeared. This did not mean that the whole culture was actually reduced to a family level. The families ceased to be related to one another through band institutions and became partially integrated into the economic and to some extent into the religious and political institutions of the colonial or national states. These institutions were mediated to them through the trader, the missionary, and government officials.

The Mundurucú of the Cururá River in the Amazon Basin, according to Robert Murphy's recent, unpublished studies, have tended to lose their band and tribal organization and to split into family units for similar reasons. Since they have become gatherers of wild rubber, each family works the trees within delimited sections of the rivers.

Family contacts are increasing with the rubber trader and to some extent with church and government officials rather than with one another. A similar pattern was found by Wagley among the rubber gathering Caboclos on the lower Amazon, although social and religious ties were stronger among them owing to their access to more developed communities (Wagley, 1953).

The Shoshoneans developed a higher level of sociocultural integration and a cross-culturally significant type only after the whites entered their country and horses were introduced. The multifamily, mounted, predatory bands depended upon raiding the new resources brought by the whites. In this respect they differed from the mounted Plains tribes, which subsisted by hunting bison, and resembled such peoples as the Apache, whose forays made them the scourge of the Southwest, the Puelche and certain tribes of the southern Gran Chaco in South America, and perhaps some of the Asiatic horse nomads, whose existence was at least quasiparasitic through raiding activities.

The full significance of the predatory band as a cultural type warrants detailed comparative study, for it is not now possible to say what people belong to this type. There is no doubt, however, that the type has conceptual validity. Moreover, it should be stressed that the cross-cultural significance of this type consists of form and function rather than element content. The Shoshoneans, Apache, Puelche, and Asiatics were very unlike in specific details of behavior. They belonged to different culture areas, but they had the same type of culture.

The final phase of Shoshonean culture history has been sketched in Chapter 3. When the Indian wars ended, the people who did not enter reservations rapidly adapted themselves to the new white society by working for ranches, mines, or taking odd jobs in the new towns. The very absence of aboriginal band or community institutions made this adjustment easier. The principal obstacle to rapid and complete assimilation into the subculture of the local white American communities was and still is race relations, which bar the Shoshoneans from full participation in many crucial aspects of the American way of life.

7

The Patrilineal Band[1]

Loose aggregates of comparatively independent families such as those of the Shoshoni occur only rarely because in most parts of the world subsistence patterns required sufficient regularity of co-operation and leadership to give definite form and stability to multifamily social groups. There are many kinds of such multifamily groups of which the patrilineal band is but one.

The patrilineal band illustrates several concepts. First, it is a cultural type whose essential features — patrilineality, patrilocality, exogamy, land ownership, and lineage composition — constituted a cultural core which recurred cross-culturally with great regularity, whereas many details of technology, religion, and other aspects of culture represent independent variables, the nature of which was determined by diffusion or by unique local circumstances. Second, its cultural core resulted from ecological adaptations which, under the recurrent conditions of environment and subsistence technology, could vary only within minor limits. Third, it represents a level of sociocultural integration slightly higher than that of the Shoshoni family; for its multifamily aggregates found cohesion not only in kinship relations

[1] This is an adaptation and expansion of the article, "The Economic and Social Basis of Primitive Bands," in *Essays in Honor of A. L. Kroeber* (University of California Press, 1936), pp. 331-50.

122

but in co-operative hunting, in common landownership, and to some extent in joint ceremonies.

I shall analyze the cultures of these bands as they occurred among the Bushmen of South Africa, some of the Congo Negritos of Central Africa, some Philippine Negritos, the Australians, the Tasmanians, some southern California Shoshonean-speaking groups, and the Ona of Tierra del Fuego. Other tribes besides those covered in the present survey no doubt had the same pattern.

The essential features of these bands are most readily explained as the independent product of similar patterns of adaptation of technology and certain social forms to the environment. There are only two other possible explanations of the patrilineal band. First, that the pattern was borrowed from neighboring tribes. This explanation is untenable since their neighbors did not have the pattern. Second, that the pattern is the heritage of some archaic culture which developed at an early period of human history and has been preserved ever since. Perhaps some social patterns do have great persistence, but they must meet some need. It would be stretching credulity much too far to suppose that a pattern which is closely adapted to a special kind of subsistence had persisted for thousands of years among tribes who had wandered through dozens of unlike environments to the remotest corners of the earth, especially when other hunting and gathering tribes had lost these patterns and acquired types of society appropriate to their mode of life. Moreover, like most cultural historical theories, neither the hypothesis of diffusion nor of archaic heritage provides an explanation of how and why the patrilineal band developed in the first place. The cultural ecological hypothesis on the other hand is not only explanatory but it is by far the simplest and most consistent with the facts.

The cultural ecological explanation of the patrilineal band hinges on an identity of exploitative patterns rather than of technology or environment. Technology and environment were similar in crucial respects, but they were not identical in their totality. Cultures do not exploit their entire environments, and it is, therefore, necessary to consider only those features which bear upon the productive patterns. The environments of the patrilineal bands were similar in that, first, they had limited and scattered food resources, which not only restricted population to a low density but which prevented it from assembling in large, permanent aggregates. Second, the principal food resource was game, which unlike wild seeds, may be profitably taken collectively. Third, the game occurred in small, nonmigratory bands rather than in large, migratory herds. This kind of game can support only small aggregates of people, who remain within a restricted territory. Large herds, on the other hand, support much larger aggregates who can remain together as they follow the herds. These latter aggregates were bilateral or composite bands.

Dispersed and small game herds are, therefore, a condition of patrilineal bands, but this does not mean identity of environment, for deserts, jungles, and mountains tend to limit the number of game and the distance it could wander. Of the tribes examined here, the Bushmen, Australians, and southern California Shoshoneans lived in areas which had sparse game because of extreme aridity. Moreover, all were affected by the limited sources of water. In Tierra del Fuego, the habitat is one of wet plains but guanaco and small rodents, the principal foods, were scattered and nonmigratory. The Congo Negritos and the Philippine Negritos lived in the tropical rain forests, the former in lowlands and the latter in mountains.

Exploitative technology of these societies varied considerably in detail, but in all cases it included weapons of about equal efficiency and hunting patterns which entailed as much co-operation as circumstances permitted. The Bushmen used bows, poisoned arrows, clubs, pitfalls, poisoned springs, grass fires, dogs, and surrounds. The Congo Negritos employed bows, poisoned and nonpoisoned arrows, spears, knives, and long game nets. The Shoshoneans had bows, thrown clubs, traps, nets, surrounds, and drives. The Ona used bows, spears, clubs, slings, and spring pole nooses. Australian technology may have been less efficient in that it lacked the bow, but it included clubs, spears, and the spear-thrower. The sociological effect of hunting scattered game individually or collectively was the same everywhere.

The interaction between a bow-spear-club technology and a small, nonmigratory herd food resource tended to produce the patrilineal band. This type of band was the normal result of the adaptive processes of cultural ecology, and though various factors constantly operated to destroy the ideal pattern, as will be shown, interaction of technology and environment was such as to restore it. Only a basic change in environment or technology could have eliminated the patrilineal band. The inevitability of such bands under the given conditions is shown by its persistence along with clans, moieties, and other special patterns in the different groups, and, in the case of the Congo, an interdependence of the hunting Negritos and farming Bantu tribes who inhabited the same area.

With a given population density, the size of the territory and of the band which owns it are direct variables. If the group is enlarged the territory must also be increased in order to support it. Among the ethnic groups in question, however, the population is sparse, ranging from a maximum which seldom exceeds one person per 5 square miles to one person per 50 or more square miles. This prevents indefinite enlargement of the band because there would be no means of transporting the food to the people or the people to the food. The area which the band can conveniently forage averages some 100 square miles and seldom exceeds 500 square miles, a tract roughly 20 miles to a side. Consequently, the band averages 50 individuals and seldom exceeds 100.[2] Only in regions of unusual resources — for example, where there are herds of migratory game — does the group size surpass these figures.

We now have to consider why these bands are patrilineal. First, it is characteristic of hunters in regions of sparse population for postmarital residence to be patrilocal. This has several causes. If human beings could be conceived stripped of culture, it is not unreasonable to suppose that innate male dominance would give men a commanding position.[3] If, in addition to native dominance, however, the position of the male is strengthened by his greater economic importance, as in a hunting culture,[4] or even if women are given greater economic importance than men, it is extremely probable that postmarital residence will be patrilocal.

But in these small bands patrilocal residence will produce the fact or fiction that all members of the band are patrilineally related[5] and hence matrimonially taboo. Band exogamy — that is local exogamy —

---

[2] Wilhelm Koppers observes that 15 to 20 individuals is common and about 100 the probable limit. See Wilhelm Koppers, *Die Anfänge des menschlichen Gemeinschaftslebens* (Vienna, 1921), p. 72.

[3] Bingham observed gorillas in a state of nature in groups of eight to twenty-two individuals, each group under a dominant male; chimpanzees are said to be similar; and it is probable that the males among the baboons observed in nature by Zuckerman had a comparable dominance. See Harold C. Bingham, *Gorillas in a Native Habitat*. Report Joint Expedition of 1929-1932 by Yale University and Carnegie Institution of Washington for Psychobiological Study of Mountain Gorillas (*Gorilla berengei*) in Parc National Albert, Belgian Congo, Africa (1932). Also see S. Zuckerman, *The Social Life of Monkeys and Apes* (New York: Harcourt, Brace and Company, 1932).

[4] E.g., the extraordinarily low status of women in the arduous hunting area of northern Canada. Radcliffe-Brown has observed that Australian hunters would be much less successful in territory which was not known to them from childhood.

[5] Relationship is seldom traced beyond three generations among these people.

is therefore required. Probably at one time or another such bands have actually consisted of relatives with traceable connection. Genealogical data on the tribes of southern California, for example, show that more often than not the band comprises a true 'patrilineal lineage. Because life is so precarious that increase of the total population is impossible and budding collateral lineages often become extinct, the possibility is small that several independent families which have no traceable connection will develop in any band. Such families will occur only if the band is extraordinarily large. And even in this case, the fiction of relationship may be perpetuated after the connection is forgotten if group unity is reinforced by patronymy, myths, and other factors.[6]

For these reasons, the bands of hunters who live in sparsely populated areas must ordinarily be patrilineal. But special factors may make them temporarily composite. Thus, if unrelated and hence intermarriageable families exist within a band, local exogamy and patrilocal residence with respect to the band are unnecessary. This will occur when parallel-cousin marriage is permitted or where bands have, for various reasons, become unusually large and lack any factor that would create or perpetuate a fiction of relationship between its members. Occasionally, matrilocal residence will introduce families which are not related patrilineally into a band. This will prevent strictly patrilineal inheritance of band territory and tend to weaken the fiction of relationship between band members. For these reasons, patrilineal bands at certain times or places deviate from the ideal pattern and consist of unrelated families. In this respect, they resemble composite bands, but whereas the latter normally must remain composite, patrilineal bands tend to return to their typical pattern. The factors which produce composite bands will be analyzed subsequently.

Political unity in all bands is very similar. Centralized control exists only for hunting, for rituals, and for the few other affairs that are communal. Consequently, the leader has temporary and slight authority. In patrilineal bands, he is usually the head of the lineage, which, being a status based on kinship, is usually not formally institutionalized. The shaman, however, controls many collective activities, and he is feared and respected for his supernatural power, which often gives him more influence than the other leaders. Bands which are

---

[6] I make no effort to solve the very difficult problem of why there are incest laws at all. Marriage with relatives to the third generation, i.e., cousins, is taboo in most of these cases, although cross-cousin and even parallel-cousin marriage is permitted among several.

ordinarily autonomous may temporarily unite for special occasions such as Australian and Fuegian initiation ceremonies. Although the reason for this larger unity is religious and social, food supply strictly limits the duration of multiband gatherings.

The occurrence of clans among Australians, Ojibway, and others, of moieties in Australia and in southern California, and of other social forms in no way affects the cause-and-effect relationships involved in the formation of the patrilineal band. Such institutions are variables with respect to the pattern we have analyzed. Their presence or absence is to be explained by diffusion or by some special local factors and not by adaptations of technology to environment.

TRIBES WITH THE PATRILINEAL BAND

In the following pages some patrilineal bands will be discussed in detail, showing reasons in each case for departures from the ideal pattern.

The Bushmen[7]

A hunting and gathering culture imposed upon an arid and unproductive native environment produced a sparse population among the Bushmen. Population aggregates were necessarily small,[8] and the group that co-operated in various undertakings was a politically autonomous patrilineal lineage. Although the band or lineage split seasonally into smaller units, probably family groups, it owned and communally utilized a definite territory. Some hunting required joint effort of all band members, and game was often shared by all.

The bands of the Northwestern Bushmen, including the Heikum, were ordinarily patrilineal owing to patrilocal residence and local or band exogamy. The Naron bands, however, were sometimes composite

---

[7] This section is based on I. Schapera, "A Preliminary Consideration of the Relationship between the Hottentots and the Bushmen," *South African Journal of Science,* XXIII (1926), 833-66; I. Schapera, *The Khoisan Peoples of South Africa* (London, 1930); S. S. Dornan, *Pygmies and Bushmen of the Kalahari* (London, 1925); E. J. Dunn, *The Bushman* (London, 1931); George W. Stow, *The Native Races of South Africa* (New York, 1905); S. Passarge, *Die Buschmanner der Kalahari* (Berlin, 1907).

[8] Schapera, *The Khoisan Peoples of South Africa,* pp. 67-81, has gleaned a few figures on band size from various sources: Cape Bushman, who were seriously affected by foreign contacts, 100 to 150, according to one estimate, and 3 to 4 families each, according to a more recent figure; Heichware, 20; Kalahari, 30; !Okung, not exceeding 30; Northwestern Bushmen, ranging from 20 to 150 and probably averaging 50 to 60 each.

because matrilocal residence, which was practiced occasionally in order that the wife's mother might help the wife with her children, introduced families which were not related patrilineally into the same band. This weakened patrilineal inheritance of the estate and tended to obviate the necessity of band exogamy, which, however, was preferred (Schapera, 1930: 81-85). The Cape, Namib, and !Okung bands also tended to be composite because, although band exogamy was preferred, matrilocal residence, for a reason which has not been revealed, was sometimes practiced. Band endogamy, moreover, was facilitated by cousin marriage, parallel or cross, which was barred among the Northwestern groups (Schapera, 1930:82-83; 102-07).

Schebesta (1931) reports what appears to be an identical pattern. The Bambuti, Efe, Bac'wa, and Batwa of the Belgian Congo had exogamous, patrilocal, and generally autonomous sibs ("sippe") or families of male relatives numbering sixty to sixty-five persons each. Apparently, the "totemic clans" of these people were the same as lineages, that is, they were localized clans or sibs.

Central African Negritos

Several scattered groups of Negritos or pygmies living in the dense tropical rain forests of the Congo in equatorial Africa also belonged to the patrilineal band type. The bands were predominantly hunters, and the exploitative patterns produced the features typical of the patrilineal band despite the fact that the pygmies lived in a close dependency relationship with the Bantu Negroes.

In the Ituri Forest (Putnam, 1948:322-42), a Negro village and a pygmy band jointly owned about 100 square miles of country. The Negroes were largely farmers, and the pygmies were entirely hunters, the latter supplying the former with meat in exchange for vegetable foods. The dependence of the pygmy upon the Negro might account for the cohesion of the pygmy band and for the pattern of land-tenure, but it would not account for the patrilineality and exogamy, which must be explained by the low population density, the small band size, and the predominance of hunting.

The bands ranged in size from 100 to 200 persons, 150 being the average. All families were normally related through the male line, and the band, therefore, constituted a locally exogamous and patrilocal group. The cohesion of the lineage or band was reinforced by the belief that a totemic animal was the ancestor of the band and by myths. The band contained unrelated families only when exceptional circumstances introduced a man from some other band, for example, when a man could not get along in his own band or when he had trouble with his Negro group. The patrilineal features resulted from the hunting pattern. The men spent all their time hunting for game which was normally scattered. They used nets in collective drives or else bows, spears, and knives in individual stalking. The game was varied and included turtles, rats, antelope, buffalo, and elephants. Hunting was restricted to the band's territory, the size of which must be interpreted as the optimum which can be exploited. Had the territory been substantially larger, the band would have surpassed a kin group in size and therefore ceased to be exogamous and patrilocal. However, the sparse population, the limitations upon the area which could be hunted, and the patrilocality after marriage produced localized lineages.

These bands sometimes tended to be composite for two reasons. First, it was customary at marriage for the husband's band to furnish a woman who married a member of his wife's band. When no woman was available, the man lived with his wife's people. Second, band endogamy, that is, marriage between related members of the band, though felt to be a breach of incest laws, was often practiced when other bands were remote and inaccessible (Schmidt, 1910:173).

The Negritos of Gabon in French Equatorial Africa were grouped in some 100 or 150 villages, each of which usually comprised one family "rangée sous l'authorité d'un seul chef, le père du clan, généralement de 30 a 35 individus males." These seemed to be independent, patrilocal, and exogamous, and therefore true patrilineal bands. But they belonged to some kind of larger patrilineal totemic clans, which were preferably, but not always, exogamous (Trilles, 1932: 20-23, 143-51, 409-18).

Semang

The more or less inadequate information now available indicates that many of the Negritos of the Malay peninsula possessed the patrilineal band. Largely hunters and gatherers and more or less isolated in the sparsely settled mountain forests, the Semang groups were small, ranging, according to fragments of evidence recorded by Schebesta (1929), from individual families which were probably temporary subdivisions to groups of 50 or more persons. These seem to have been politically autonomous, landowning bands. Skeat and Blagden (1900: 495-97) say that the Kedah Semang band often amounted to an enlarged family and, somewhat obscurely, that the chief was practically "the head of a family, which in this case is represented by a larger family, the tribe." It may be, however, that band territory was some-times further subdivided among bilateral families so that each owned an area for its durian trees. Schebesta says (1929:83, 234, 279) that "the individual groups wander within the tribal boundaries but always return to their family territory, especially at the time of the durian crop" and that the trees are owned by men as family heads. These family tracts were, perhaps, comparable to the Algonkian and Althabaskan beaver-trapping territories.

That these bands were truly patrilineal is indicated by Schebesta's statement (1929) that the unit of society was the "sib" like that of the Congo Negritos, but he does not particularize its characteristics. Elsewhere he observes that there was considerable band exogamy and patrilocal residence, although he recorded one band that was com-posite. One reason for the occurrence of the latter among the Kenta Semang was that durian trees were sometimes inherited matrilineally. This would, of course, favor matrilocal residence and tend to set up a composite band.

Philippine Negritos

The predominantly hunting and gathering Philippine Negritos lived in comparative isolation from the Malaysians. They were clustered in bands which Vanoverbergh (1925:430-33), says comprise "a certain group of families." These remained in the same portion of the forest and seasonally exploited different parts of an area which had a radius of not over twenty miles. Trespass on the land of neighboring bands was not forbidden but was avoided. The land was hunted communally by its owners, but cultivated trees and honey nests were privately owned. It is not recorded, however, how trees were inherited. Bands seem to have been politically autonomous, but the lack of an institu-tionalized band chief is implied by the somewhat vague statement that authority rested in the father of the family.

There is some indication that Philippine Negrito bands have re-cently changed from patrilineal to composite. Schmidt (1910:72-73), quoting Blumentritt on the Zambales-Bataam, says that the bands are now endogamous but at the end of the eighteenth century were exogamous. Present-day endogamy is further shown by the presence of unrelated families in the same band.[9] Nevertheless, patrilocal residence

---

[9] Morice Vanoverbergh, "Negritos of Northern Luzon," *Anthropos*, XXV (1930), 538-39, found that some bands contained related males and also that related males occurred in different bands.

is recorded, although it is not clear whether residence is patrilocal with respect to the band or the family.

There is, therefore, some doubt as to the frequency of the two types of bands and the customs concerning residence and other matters which would produce them. It appears, however, that some factor has tended to produce a change from patrilineal to composite bands during the past century. At least one important cause of composite bands today is the practice of marrying cousins. Although marriage was preferably between cross-cousins, parallel-cousins were eligible for matrimony (Vanoverberg, 1925:425-28).

Australians[10]

The relatively low productivity of Australia permitted but a sparse population which averaged only 1 person per 12 square miles for the entire continent.[11] The population was grouped into relatively small, autonomous bands which Radcliffe-Brown calls hordes. Each band comprised 20 to 50 individuals and owned 100 to 150 square miles of land. The male members of the band inherited and communally hunted their tract, which was definitely bounded and protected from trespass.[12]

These bands were truly patrilineal, and they approximated male lineages. They were almost universally exogamous and patrilocal. The idea of relationship between band members was further reinforced by kinship terminology. Even those ethnic groups which had moieties, sections (formerly called "marriage classes"), and matrilineal clans and totems had not, except in a portion of western Australian, lost the patrilineal band (Radcliffe-Brown, 1931:438).

---

[10] This material is largely from A. R. Radcliffe-Brown, "Former Numbers and Distribution of the Australian Aborigines," *Official Yearbook of the Commonwealth of Australia,* No. 23 (1930), pp. 671-96; and Radcliffe-Brown, "The Social Organization of Australian Tribes, I-III," *Oceania,* I (1930, 1931), 34-63, 204-46, 426-56 (especially pp. 436-39, 455).

[11] Radcliffe-Brown, *Official Yearbook of the Commonwealth of Australia,* No. 23 (1930), p. 696. The population range was 1 person per 2 square miles in the most fertile section to 1 per 38 square miles in the more arid regions.

[12] D. Sutherland Davidson, "The Family Hunting Territory in Australia," *American Anthropologist, n.s.,* XXX (1928), 614-32. Davidson has collected evidence that in some localities the landowning group was the bilateral family. It is the opinion of Radcliffe-Brown, *Oceania,* I (1931), 438, however, that "the particularism of the family whereby it might tend to become an isolated unit is neutralized by the horde [i.e., band] solidarity."

Tasmanians

Information on the Tasmanians, though incomplete, indicates the aboriginal presence of the patrilineal band. The scant population[13] was divided into autonomous bands of 30 to 40 persons each. Each band owned a tract of land on which it wandered seasonally in search of food. It protected its hunting rights against trespass, which was a common cause of war (Roth, 1899:58-59, 104-07).

The Tasmanian band must have been patrilineal, for evidence assembled by Roth indicates, although it does not prove beyond question, that the band was exogamous and marriage patrilocal.

The Ona of Tierra del Fuego

The Ona of Tierra del Fuego fall strictly into the patrilineal band pattern. The low subsistence level, based largely upon guanaco hunting, produced a population of only one individual to 4.5 or 5 square miles. This was grouped in politically independent bands of 40 to 120 persons, each owning an average of 410 square miles. Gusinde (1931) believes that the manner of life would not have supported larger aggregates. Each territory was named, band rights to it were sanctioned by myths, and hunting privileges were protected against trespass. Although each band was politically autonomous, there was no institution of chief.

The band was patrilineal because it was exogamous and patrilocal. Local exogamy was required even among the large bands in which relationship between members was not traceable, for native theory held that each band was a male lineage.

Tehuelche of Patagonia

The Tehuelche of Patagonia, although very incompletely known, are instructive when compared with the Ona. Also dependent largely upon herds of guanaco, their economic life appears formerly to have resembled that of the Fuegians. There is evidence that they were divided into bands, each having some degree of localization[14] and led in its travels, etc., by a patrilineal chief (Outes and Bruch, 1910:126;

---

[13] Radcliffe-Brown, *Official Yearbook of the Commonwealth of Australia*, No. 23 (1930), p. 695, gives the aboriginal total as probably 2,000 or 3,000, which is one person to 8 or 13 square miles.

[14] Antonio Serrano, *Los Primitivos Habitantes del Territorio Argentino* (Buenos Aires, 1930), p. 157. Nuñoz, quoted by Serrano, says that among the Northern Tehuelche the head chief owned the land and that the lesser chiefs could not change their land without giving notice to him.

Beerbohn, 1881:93) who was called "father" (Musters, 1873:194). The band chief, however, acknowledged a general cacique, who, according to Musters, had very little authority. The institution of general or tribal cacique may easily have developed subsequent to the arrival of the European.

The introduction of the horse about a century and a half ago completely altered ecological conditions in Patagonia. It enabled people to move widely in pursuit of guanaco herds and to transport foods considerable distances. This would, of course, have tended to eliminate band ownership of small parcels of territory, even had it existed. It also permitted enlargement of population aggregates far beyond the size of the usual lineage. Further motivation for amalgamation of formerly separate bands was provided by internecine strife, which was stimulated by competition for foods and war against the white man. The political unit consequently increased in size and had a single, although not absolute, chief. Thus, in 1871, bands numbered as many as 400 or 500 persons, although they occasionally split into smaller groups (Musters, 1873:64, 70, 96-97, 117, 188). As there is no mention of exogamy of any form, it must be assumed that these bands were composite. This is common elsewhere in bands of such size.

Southern Californians

The Shoshonean-speaking Serrano, Cahuilla, and Luiseño, and some of the Yuman-speaking Diegueño of southern California were divided into patrilineal bands. This region is exceptional in that abundance of acorns and other wild seeds permitted the unusually dense native population of one person per square mile. But this great density was accompanied by small territory size rather than large band size, probably because the very few and small sources of water prevented greater concentration of people. Therefore, bands averaged only fifty individuals and the territory only fifty square miles.

The other factors producing the patrilineal bands were those which operated elsewhere. Because of patrilocal residence coupled with the small size of the bands, most of them were actual patrilineal lineages, so local exogamy was required. In addition, a band chief, "priest," ceremonies, ceremonial house and bundle, and myths contributed to group cohesion (Strong, 1927, 1929; Gifford, 1918, 1926, 1931; Kroeber, 1925, 1934). This strongly fortified patrilineal pattern may also have served to maintain the band at lineage size.

The culturally similar neighboring Cupeño provide an illuminating contrast to these groups. Because the local abundance of food and water permitted greater concentration, they were able to live in two permanent towns, each numbering some 250 persons. Each village contained several lineages and had a chief. Bands were, therefore, of the composite type (Gifford, 1926:394-96; Strong, 1929:188-90, 233).

CAUSAL FORMULATION FOR PATRILINEAL BANDS

In any society there are certain cultural factors which potentially give cohesion to aggregates of several families: marriage, extension of kinship ties and corollary extensions of incest taboos, group ceremonies, myths, games, and other features. These features may be derived from cultural heritage of the group or they may be borrowed from neighboring tribes. In each group they are integrated in a total socio-cultural system, but the nature of this system is not explained merely by tracing the diversified history of the features or by describing the functional interdependency of the parts. These features must be adjusted to the subsistence patterns that are established through the exploitation of a particular habitat by means of a particular technology; and the subsistence patterns are only partly explainable in terms of culture history. The use of bows and arrows, traps, hunting nets, game drives, or grass firing can generally be traced to diffusion, but the hunting patterns and the social effect of these patterns are quite unlike in areas of sparse and scattered game and in areas of large herds of migratory game. Among societies which devote a very great portion of their time and energy to food-getting, these differences in hunting patterns will greatly affect the size, permanency, composition, and general behavior patterns of the group. The extent and degree to which subsistence patterns affect the total structure of the society and the functional integration of its various parts are questions to be answered by empirical procedure.

The patrilineal band represents a social type the principal features of which are determined within exceedingly narrow limits by the cultural ecology — by the interaction of technology and environment. Other features, such as clans, moieties, age-grades, men's tribal societies, group ceremonialism, totemism, and mythology may or may not also be present. If they do form part of the cultural inventory of the band, they are integrated to the patrilineal pattern. A causal formulation of the factors producing the patrilineal band may therefore omit these various historically-derived features, for the latter are of interest only when attention is shifted to the uniqueness of each culture and they do not help explain the patrilineal features which are the subject of inquiry.

The factors which produce the patrilineal band are:

(1) A population density of one person or less — usually much less — per square mile, which is caused by a hunting and gathering technology in areas of scarce wild foods;

(2) An environment in which the principal food is game that is nonmigratory and scattered, which makes it advantageous for men to remain in the general territory of their birth;

(3) Transportation restricted to human carriers;

(4) The cultural-psychological fact, which cannot be explained by local adaptation, that groups of kin who associate together intimately tend to extend incest taboos from the biological family to the extended family thus requiring group exogamy.

These four factors interact as follows: The scattered distribution of the game, the poor transportation, and the general sparsity of the population make it impossible for groups that average over 50 or 60 persons and that have a maximum of about 100 to 150 persons to associate with one another frequently enough and to carry out sufficient joint activities to maintain social cohesion. The band consists of persons who habitually exploit a certain territory over which its members can conveniently range. Customary use leads to the concept of ownership. Were individual families to wander at will, hunting the game in neighboring areas, competition would lead to conflict. Conflict would call for alliance with other families, allies being found in related families. As the men tend to remain more or less in the territory in which they have been reared and with which they are familiar, patrilineally related families would tend to band together to protect their game resources. The territory would therefore become divided among these patrilineal bands.

It is worth noting that the nature of Great Basin Shoshonean land-use precluded the banding together of patrilineal families and land-ownership. For two reasons, the pine nut, which was the principal food, had a very different sociological effect than game hunting. First, good crops were so abundant that there was never competition for it. Second, abundant crops occurred each year in very different localities and they brought different groups together each time.

Among the patrilineal bands, the component biological families associated together sufficiently often to permit an extension of incest taboos to all members. Prohibition of marriage within the immediate biological family is universal among mankind. There are generally extensions of marriage restrictions to collateral relatives of the second or third degree, though cross-cousins may marry in certain cultures. The patrilineal bands were so small that they usually consisted of known relatives who commonly fall within the prohibited degrees of relationship, and cross-cousins — the father's sister's daughter or the mother's brother's daughter — would normally be in another band. Band exogamy is therefore required.

The several features of the patrilineal band reinforce one another. Patrilocal residence after marriage because the male wishes to remain in country he knows causes an area to be habitually occupied, utilized, and defended by patrilineally-related families. Local exogamy prevents the introduction into the band of unrelated families, so that the band becomes in fact, a patrilineal lineage.

The requirement that the band be exogamous may persist after traceable kinship relations in the group are forgotten if the patrilineal complex is reinforced by other features, such as names, kinship terminology, myths, ceremonies, totems, and the like. Thus, the bands of Australia, southern California, and Tierra del Fuego conform more rigidly to the pattern because they possess such supports. Among the Bushmen and Negritos patrilineal bands may often temporarily become composite bands when special conditions exist.

A theory of the patrilineal band which sought its origin in purely cultural-historical terms would be confronted by insuperable difficulties. Such a theory would have to assume either that the band inherited the basic patrilineal pattern from some archaic world-wide culture or that it borrowed it from some neighboring tribes. As we have seen, primitive nonagricultural peoples in areas of seed resources, of fish, or of large game herds do not have the patrilineal band because these areas are not conducive to the exploitation of a certain restricted territory by small groups of men in the manner found among the patrilineal band peoples. It is inconceivable that this pattern could have survived the migrations of mankind over dozens of unlike environments during thousands of years. The theory of borrowing from neighbors will not stand up because the neighbors of these tribes simply do not have patrilineal bands.

A holistic or functional explanation minimizes the importance of cultural ecology by insisting that all features of the culture are equally cause and effect. This simply evades the issue of causality. As we have seen, the clans, moieties, men's tribal societies, and other special features occur with only some of the patrilineal patterns and they also occur among quite different kinds of societies. There is a functional interrelationship between hunting in a restricted area, the male's continued residence in that area, patrilocality, and local exogamy. Exogamy within a localized patrilineal group causes the men to hunt scattered game in certain ways. The groups hunt what is available with devices at their command; men best remain in the territory where they were raised; their wives come to their territory after marriage; and the bands are so small that people are related and, given concepts of incest, local exogamy is practiced. It is not claimed that the cultural ecological factors explain everything about the patrilineal band. They explain why these bands differ from other bands which have a similar technology and similar potentialities for extending incest taboos outward from the biological family.

A common explanation of the patrilineal band is that it is merely a localized clan, and diffusionists seek to trace its source to clans elsewhere. Societies which have clans may influence patrilineal bands in two ways; first, borrowed clans may crosscut the bands but fail to change their basic patterns; second, clan myths, ceremonies, and other features may be borrowed by the band and reinforce its local unity. But diffused unilateral structure and exogamy cannot explain the adjustment of male lineages to exploitative activities. In fact, the concept of the patrilineal band has greater value in explaining the clan than vice versa. If, for reasons stated here, a localized patrilineal group develops, it is in effect a localized clan. Whether it should properly be called a clan, however, would depend upon whether it is exogamous regardless of locality. Those groups which have reinforcing features, such as the southern California Shoshoneans, the Australians, and others, would be clans if exogamy continued after they were dislocated from their territories and the different bands mixed up. Evidently this has happened often in human history, and clans have developed in many places. We shall subsequently show how the data of archaeology and ethnology support such an interpretation of the origin of clans among the Pueblo Indians of the Southwest.

CULTURAL VARIABLES AND THE PATRILINEAL BAND

The features of the patrilineal band which must be explained by ecological factors are patrilineality, patrilocality, exogamy, landownership, and informal and limited leadership. Many other features, however, were fairly variable in form despite this basic pattern. A substantial range of possible alternatives made diffusion a more direct explanation of their presence.

Some of the technological traits secondary to the main hunting patterns were extremely variable. Containers used in transporting, preparing, and storing food, for example, could not be elaborate, heavy, or numerous because of the nomadic life, but the materials of which they were made, their specific forms, and their decorations were quite variable. The Congo Negritos, Semang, Shoshoneans, and Ona used basketry of various weaves, shapes, and ornamentation; the Bushmen and Congo Negritos employed some pottery; the other areas utilized skins, shells, bark, or other convenient materials. Fire was made with the wooden drill by the Bushmen and Shoshoneans, with the fire saw by the Semang, and with pyrite and stone by the Ona. The Congo Negritos had no means of making fire and were forced to borrow it if their own went out. Shelters were limited by the requirement that they be quickly and easily put together of materials available. These bands used natural shelters, such as caves, when possible. Otherwise, they built mere windbreaks, brush- or skin-covered conical lodges, or dome-shaped brush houses. Similar huts are found scattered throughout the world among primitive peoples, and it would be rather profitless to speculate as to whether they diffused or not, for they are so elementary that it would require no great ingenuity to invent them. Clothing was scant and made with simple skills, but styles varied locally: string skirts or aprons, wrap-around skin skirts, breechclouts, robes, and the like, or perhaps nothing but a few smudges of paint.

Musical instruments and games were generally simple, for extensive paraphernalia was out of the question. The former were generally learned from neighboring tribes. For example, the Semang used flutes, jew's-harps, guitars, and drums borrowed from their Malay neighbors; and the Bushmen had musical bows, flutes, cocoon rattles, and drums, all probably acquired from the Bantu; while the southern California Shoshoneans used only flutes and rattles; the Australians swung bull-roarers and pounded sticks on rolled-up hides; the Ona struck sticks together; and the African Negritos thumped hollow logs.

A certain distinctiveness is evident in many features of social organization. While the formal aspects of these are attributable to diffusion, their functional significance was very similar because of their role in the total culture. Several of the bands had men's tribal societies — religious organizations into which young men were initiated during rites from which women and children were barred. The neophytes were scarified, given hunting tests, and made to observe food taboos, while religion was explained to them. The Australian societies used bull-roarers in their ceremonies, whereas the Ona used masks and special huts and had rites based on the concept of death and resurrection of the initiate. Southern California Shoshoneans lacked such societies, but their group fetish bundle, ritual, and ceremonial leader had a similar function in reinforcing group cohesion. These and other social features, however, were not necessary to existence of the patrilineal band pattern, and they can hardly constitute the primary basis of cultural typology. The Semang have no men's society.

The presence in any society of the patrilineal band and the tribal society must be "explained" in different terms. The secret society is scattered throughout the world in many kinds of cultures and there is little doubt that it represents a very ancient pattern which has fitted certain psychological-cultural needs as well as a variety of cultural functions so well that it has persisted in spite of tremendous cultural change and that it has even diffused from one type of culture to another. The secret society can in no way be considered a cause of the patrilineal pattern or of the type of land use that underlies this pattern.

There were other social features which, from the point of view of the patrilineal pattern, were secondary or variable and which were found also among tribes lacking the patrilineal band. Some of the northern Australians had matrilineal moieties, which were probably diffused from Melanesia. The combination of these with localized, patrilineal, exogamous groups created a very complex organization. The uniqueness of this organization — the fact that it consisted of functionally interrelated parts — does not mean that the origin of its parts cannot be treated separately and in causal terms. The southern California Shoshoneans had moieties which cut across localized patrilineal bands, but these functioned primarily at death ceremonies.

The religious patterns of these tribes were affected by the ecological adjustments principally in a negative sense: they lacked complicated and institutionalized worship of the kinds found among more developed cultures, there being little ceremonialism dedicated to group purposes. Rites were concerned primarily with birth, puberty, sickness, death, and other crisis situations of individuals. The patterns of these crisis rites and of shamanism show certain general similarity to one another and very probably they represent in large part an ancient heritage which survived throughout the world in cultures of

Table 1. PATRILINEAL BANDS

	Number of persons per square mile	Average size of band	Average number of square miles in band territory	Permanent residence patrilocal with respect to band	Exogamy of band, i.e., locality, required	Band politically autonomous, weak chief	References and remarks
N.W. Bushmen	?	50-60	?	X	X	X	Schapera, 1926, 1930; Dornan, 1925:85; Stow, 1905:33, 229-30; Dunn, 1931:7, 22
Congo Negritos-Bambuti, Efe, Bac'wa, Batwa	?	60-65	?	X	X	X	Schebesta, 1931; Schmidt, 1910
Negritos-Gabon	?	20-70	?	X	X	X	Trilles, 1932
Semang	½-⅛	35?	?		(X)	X	Schebesta, 1929; Skeat and Blagden, 1900
Australia—W	⅕	30	150	X	X	X	Radcliffe-Brown, 1930:688
—S	?	40 —	?	X	X	X	Radcliffe-Brown, 1930:690
Victoria	⅟₁₅	50+	750	X	X	X	Radcliffe-Brown, 1930:691
Queensland	³⁄₁₀	30	100	X	X	X	Radcliffe-Brown, 1930:694
Herbert R.	⅕	20-25	100	X	X	X	Radcliffe-Brown, 1930:696
Average	⅟₁₂	35	420	X	X	X	
Tasmania	⅛-⅟₁₃	30-40	350	X	X	X	Radcliffe-Brown, 1930:695; Roth, 1899
Ona	¼-⅕	40-120	410	X	X	X	Gusinde, 1931
California: Miwok, Luiseño, Serrano, Cahuilla, Cupeño	1	50	50	X	X	X	Gifford, 1926 Kroeber, 1925: 883, 58; Strong, 1927, 1929; Gifford, 1926
Diegueño (N&S)	½	50?	50?	X	X	X	Gifford, 1926

many kinds. That is, these rites show a great deal of stability, their basic patterns persisting in many cultural contexts which are quite dissimilar. This fact makes it obviously quite absurd to conceive that religion could be the starting point, the primary factor, in an investigation of the origin of social forms and economic patterns. Religion was a functional part of each culture, but from the point of view of the basic social types and cultural ecological determinants its form was a relatively independent variable.

The local forms and functions of the puberty rites are an illustration of the considerable range of variations that could be woven into the basic pattern of the patrilineal band. We have already seen how puberty rites stressed the maturing of young men among the Northwest Bushmen, the Australians, and the Ona to the extent that the adult males constituted a secret organization. The Congo Negritos may also have had such societies; at least, it is clear that in the Ituri Forest young Pygmy men together with the sons of their Negro overlords were circumcised in groups every few years, each group becoming an age-grade society. The other tribes wholly lacked any such formal grouping of their males. Among the Semang, children of both sexes were merely inducted into the status of puberty by a simple rite at which they were painted, tattooed, scarified, and had their teeth filed. The Shoshoneans of southern California, like their nonpatrilineal neighbors, had observances for both sexes. Pubescent girls were "roasted" in a pit and required to race each day, to scratch themselves only with a stick, and to refrain from drinking cold water. Boys were drugged, lectured on tribal lore and morality, subjected to biting ants, and required to dance. Among the Semang both sexes were painted, scarified, and tattooed at adolescence.

In all these tribes, as in hundreds of others throughout the world, the shaman's chief function was to cure disease by supernatural means, generally through singing and sucking out the supposed cause of disease. He had certain other functions, however, which varied with the special local patterning of religion. Among the Bushmen, for example, he officiated at puberty ceremonies, and among the Semang he mediated between mankind and the thunder god.

Death observances were matters of private ritual among most of these bands, but the Shoshoneans of southern California developed them into a ceremony which greatly strengthened group cohesion. An annual mourning ceremony was held under the direction of a special ceremonial leader, while images of the deceased were burned and myths were recited to commemorate the dying god. This ceremony seems to have contributed greatly to the cohesion of Shoshonean bands, and it may partly explain why the bands continued to regard themselves as kin groups and to practice exogamy after they became dislocated from their territories, scattered, and lost geneological knowledge of their relationship to one another.

8

The Composite Hunting Band[1]

The term "composite" is used in contrast to the term "unilineal" — patrilineal or matrilineal — to designate certain primitive societies which consist of many unrelated nuclear or biological families. These are integrated to form villages or bands of hunters, fishers, gatherers, and simple farmers on the basis of constant association and co-operation rather than of actual or alleged kinship. The present chapter describes the composite hunting band found among the Algonkian and Athabaskan Indians of Canada. This band illustrates but one of many types of multifamily organization found among primitive people. It is of theoretical importance to the discussion in the present volume for two reasons. First, although it represents about the same level of sociocultural integration as the patrilineal band, it is typologically different because it is produced by distinctive cultural ecological processes. In Canada, the composite hunting band occurred in an area of low population density and of primary reliance upon large

---

[1] This, like the last chapter, is an adaptation of a portion of the article, "The Economic and Social Basis of Primitive Bands," in *Essays in Honor of A. L. Kroeber* (University of California Press, 1936), pp. 331-50. It is separated from Chapter 7 because the composite band is typologically different from the patrilineal band.

herds of migratory game. Like the patrilineal band, it is politically autonomous and controls the principal resource in its hunting territory, but it is much larger than the patrilineal band and hence lacks band exogamy, patrilocal residence after marriage, and patrilineality. It consists of many unrelated families which may intermarry within the band.

The Canada hunting bands are of theoretical interest second because among many groups there co-existed family ownership of fairly small and precisely bounded areas for trapping fur-bearing animals, especially beaver, and band ownership of large areas for hunting game. While some authors, notably Speck, have contended that family trapping territories were aboriginal, the weight of evidence is fairly conclusive that they developed in response to the fur trade which created a market for beaver and other pelts and a source of much desired steel axes, pots, traps, guns, and other hardware.

As dependence upon the fur trade increased, the former hunting bands become rather permanently fragmented into family groups, each subsisting primarily upon trade goods acquired in exchange for the produce of its trapping area. Among the Montagnais of Labrador, as Leacock's study (1954) shows, each family is now linked to the larger Canadian society through the trader, missionary, and government officials more than to other Montagnais families through native band activities. These Indians now form a subcultural group within a contemporary national level type of sociocultural system. The Carrier Indians of British Columbia (Chapter 10) have undergone similar modification for the same reasons.

THE NORTHERN ALGONKIANS

The relatively unproductive environment of the nomadic hunting and gathering Algonkian-speaking tribes of Canada limited the population to one person per 5.3 square miles north of the Great Lakes and to one person per 34.6 or more square miles in the eastern sub-Arctic region (Kroeber, 1934:3-4). The political unit was the band, which generally numbered several hundred individuals. Each band had a patrilineal chief, usually it held seasonal festivals, and often it was slightly distinctive dialectically (Speck, 1915a, 1915b, 1917a, 1917b, 1922, 1923, 1927, 1928[2]). Fur-trapping territory, however, was

---

[2] In this excellent series of papers, Speck has recorded such bands, and the landowning families into which they are divided, among the Mistassini, Dumoine River and Kipawa Algonquins, the Timiskaming, Timagami, and White

owned by the family, which, according to Speck (1917a:85), consisted of the "individuals of one family connection, primarily through blood but also through marriage relationship, who hunt together as a herd within the confines of a certain tract of country." The family tract was and still is inherited patrilineally.

This family landownership bears an intimate functional relationship to the highly specialized economy introduced by the fur trade. Fur-bearing animals, especially the beaver, may be husbanded in relatively small areas (Speck, 1915b:293-95). Barter of pelts with the white man for other goods enables a group to subsist on an area which is smaller than would otherwise be possible. Jenness suggests that title to land originally rested in the band and that the family subdivision is a post-European development. He records, for example, that partition occurred among the Athabaskan-speaking Sekanni on the headwaters of the Peace River during the last hundred years, "after the necessities of the fur trade compelled the families to disperse among the different creeks and rivers." The author found in 1939 that the Carrier Indians of British Columbia had abandoned moiety-owned hunting territories in favor of individually owned trapping territories after the white man had stimulated the fur trade. It is understandable, therefore, that Montagnais families were apportioned their land in the time of the Jesuit missionaries (Jenness, 1932:124), and that Micmac family territories should be "less permanent, less hereditary . . . and the judicial power of the chief in the reassignment of territory . . . rather more definite" than elsewhere (Speck, 1922: 85-86). Among the Canadian Algonkians, the subsistence and land-owning unit has usually been the bilateral family in historic times. In aboriginal times, however, when hunting of large game, which ranges in herds far beyond the limits of the family trapping territories, was the principal subsistence activity, the multifamily, composite band was probably not only the political unit but also the landowning subsistence and social unit.

These bands are composite rather than patrilineal for several reasons. First, the segregation of family units, each of which is preferably patrilocal, prevents the band as such from being patrilocal. Second, each band is so large that any kinship connections of all

Earth Lake (Minnesota) Ojibway, the Montagnais, Abnaki, Penobscot, Micmac, Naskapi, Narragansett, Northern Salteaux, Passamaquoddy, Malecite, some Cree and even Pamunkey of Virginia. McLeod also attributes band organization to the Lenape of Delaware.

members of the band to one another would be forgotten, even if such connections had once existed, unless special factors were present to preserve the fiction.

The larger of the families[3] owning trapping territories may sometimes become patrilineal bands because patrilocal residence, if consistently practiced, would mold each into a male lineage. No doubt many are patrilineal bands, but supporting conditions have been too unstable to make this very frequent. Speck states that patrilocal and matrilocal residence depend "upon the number of sons or daughters in the family group, the conditions of physical ability of its members, whether the father is living, and the circumstances of the uncles, the conditions of the game . . . the conditions of the hunting district . . . upon temporary climatic conditions, and even upon personal circumstances." Therefore, although residence was preferably patrilocal and it was common for the oldest son to inherit the paternal hunting tract, his brothers often joined their wives' families (Speck, 1917a:97-98).

THE CANADIAN ATHABASKANS

The habitat of the Athabaskan-speaking tribes of the Canadian far north is so unfavorable that the population varied from only one person per fifty square miles to one person per eighty or more square miles, and some regions were virtually uninhabited. The population was nevertheless grouped in politically independent bands[4] which seem to have been definitely localized.

Speck (1928:329) quotes various sources to demonstrate that "segregated family hunting, trapping and fishing grounds exist among many of the tribes," especially in the west. Jenness, as already noted, believes that this is the result of the fur trade and that the entire band formerly utilized the land communally. Morice's observations bear the same implication. He says that "sedentary" game, chiefly the beaver, is

[3] The families are variable in size. Among the Mistassini they average 6 individuals, owning 15 square miles each (a greater per mile density than is given by Kroeber, probably owing to unusual local productivity); among the Toudasac and Escoumains Montagnais, 5 individuals owning 141 square miles; among the Penobscot, 18 individuals owning 500 to 2,000 square miles; among the Timiskaming, 34.4 individuals. Micmac family territory ranges up to 2,000 square miles.

[4] There were no chiefs. Prestige, skill, and other qualities gave temporary authority when leadership was required. See, e.g., Cornelius B. Osgood, "The Ethnography of the Great Bear Lake Indians," *National Museum of Canada Annual Report,* 1931, pp. 31-92; 1933, pp. 73-75.

regarded "as the object of a strict proprietorship as the domestic animals or personal chattels," whereas "nomadic" game, the larger animals which are taken primarily for their meat, is usually shared within the band when killed.[5] Osgood says that individual beaver-hunting territories exist now among the Satudene and Slave though they did not formerly (Osgood, 1931; 1933:41, 71). Birket-Smith (1930:69) believes that the collective nature of caribou hunting among the Chipewyan would preclude family hunting territory.

The Athabaskan band seems usually to have been composite, for Jenness (1932:123, 380, 381-84) observes that marriage in general "depended on blood relationship only, and often occurred within the bands; but many were so small that they were practically exogamous units."

The bands of the eastern Athabaskans living mainly in the Mackenzie Basin were extraordinarily large in view of the sparse population, numbering several hundred persons each.[6] This surprising size must be explained by the local economy. There were large herds of migratory musk ox and often of caribou in much of the area. These were hunted more or less seasonally and collectively by large groups of people. Population, which otherwise had to be distributed over an enormous area, was able to concentrate during these hunts in a group having some temporary centralized control and thus constituting a political unit. The bands were generally so large that they comprised unrelated families. Local or band exogamy was unnecessary and consanguinity was the only bar to marriage.

The Western or Cordillera Athabaskans had a much denser population and more settled life, owing to the presence of excellent fishing streams. They were also profoundly affected by influence from the Northwest Coast, which introduced not only much material culture but a caste system, potlatching, and matrilineal clans and moieties to many groups. A patrilineal or composite band is not necessarily destroyed by the introduction of clans, but it can hardly survive a shift

---

[5] A. G. Morice, "The Great Déné Race," *Anthropos,* V (1910), 130-31. Among the Western Déné, however, the hunter has greater freedom in disposing of his game.
[6] The Slave had five bands, averaging 220 individuals each; the Hare had five, numbering 120 or more each; the Dog Ribs had three, numbering 380 persons each (Osgood gives four bands); a Yellow Knife band is stated to have numbered 190 persons. These figures are based largely on A. G. Morice, "The Great Déné Race," *Anthropos,* I, 265; also see Diamond Jenness, "The Indians of Canada," *Canada Department Mines National Museum,* Bulletin 65 (1932), pp. 390-91; Osgood, *National Museum of Canada Annual Report,* 1933, p. 3.

to matrilocal residence and matrilineal property rights. Prior to the Northwest Coast influence the Western Athabaskans probably had composite bands; afterwards their society was radically altered. Many of the Carrier adopted matrilineal, landowning moieties and phratries, each of which apportioned tracts to its component clans. The neighboring Babine had matrilineal clans and matrilocal residence. The Chilcotin acquired a somewhat obscure system of clans and a stratified society. The Tahltan had moieties, each subdivided into three clans, which were said formerly to have claimed distinctive territory but now share land communally. The Nahani and Kutchin or Loucheux had, in addition to independent bands, matrilineal moieties, the relationship of which to the economic system is not clear. Thus ecological conditions favored patrilineal or composite bands but allowed latitude for other patterns, and Northwest Coast influence seems to have destroyed the composite bands among most of the Western Athabaskans. (See also Chapter 10.)

THE ANDAMANESE

The Andamanese are instructive by way of illustrating several special conditions. The unusual productivity of the natural environment permitted the relatively dense population of three persons per square mile in spite of the hunting and gathering culture. Although the people undoubtedly could, as far as ecology is concerned, have lived in fairly large bands, each band actually averaged only fifty individuals and the territory it owned averaged only sixteen square miles. The reason for this is not clear, but it may be noted that each band tract afforded an ample variety of foods so that a motive for ranging over a wider territory was lacking. The bands were politically independent but had no definite chiefs.[7]

Some tendency of the bands to be patrilineal is indicated by Radcliffe-Brown's statement that probably a "majority of marriages, or at any rate a large proportion, were between persons belonging to different local groups (Radcliffe-Brown, 1922:72; see also Man, 1882). Otherwise, the bands were composite despite their small size. The

[7] A. Radcliffe-Brown, The Andaman Islanders (Cambridge University Press, 1922), pp. 22-25, 43-48. H. R. Man, "On the Aboriginal Inhabitants of the Andaman Islands," Journal Royal Anthropological Institute, XII (1882), 108-109. Radcliffe-Brown disagrees with Man's assertion that each group of bands forming a "tribe" had a superior chief and states that the bands were entirely independent, authority being vested in elders. If sufficiently persuasive, a man or woman might exercise some influence over neighboring bands.

Table 2. COMPOSITE BANDS

	Number of persons per square mile	Average size of band	Average number of square miles in band territory	Permanent residence patrilocal with respect to band	Exogamy of band, i.e., locality, required	Band politically autonomous, weak chief	References and remarks
S. Bushmen	?	100-150	?	0	0	X	Schapera, 1930
Andaman	3	50	16	0	0	X	Radcliffe-Brown, 1922:22-87; Man, 1882
Algonkian	⅓-⅕	25?	?	0	0	X	Patrilineal family territory. Speck, 1915a:9-10
Ojibway	⅕	95-240	100-1,000?	0	0	X	Patrilineal family territory. Speck, 1915b:298-99; 1917a:89
Montagnais	⅕-⅟₃₅	44-700	250-10,000	0	0	X	Patrilineal family territory. Speck, 1927

reason for this is apparently the great frequency of child adoption, which Radcliffe-Brown says was usually between bands. Even though marriages between foster brothers and sisters were forbidden, it is evident that several unrelated and hence intermarriageable families would be established in such bands. Consequently even if consistent patrilocal residence should tend to convert these small bands into patrilineal lineages, adoption would constantly offset its effect and obviate the necessity of local exogamy.

CAUSAL FORMULATION FOR THE COMPOSITE BAND

Composite and patrilineal bands occurred among hunting tribes in areas of scarce foods, low population density, and poor transportation. In both, the prohibition of marriage with relatives may potentially take various forms. But the band was composite rather than patrilineal if (1) the chief food was game which occurred in large herds; or (2) if certain social practices temporarily introduced unrelated families into the patrilineal band.

The large game herds made social aggregates of several hundred persons possible. In bands of this size, knowledge of relationship between band members was lost after several generations, and band endogamy may have been practiced.

Social factors which made for composite bands where patrilineal bands normally occurred include: adoption of children between bands (Andamanese); endogamy caused by legitimacy of parallel-cousin marriage (several Bushman groups and Philippine Negritos) or by remoteness of bands into which to marry (Congo Negritos, Philippine Negritos); matrilocal residence practiced because of a shortage of men in the wife's family or more favorable subsistence in the territory of the wife's family (Algonkian); desire to secure assistance of the wife's family in child-rearing (Naron Bushmen); lack of a woman to exchange with the wife's band in marriage (Congo Negritos). These social factors may introduce unrelated families into patrilineal bands and make them temporarily composite, but such bands normally tend always to resume their typical patterns which are induced by cultural ecological factors.

There are many social groups other than composite hunting bands which consist of unrelated families, but these are beyond the present scope of inquiry. A greater population density produced by more abundant wild resources, such as acorns in native California, or by domesticated plants and animals may cause large composite groups of many kinds.

9

Lineage to Clan: Ecological
Aspects of Southwestern Society[1]

INTRODUCTION

A society consisting of a lineage represents a higher level of socio-cultural integration than one fragmented into individual families, such as the Shoshoni or Eskimo, because it ordinarily derives cohesion from such common group activities as ceremonialism and economic pursuits as well as from kinship bonds. A lineage, however, is not necessarily the historical successor of a family level society. Possibly some of the very earliest hunters consisted of lineages when collective activities made such organization feasible. On the other hand, some societies doubtless developed directly from a family level to that of a composite society consisting of many unrelated kinship groups. The composite bands of the northern Canadian hunters, for example, probably developed from loose family aggregates, not from bands consisting of lineages.

A lineage is higher level than an individual family in a conceptual sense but it is not necessarily a stage in evolution. Moreover, despite

---

[1] This chapter is a modification of "Ecological Aspects of Southwestern Society," *Anthropos,* Vol. XXXII, (1937), 87-104. The past eighteen years of research will modify the substantive but not the theoretical aspects of the material.

the several features which usually accompany unilineality — local exogamy, postmarital residence rule, and consistent reckoning of kinship in either the male or female line — the lineage does not represent a cultural type. Instead, there are many kinds of lineage-based societies which have not yet been classified but which differ in subsistence, settlement pattern, social composition, and group functions. There are significant differences, for example, between the matrilineal and patrilineal lineages in the tropical rain forests of South America, Oceania, Southeast Asia, and Africa, in the various environments of the temperate latitudes, and in the arid regions where irrigation is necessary for farming.

All primitive societies consisting of a single lineage probably represent about the same level of sociocultural integration despite their divisibility into many cultural types, which result in part from a somewhat distinctive ecological adaptation and which in many cases constitute special stages or periods in a particular cultural continuum. Such societies have great significance for analysis of cultural development, first, because they are found so commonly in the primitive world (Murdock, 1949) and second, because under certain conditions they have been superseded by larger and more complex multilineage societies. In these larger sociocultural systems, the lineage may retain certain of its former functions but it surrenders others to the new institutions of the total society.

The transition from a society consisting of a single lineage to one having several is not a universal phenomenon of cultural development and therefore does not represent unilinear evolution. Conceptually, it represents a succession of levels of sociocultural integration. Empirically, it represents the transition from certain types of lineages to certain types of multilineage societies. The sequence from one level to another involves certain very general processes, while the sequence from one type to another involves more specific and concrete processes. The present chapter examines the particular processes through which three kinds of localized lineages amalgamated to form special types of multilineage societies. The first type is the patrilineal band, discussed in Chapter 7, which occurred in parts of California and which under certain conditions of European influence occasionally became a multilineage society. The second type is that of the Yuman-speaking tribes of the lower Colorado River and of southern California which seem to have developed in prehistoric times through a sequence ranging from localized lineage through multilineage and multiclan villages to multivillage "nations." The third is that of the Western Pueblo area,[2] where localized lineages of horticultural groups of Basket Makers and early Pueblo were superseded by large, socially complex villages consisting of many lineages and clans.

Since the developmental processes discussed involve social groupings which have been variously and loosely subsumed under the terms "lineage" and "clan," more precise definitions are needed.

In the present chapter, *lineage* designates a consanguinal group which perceives kinship ties as stronger in one line of descent than the other. Thus, if the lineage is patrilineal, the sons, the son's sons, etc., are reckoned as closer relatives than the daughters, who normally marry into another lineage, the daughters' children, etc. Since a complex society may have a strong feeling for unilinear descent, the functional and developmental significance of a lineage depends upon its larger context, and further discriminations are therefore needed.

A *localized lineage* is a local society consisting of persons whose relationship is reckoned either in the male or female line and who, because relationship within the lineage constitutes a bar to marriage, are exogamous with respect to both the kinship group and the locality. Since, however, societies which are exogamous by locality are frequently designated "clans," whether or not relationship between members is known and traceable, it is important to distinguish clan from lineage.

Even if in the course of time a localized lineage becomes very large its members may still preserve a sense of kinship. This does not necessarily mean that they can trace geneological relationships but rather that a belief in common descent is perpetuated by such factors as the myth of a totemic ancestor, joint participations in ceremonies, common residence, and other factors creating an emotional bond. Any localized lineage tends to split into sublineages in successive generations, and, unless there is a strong geneological sense, as in Polynesia, a fairly large local group — empirically, a group usually consisting of 150 to 200 or more persons — will lose sight of known relationship while retaining the sense of kinship because of cultural factors. When, therefore, the local group consists of several lineages whose members cannot trace their relationships geneologically but is nevertheless exogamous, it is designated as a *localized clan*.

---

[2] For an excellent synthesis of archaeological and ethnographic data see Fred Eggan, *The Social Organization of the Western Pueblo* (University of Chicago Press, 1950).

This definition of clan is based primarily upon its function as an exogamous unit. Whereas the *lineage* is exogamous because of known kinship relations which proscribe certain marriages within the culturally determined concept of relationship, the *clan* prohibits marriage between its members on the basis of a culturally determined fiction. For this reason, a clan tends to be exogamous whether or not it is localized. By *clan,* therefore, is meant any group which is exogamous because of a common name, belief of descent from a common ancestor, common ritual, or other factors which create a feeling of kinship between its members. It is only when a clan consists of a single lineage that actual kinship is traceable.

It is the clan rather than lineage or local group, however, which determines exogamy; for if a clan occurs in several localities its members still may not intermarry, whereas lineages are normally so small that they are strictly localized and therefore may marry into any group outside their locality. These localized clans and lineages may or may not be parts of larger sociocultural systems. Among primitive farmers, such as the Navaho and many of the Amazon tribes, they are virtually autonomous. In modern civilized societies, such as China and Yugoslavia, they retain certain local functions but have surrendered others to the larger society. There are primitive societies in which the autonomous local community consists of several clans rather than one. In such communities, the clan retains sufficient functions to maintain its identity — else it would dissolve into lineages and families — but it surrenders other functions to the larger society.

The following analysis of cultural, historical, and ecological factors in the development of several societies in the Southwest is not so much an effort to establish a cultural typology — although three different types are represented in the area — as to utilize the concept of levels of sociocultural integration in the analysis of processes of cultural change.

Native society in the Southwest and southern California has been treated largely in terms of sociological and ceremonial patterns. Comparative analysis has shown that several cultures have certain similarities in exogamous institutions, which have been classed under the general heading of "unilateral organizations." This in turn has lead some students to assume that unilateral reckoning is such an arbitrary and artificial type of kin segregation that its independent development in several areas is improbable. On this assumption, Gifford (1918: 217-18), Kroeber (1925), and Olson (1933) have inferred that the unilateral, patrilineal societies in southern Califorina must have been derived from a Pueblo source. Gifford, in a later paper (Gifford, 1926: 399-401; Kroeber, 1928), however, appears to modify his position. Emphasizing the autochthonous nature of the localized California "lineage," he supposes that the Colorado and Gila river Yuman clans may have developed from such prototypes. Strong (1929: 344-49) concurs in regarding the localized lineage as a native California institution. He focuses attention, however, upon the ceremonial functions of these organizations and concludes that the group priest, ceremonial house, and fetish bundle complex, which was unquestionably borrowed from the Pueblo, were so powerful in producing unilateral groups that separate origins of the clan in the Southwest and southern California are conceivable (Strong, 1927).

Forde (1931a) suggests an independent origin of Yuman clans in Mexico. Pueblo clan origins were first postulated by Stephen, Fewkes, Mindeleff, and others in terms of native clan migration legends.[3] This is an impossible interpretation of the data and has been amply refuted by various recent writers (Kroeber, 1917). The more common explanation of Southwestern clans avoids the question of ultimate origins by assuming an outside source (Olson, 1933; Beals, 1932a), although Lowie (1925:127, 183) argues local origin connected with female house ownership and Kroeber (1928) and Strong (1927:54) postulate development from small villages, which were at first patrilineal and resembled those of southern California, then shifted to matrilineal descent approximately during the consolidation of population into communal villages in the Pueblo II-III periods.

The present analysis of Southwestern society assumes that cultural process, and therefore sound historical reconstruction, can be understood only if due attention is paid to the economic and ecological factors that shape society. This requires analysis of the degree and manner in which economic factors have combined with kinship, ceremonialism, inheritance, and other factors to produce observed social patterns.

Lowie (1925) has paved the way for the treatment followed here by suggesting various economic interpretations of clan origins. I shall reconsider the problems of the Southwest in the light of new data, insisting not only that somewhat comparable processes have operated to produce the patrilineal clans of the Yuman tribes and the matrilineal clans found among the Pueblo, but that this is entirely under-

---

[3] "Clan" was used without entire consistency or clarity.

standable in ecological terms. I suggest, in fact, that although these need not be the sole factors that have produced clans, very comparable development has occurred independently in many parts of the world.

SOUTHERN CALIFORNIA

Gifford (1926) has shown that the fundamental social grouping of many recent and possibly of all ancient California tribes is the localized patrilineal lineage. Among the Cahuilla, Serrano, Cupeño, Luiseño and perhaps other tribes of southern California, band solidarity is reinforced by possession of a common ceremonial house, priest, fetish bundle, various ceremonies, and a name which is usually taken from a locality (Strong, 1927 and 1929). Most of these tribes and the similarly organized Miwok and Western Mono (Gifford, 1926) have, in addition, patrilineal, exogamous moieties, which, however, are irrelevant to the thesis of this chapter and may be ignored. The patrilineal band is not peculiar to California, for it appears to have existed among certain primitive tribes of Mexico: Yaqui, Tehueco, Mayo, Acaxee, Colima, and perhaps others (Beals, 1932a, 1932b). Even the semi-horticultural Havasupai have not lost a form of it.

Chapter 7 has shown that the patrilineal band is common,[4] indeed expectable, among tribes whose ecology is such that because of an extremely low material culture and/or inhospitable environment, the per mile population is small (usually less than one person per square mile and as low as one person per twelve to thirty-eight square miles in Australia). Barring factors which prevent population from reaching an equilibrium within an area, ecological conditions limit aggregates to 50 or 100 persons. Patrilocal residence is the rule, for in a hunting culture a man can secure food more efficiently in his own than in his bride's territory. Innate male dominance may, of course, also produce patrilocal residence if the society possesses no factors to strengthen the position of women. In these small bands, exogamy is a necessary consequence of patrilocal residence, because, granting the social factor of incest taboos of some kind, the band comes to consist of relatives connected in the male line.

------

[4] Many German anthropologists long ago drew attention to the prevalence of the features of the patrilineal band among the world's most primitive peoples and interpreted them as representative of primeval "kulturkreise." For an excellent summary of these theories, see Wilhelm Koppers, *Die Anfänge des menschlichen Gemeinschaftslebens*.

The assumption that the patrilineal band of California was derived from the Pueblo matrilineal clan fails to explain the postulated changes in its several important features. Lowie has asked how observation of matrilineal descent could inspire a bilateral people to become patrilineal but positively not matrilineal (Lowie, 1934). Passing over this difficulty, which arises from stressing the abstraction of unilateral descent, the other features of the patrilineal band cannot be reconciled to the theory of borrowing. The modern Pueblo clan is not politically autonomous and does not inhabit a separate tract; it is part of a village and never owns more than agricultural land. There is nothing about the clan, therefore, to suggest the territorial and political independence of the patrilineal band. Next, it is inconceivable that Pueblo matrilocal residence, which is generally within the same village, could implant among Californians the desire for patrilocal residence in a village often ten or fifteen miles from the bride's home. Third, exogamy is practiced because of the theory that all members of a group are related. But if the local group consisted of unrelated, bilateral families, what observation of a Pueblo village of mixed clans would suggest that it was desirable to regard all of these as relatives and reckon their relationship through the men only? It appears, in fact, that diffusion of patrilineal clans to the Pima and Papago not only failed to affect the local exogamy of these tribes but that the clans even lost their exogamy. Precisely what, then, is diffused? Certainly none of the essential features of the patrilineal band.

Strong (1927: 56) states the case somewhat differently. He stresses the importance of the group-house, priest, and fetish bundle complex in the Southwest and southern California "as the most important single factor in shaping their social organization." This complex, of course, reinforces the cohesion of the group possessing them, but does not predetermine what that group shall be. Most probably the complex would be borrowed by any group which is politically and ceremonially autonomous. In this case it was borrowed by a pre-existing patrilineal band.

The formation of clans from patrilineal bands, far from requiring the miracles of diffusion, is remarkably easy; it occurred repeatedly in a small way in California. The first condition necessary for the emergence of clans is any factor that will increase the population — empirically usually to approximately one person or more per square mile — so that several bands may exist together in larger communities. These will usually be permanent villages, not seasonal camps. This alone is not sufficient, however, for instead of bands moving together the area utilized by each may be decreased. Thus, the Havasupai in their canyon home have reduced the social unit to a patrilineal family averaging 4.7 persons (Spier, 1928). Likewise, it is evident in the distribution of many early Pueblo sites (see below) that larger population clusters than actually existed were ecologically possible.

The second requirement, therefore, is some factor, such as war or tribal movements which makes for dislocation of the bands and concentrates them in large, multiband communities. At this point, therefore, economic determinants are supplemented by historical or sociological factors.

Third, the solidarity of each band must be such as to preserve its exogamy and identity. Group names, totems, ceremonies, and the like will serve this end. If this condition is not fulfilled — if lineages branch off and lose their sense of relationship — clans will not form.

Records of incipient clans are available from several California tribes. When the Miwok patrilineal bands were dislodged from their lands by pressure from the white man and forced together in larger villages, each retained its identity, even after seventy years (Gifford, 1926:389-92). The bands of southern California usually remained more or less intact in spite of dislocations initiated in the Mission period; a number of recent villages contained several such groups. This was brought about sometimes by reduction in the membership of each band which enabled several to come together and at other times by a shift to the white man's economy or by an unusual abundance of water which permitted an increased population at certain sites. Examples are the Cupeño, having seven lineages in one village; one Serrano village with four lineages and another with two (Gifford, 1926:394-96; Strong, 1929:188-90, 233); a Cahuilla village with several independent lineages (Gifford, 1918: 187). It is doubtful that a true clan system could crystallize in any of these villages, for Caucasian influence, which is bringing about the present collapse of the Yuman sibs, would no doubt destroy it.

Similar events have occurred in Mexico. Among several central and western tribes patrilineal bands, which had originally been independent and even spoke different dialects, came together in villages, where, however, they continued localized in "barrios" or divisions of the town. There is some suggestion that true patrilineal sibs existed in a number of tribes (Beals, 1932a: 474; 1932b).

It is not essential to this theory that clans come into existence wherever factors are favorable; bands assembled in villages may for various reasons lose their exogamy. If clans develop at one place in an area, they may spread to neighboring villages, especially where the culture is congruent.

THE YUMAN TRIBES

The case for deriving the patrilineal Yuman clans of the Colorado River from patrilineal bands rests, first, on the fact that a local origin of these clans is the only conceivable interpretation of present data, second, on the existence of every gradation between patrilineal bands and nonlocalized clans among the Yuman tribes.

Local origin of the Yuman clans must be postulated because they cannot have developed prior to the location of the Yumans in their present habitat. The Walapai, Havasupai, Diegueño, Seri, and most Yavapai lack clans, and there is no evidence that they developed in Sonora which was very probably the earlier abode of these tribes. Diffusion from the Pueblo area is equally untenable, for apart from the insuperable difficulties in the way of derivation of a patrilineal from a matrilineal system, there is little evidence of contact with the Pueblo. It is impossible to accept Olson's implication that the occurrence among the southern California Shoshonean tribes of such Southwestern traits as priest, fetish bundle, and other ritual elements prove the Southwestern origin of Yuman sibs (Olson, 1933:362); for these traits are unknown to the Yumans, who entered territory in which Pueblo culture had existed from Pueblo I to III periods.

Yuman sibs may be regarded simply as localized patrilineal lineages which become dislocated, clustered in large villages (ranging around 500 persons), and acquired special features of nomenclature, totemism, etc. The change was probably brought about by the practice of relatively intensive horticulture in a favorable environment, which produced among the Mohave, Yuma, Cocopa, Halchidhoma, Maricopa, and other river tribes a population averaging three persons to four square miles as against the Walapai, Havasupai, and Yavapai population of one person to sixteen square miles. The important point, however, is that horticulture permitted the concentration of population in large villages. The coastal California tribes had a population of one to two persons per square mile and even the inland desert dwellers are estimated at one per square mile (Kroeber, 1934), but, with the possible exception of the Chumash, among whom Harrington is said to have found totemic clans (Harrington, 1917), all California tribes lacked clans. In southern California, therefore, increased population density brought about decrease in the size of the territory occupied by each group instead of enlargement of villages; bands averaged only fifty persons.

Among the Colorado River tribes, however, some further factor must have disrupted localization of the bands. The most probable cause was warfare, which in recent times has dislodged entire tribes (Spier, 1933:1-18) and caused people to concentrate in villages for protection. Relocation because of the epidemics (Spier, 1933:38) or death customs may have furthered this concentration.

Between the patrilineal bands of the southern California Shoshoneans and the nonlocalized river clans are several Yuman tribes with intermediate patterns. It is possible that these are broken-down clans, but more probable that they are incipient, unformed clans. Although their departure from the patrilineal band pattern may be due to partial borrowings from the river tribes, their economic similarity to the Shoshoneans favors the hypothesis that they are incipient clans.

The Southern Diegueño (Spier, 1922) resemble the Shoshoneans except that band names are taken not from places but often from animals. At least one name is shared with the Northern Diegueño and several with the Kamia. It may be suggested that in this case preliminary diffusion of nomenclature created some cohesion among similarly named bands and contributed toward a growing sense of nationalism. (A parallel is suggested in the Southeastern and Iroquoian tribes, where similar clans in different groups facilitated growth of tribal confederacies, though contrary instances could also be cited.) The Southern Diegueño, like the Shoshonean bands, have been dislocated for various reasons, but retain their identity.

Northern Diegueño (Gifford, 1918:155-78) groups differ only in being less definitely localized, which may be explained by greater mission influences. The village of Pamo, for example, has a cluster of lineages with an elected village chief — a step toward a clan system.

The Kamia (Gifford, 1931) bands are much less localized and two are even horticultural. A sense of multicommunity nationalism is shown by the possession of a tribal chief.

The Akwa'ala (Gifford and Lowie, 1928) have completely nonlocalized clans, although many of the clan names resemble those of the Diegueño bands. They lack, however, the peculiar system of female-carried names found among the river Yumans.

Finally, a true clan system occurs among the Mohave (Kroeber,

1925:741-44), Yuma (Forde, 1931a), Cocopa (Gifford, 1933), Halchidhoma, and Maricopa (Spier, 1933:186-95). These clans are
nonlocalized, although they possess some traditions of former localization, and they have no chiefs or special clan functions. These tribes
are extremely nationalistic in having intervillage alliances which function under tribal and village chiefs (Gifford, 1926). Horticulture is
not exclusively a masculine pursuit among these peoples, but a definite
economic weighting of the male is indicated by landownership, inheritance, and postmarital residence. Undoubtedly, men acquired
their importance during an earlier stage of patrilineal bands, for it is
impossible to imagine that it was produced by and followed patrilineal
clans.

   With conditions favorable to a clan organization, clans could easily
have spread after a single origin. The peculiar manner in which
women bore clan names, the names themselves, and other features
distinguishing these clans indicate considerable diffusion within the
area, even to the Pima, a marginal group, where the clans failed to
function exogamously (Russell, 1908; Spier, 1933:194), and to the
Papago, where village, not clan, exogamy continued in force (Gifford,
1918:177).

   The totem names of many Yuman clans — for example, frog, corn,
tobacco, rattlesnake, and coyote of the Yuma (Forde, 1931a) — obviously resemble Pueblo clan names and are very probably of Pueblo
origin. This, however, proves nothing as to the origin of the groups
bearing those names. American fraternal orders, for example, have
often taken a system of nomenclature from the royal houses of Europe
and oriental kingdoms, but this does not suggest a community of
origin of the organizations so designated.

THE WESTERN PUEBLO AREA

   The history of clans among the Western Pueblo must rest upon a
somewhat more hypothetical basis, for the data of archaeology are not
always adequate. Nevertheless, information now available indicates a
development of unilateral organizations which, in many respects,
closely parallels that of the Colorado River and southern California
tribes. The Pueblo development differs in that its horticultural history
has had certain distinctive correlates.

   The failure of many of the Basket Maker II people to build lasting
habitations precludes knowledge of their village composition. It is
probable that the minor importance of horticulture compared with

hunting and gathering and the consequent seasonal shifting of camps prevented permanent villages.

Basket Maker III pit lodge villages seem to have been more permanent, though slight seasonal population shifting is still indicated. We know nothing, of course, of landownership, but it is certain that farm plots were becoming more important assets than hunting land, bringing new factors of property ownership to bear upon the social structure. The small house clusters of this period, in the San Juan drainage at least, are frequently located at no great distance from one another in the regions of arable land. Any landownership must have involved small farm plots, not vast hunting and gathering tracts. It would have been ecologically possible for the Basket Maker III people to have lived in fewer and larger villages rather than in many small units. That the small house clusters were unilateral groups living on or near their farm lands is consistent with their size and distribution. Motives for concentration of these clusters in larger villages were absent. It appears that population increased, small lineages budded off, and each set up a new house cluster at no great distance from its neighbors and former kin.

The Basket Maker III Shabik'eshche village in the Chaco is one of the few which is thoroughly described. This consisted of early and late settlements, each having about nine houses clustered but arranged in no special plan (Roberts, 1929). If each house sheltered an average family of five[5] the total population of each aggregate would not exceed fifty, which, if accompanied by a rule of residence and exogamy, would necessarily constitute a lineage or unilateral society. Even as far west as the Johnson-Paria district of southern Utah, Basket Maker sites similarly comprise compact clusters of one to seven slab structures sufficiently large to have served as houses.[6]

Pueblo I village composition, in spite of the population increase at this time, did not differ from that of the Basket Maker except in

---

[5] The following figures give the average house or household population of the modern Pueblo: Oraibi, 5; Mishongnovi, 5.4; Shipaulovi, 4.8; Walpi, 3.6; Sichumovi, 4.9; Hano, 4.5; Zuni, 7.5; San Juan, 4.1; Santa Clara, 5.3; San Ildefonso, 3.8; Tesuque, 5.4; Nambe, 7.1; Cochiti, 4.6; Jemez 4 to 5. See E. C. Parsons, "The Social Organization of the Tewa of New Mexico," *American Anthropological Association,* Memoir 36, 1929, pp. 9-10; A. L. Kroeber, "Zuñi Kin and Clan," *American Museum of Natural History, Anthropological Papers 18,* No. 2, pp. 134-50.

[6] Based on the writer's reconnaissance of this district in 1932. See Julian H. Steward, "Archaeological Reconnaissance of Southern Utah," *Bureau of American Ethnology Bulletin 128.*

exhibiting more clear-cut social units. During the growth of communal houses, which began in Pueblo II, the formerly separated small groups were amalgamated but did not lose their social and ceremonial integrity. The evidence for this is the relation of the kiva to the village group. If the early pit lodge sites have kivas at all, there is one to each cluster, suggesting a close parallel to the California patrilineal band, which had a single ceremonial house. In the Pueblo communal houses, the kiva-room ratio at first continued the same as in pit lodge clusters, as shown on the tabulation below. The houses, moreover, grew largely by accretion, blocks of rooms, each with a kiva, being added from time to time.

The amalgamation of separate house clusters into communal structures did not occur simultaneously throughout the Southwest. It appears to have begun in the eastern San Juan nucleus and to have spread, probably in the wake of ecological and sociological developments. But the sequence of village forms is remarkably parallel in several localities.

The Basket Maker III – Pueblo I village at Kiatuthlanna, eastern Arizona, consisted of one to a dozen groups of three to six pit lodges each, which "possibly represent family or clan units" (Roberts, 1931). Later these villages increased in size, each having a population of 20 to 300 individuals. By late Pueblo II or early Pueblo III times, the village rapidly became communal. Starting with a block of six masonry rooms and one kiva, it grew by the successive addition of seven rooms and one kiva, six rooms, six rooms and kiva, and finally, after a fire, twenty-one rooms and kiva, though never more than two kivas appear to have been used at once (Roberts, 1931:101-13).

Pueblo I villages in the Piedra district of southwestern Colorado similarly comprised one to several clusters of pit lodges, each having three to fifteen houses placed in compact crescentic arrangement around a depression which sometimes contained a kiva. Each obviously houses a clear-cut social unit. The latest type C villages consisted of only two or three dwellings each, but this appears to be a local anomaly, produced by some special factors, for similar and contemporary houses are arranged in the usual clusters in the neighboring La Plata district (Roberts, 1930).

The lineage type community evidently survived in the culture as represented by Prudden's "small house" groups (Prudden, 1918), in which the total rooms often attain considerable number. In both the "small house" unit and the much larger villages, the kiva-house ratio

Table 3. BASKET MAKER–PUEBLO VILLAGE GROWTH

Period (BM = Basket Maker. P = Pueblo.)	No. of rooms in house cluster	No. of kivas	House: kiva ratio	Site	Reference
BM III	9	..	...	Shabik'eschchee, Chaco	Roberts, 1929:146
BM III– PI	3 to 6	..	5:1(?)	Kiatuthlanna, Eastern Arizona	Roberts, 1931:15-89, 172
PI	3 to 15	..	sometimes absent	Piedra District, S.W. Colorado	Roberts, 1930
PI	7	1	7:1 (kiva or depression)	Piedra District, S.W. Colorado, A Village	Roberts, 1930:Pl. 3.
PI	12	2	6:1 (kiva or depression)	Piedra District, S.W. Colorado, B Village	Roberts, 1930:Fig. 7.
PII	6	1	6:1	Southeastern Utah	Prudden, 1918
PII	...	..	4:1	Southwestern Colorado	Martin, 1929:30-31
PII (late)	6	1	6:1	Kiatuthlanna, first house block	Roberts, 1931:111
PII	6	1	6:1	Allantown, Arizona	Roberts, 1933:68
PII	4 to 6	0	...	Chinlee, Arizona	Morss, 1927:16-21
PIII (early)	13	2	6:1	Village of Great Kivas, Zuñi Reservation	Roberts, 1932:Fig. 1
PIII	5	0	9:1	Village of Great Kivas, Zuñi Reservation, 2nd block added (large kiva not counted)	Roberts, 1932:Fig. 2
PIII	24 (total)	2	12:1	Village of Great Kivas, Zuñi Reservation, 3rd stage	Roberts, 1932:Fig. 3
PIII	53 (total)	6	8.5:1	Village of Great Kivas, Zuñi Reservation, final house	Roberts, 1932:Fig. 4
PIII	100 (occupied)	8	12.5:1	Spruce Tree House	Fewkes, 1909
PIII	100 (occupied)	14	7:1	Cliff Palace	Fewkes, 1911b:79

Table 3. BASKET MAKER–PUEBLO VILLAGE GROWTH (Continued)

Period (BM = Basket Maker. P = Pueblo.)	No. of rooms in house cluster	No. of kivas	House: kiva ratio	Site	Reference
PIII	13	2	6.5:1	Ruin 8, Kayenta district (including only circular kivas)	Kidder & Guensey, 1919:56-61
PIII	134	8	16:1	Kitsil, Kayenta (circular kivas only)	Fewkes, 1911a:Pl. 13
PIII	15	1	15:1	Olla House (circular kivas only)	Kidder and Guensey, 1919:46-56
PIII	50	3	16:1	Cradle House, Kayenta (circular kivas only)	Fewkes, 1911a:20
PIII	21	2	10:1	Kiatuthlanna, final house	Roberts, 1931:101
PIII	18	0?	?	Chinlee, Morss's #32	Morss, 1927:22-4
PIII	15	0?	?	Chinlee, Morss's #33	Morss, 1927:22-24
PIII	25	1	25-1	Chinlee, Morss's #34	Morss, 1927:22-24
PIII	20	1	20:1	Chinlee, Morss's #35	Morss, 1927:22-26
PIII	30	10	2:1	Chinlee, Morss's #36 (most rooms storage; abnormal no. of kivas)	Morss, 1927:26-29
PIV	600_	10_	60:1	Tshirege, Rio Grande	Hewett, 1906:23-4
PIV	300_	10	30:1	Tsankawi, Rio Grande (200 rooms ground floor)	Hewett, 1906
PIV	900?	10	90:1?	Otowi, Rio Grande (450 rooms ground floor)	Hewett, 1906:18-20
PIV	560?	6	92:1?	Yapashi, Rio Grande (280 ground floor rooms)	Hewett, 1906:29

Table 3. BASKET MAKER–PUEBLO VILLAGE GROWTH (Concluded)

Period (BM = Basket Maker. P = Pueblo.)	No. of rooms in house cluster	No. of kivas	House: kiva ratio	Site	Reference
PIV	240?	1?	240:1?	Kotyiti, Rio Grande (118 ground floor rooms)	Hewett, 1906:32
PV	154[a]	13	11.8:1	Oraibi, Hopi	Mindeleff, 1891:Pl. XXXVI
PV	57	5	11.4:1	Walpi, Hopi	Mindeleff, 1891:Pl. XXX; and Kroeber, 1917
PV	24	2	12:1	Sichumovi, Hopi	Mindeleff, 1891:Pl. XVIII; and Kroeber, 1917
PV	22	2	11:1	Shipaulovi, Hopi	Mindeleff, 1891:Pl. XXX; and Kroeber, 1917
PV	53	5	10.6:1	Mishongnovi, Hopi	Mindeleff, 1891:Pl. XXVI; and Kroeber, 1917
PV	35	2	17.5:1	Hano, Hopi	Mindeleff, 1891:Pl. XVI; and Kroeber, 1917
PV	191	6	31.8:1	Zuñi (family: kiva ratio)	Kroeber, 1917
PV	580	6	96.6:1	Zuñi (room: kiva ratio)	Kroeber, 1917

[a] The figures for the Pueblo V villages give the family-kiva ratio. Presumably this should be multiplied by approximately three to procure the room figure.

continues to be one to five or six. The essential difference is that in the large villages the lineages are no longer separated from one another geographically. These sites, moreover, appear to have grown by accretion, blocks of five or six rooms and a kiva having been added from time to time as at Kiatuthlanna. Even in some of the great houses of the Pueblo III period, there is much evidence of continued village growth by accretion and the kiva-room ratio at first remains the same. (See tabulation above.)

The merging of formerly localized and independent units was made possible but not caused by ecological factors. It would have been possible for the inhabitants of nearly all the sites described above to have lived in concentrated clusters of much greater size, for the distance from village to farm lands would not have been excessive. Many of the "small house" ruins of southeastern Utah are only a few hundred yards apart, and it is safe to infer that many of these closely spaced houses were contemporaneous. Similarly, the house clusters of the Johnson–Canyon–Paria district at first remained distinct and separate, although often close together, but later amalgamated into villages of several hundred rooms.

Village concentration must, therefore, have been produced by a factor of a nonecological order. Many causes are conceivable but in this instance it does not seem imperative to seek beyond the need for defense; for, whatever the danger, increasing pains taken to choose impregnable dwelling sites attest an important motive for banding together. This tendency to concentrate in large villages, aided by the development of multistoried architecture and probably stimulated by some threat, began to spread. But at this time the total Pueblo area also began to shrink. The communal dwelling has persisted to the present, but now that the motives for constructing it have vanished, the reverse tendency has set in, houses becoming more widely scattered. The unilateral organization presumed to have been created during the original concentration of the Pueblo population continues in effect to the present day.

The facts of Basket Maker–Pueblo archaeology thus accord with the theory of clan development. First, it is difficult to reconcile the division of the early villages into small house clusters with any other social unit than a unilateral lineage or band. Each house cluster is so large that it must have sheltered several families. If the families were unrelated, there would be no motive for them to build their houses close together. A rule of postmarital residence coupled with local exogamy, however, would produce lineages whose houses would fit the archaeological facts. Archaeologists have frequently called these "clan houses," but this must not be understood to mean clan in the Hopi sense. A better term is "lineage dwellings."

Second, if the twenty to fifty members of each retained their identity after merging with other similar groups in large villages — and the accretional growth of the villages as well as the continued ratio of rooms to kivas suggests that they did — a system of exogamous, nonlocalized clans would inevitably be produced in each village, as it had been in California. Whether, however, lineage exogamy — now clan exogamy — were perpetuated in these larger villages would depend upon factors making for lineage or band solidarity. Therefore, it is by no means necessary that clans should always have developed at this point. The present distribution of Pueblo clans, indeed, shows them to be essentially western and quite lacking among some of the Rio Grande villages. It is, therefore, probably no accident that among the Hopi, who have the strongest, most all-pervading clan organization, there are more features to reinforce clan cohesion. Each clan has its chief, fetish bundle, ceremonies, and even agricultural lands. These unifying features are weak among the Zuñi and generally lacking among the Rio Grande villages. Isleta, like the Pima, has merely non-exogamous named groups, Parsons' "Corn groups" (Parsons, 1932).

It is no wonder that during the interweaving of the multicolored strands that comprise modern Pueblo socioreligious fabric, the clan-kiva association should have been lost. The increased number of rooms relative to kivas, even by A.D. 1300, shows either that clans greatly increased in size, perhaps through amalgamation of similarly named lineages, or that the clan-kiva association was lost[7] though it is possible that some slight connection between clans and kivas still exists at Hopi.

The center of clan development appears to have been the eastern San Juan Pueblo nucleus. Its pit lodges had the most clearly defined grouping; the ratio of kivas to rooms in the communal dwellings was more nearly the same as in the pit houses; communal houses first developed here; population was densest.[8] The Kayenta district lagged culturally and made much less consistent use of kivas. The San Francisco mountain region pit lodges were, prior to the introduction of communal houses about A.D. 1100, irregularly distributed in variable clusters ranging from two or three lodges each to twenty-five or thirty lodges scattered in two or three square miles. The general absence of kivas here may have deprived these people of a crucial factor in integrating local social units (Colton and Colton, 1918, and 1932,

---

[7] J. Walter Fewkes, "Antiquities of Mesa Verde National Park. Cliff Palace." *Bureau of American Ethnology Bulletin 51,* 1911, pp. 79-80. Fewkes supposed that at first each "clan" had its own kiva, but that the development of religious fraternities destroyed the association. Consequently, he postulated that the older the site, the greater the number of kivas relative to rooms.

[8] A. V. Kidder, *An Introduction to the Study of Southwestern Archaeology* (New Haven, 1924), p. 54. Kidder estimated that if all the great houses of the Chaco were occupied at the same time — and these are now known to date between approximately A.D. 900 and 1100 — the total population would exceed 10,000.

maps 1-10; Hargrave, 1933). The haphazard arrangement of pit lodges in the Great Salt Lake region and of the adobe Pueblo houses in the Sevier desert region and of Utah (Judd, 1926; Steward, 1933) indicate a similar lack of the San Juan type of social unit. The failure of these and other regions to conform to the San Juan norm may, perhaps, be explained by different cultural contacts with their neighbors, a greater reliance upon hunting in their early stages, or other factors which conflicted with those making for matrilineal descent. These observations suggest that a thorough review of Southwestern archaeology to define the types of village communities and their relationship to one another and to the economic basis of life would not only have the utmost intrinsic value but would serve to correlate in some measure the now altogether too unrelated disciplines of archaeology and ethnology in the Southwest. An ethnologist, on the other hand, could undoubtedly treat of modern Pueblo clans and societies more adequately were his studies to embrace available archaeological facts about village groups, kivas, ceremonial rooms, fetishes, etc.

That the true Pueblo clans are matrilineal admits of several, though not entirely verifiable, explanations. Lowie has suggested female-owned houses to be the cause (Lowie, 1925). Female landownership is probably another cause; for at Hopi First and Second Mesas, at least, female lineages within clans possess sections of the clan-owned land (Forde, 1931b). In view of Pueblo prehistory, it is much easier to interpret female landownership as a cause rather than effect of the matrilineal clan system. It is true that field cultivation today is done by men for their wives: but, although the historical relationship of men's recent farming activities to a society so completely matrilineal in every other way can never be wholly explained, it may be pointed out that had women formerly tilled the soil, as among so many primitive horticulturists, the Pueblo would nevertheless almost inevitably have shifted this task to men. In Pueblo II times and perhaps earlier, the amalgamation of the population in large villages caused the people to live considerable distances from their fields, an arrangement which made it very hazardous for women to farm. Thus matrilineal descent was probably established early in Pueblo development, when the inhabitants of each small house cluster probably constituted a localized, matrilineal, landowning lineage.

A comparison of the eastern and western Pueblo villages shows that there were such strong factors making for patrilineal descent among the former that neither diffusion nor local development served to implant matrilineal clans among many of them.

The social organization of the remaining Southwestern tribes may be explained partly in terms of diffusion. Sufficient intertribal marriage may introduce clans into any group unless its native organization has features adverse to it. In parts of Australia, exogamous matrilineal totem and moiety groups and exogamous patrilineal bands appear to co-exist (Radcliffe-Brown, 1931:438); in southern California patrilineal moieties and localized lineages occur together; and among the Algonkian bands of the Ottawa Valley, totemic clans have been added to localized patrilineal families (Speck, 1915a:1-30). The matrilineal clans of the Navaho, Apache, and Southeastern Yavapai could readily have been borrowed from the Pueblo. The Navaho system of clan nomenclature, which is based on place names, however, may indicate that a precondition of clan development was an absorption of many Pueblo economic traits which provided a pattern favorable to clans.

The departure of the other Yavapai (Gifford, 1932:177-81, 190) and the Walapai (Kniffen et al., 1934) bilateral bands from the usual Yuman pattern may be interpreted as the result of their position between matrilineal and patrilineal societies, no set of factors having been strong enough to produce either kind of unilateral organization.

SUMMARY

The theory developed here cannot admit of rigid proof. Its merit lies in providing an explanation in terms of cultural dynamics and raising a series of problems of ecological adaptations and historical processes which may be subject to analysis in other areas. The alternative theory of diffusion offers no explanation of origins, no understanding of culture change, and bases its case upon the unproved and highly dubious assumption that similarity in "arbitrary" features is proof of community of origin of unilateral institutions (Olson, 1933: 412-13). Arbitrary features, however, are those which by definition are not functionally connected with the core of the institution and are therefore unfixed in nature and capable of considerable independent variation in time and space. Consequently, the addition of a system of nomenclature to clans — e.g., the Yuman clan totems which are Puebloan in nature — or possession of common ritual elements in no way bears upon the problem of origin of such unilateral groups.

Social and political groups are shaped by sociological, historical, and ecological factors. This chapter has attempted to show the need of considering the last in relationship to the other two. The initial development of patrilineal bands and of localized, exogamous matrilineal lineages is a simple cutural ecological adjustment. The later transformation of such societies into clans is explainable by historical processes operating within the framework of the possible ecological adaptations. The processes may be formulated as follows:

First, a technology of low productivity and/or an unfavorable environment prevents a dense population and precludes large population aggregates. Conditions under which the social groups are patrilineal, localized, exogamous, and landowning, have been formulated in Chapter 7. If the societies are horticultural, the village may consist of a localized, exogamous and perhaps landowning lineage, which is matrilineal or patrilineal according to its cultural type.

Second, increased food supply or other factors making for a denser population will produce either larger social groups (bands or lineages) occupying the same territory, more groups each of which occupies less territory, or else multilineage villages in which several formerly localized groups live together.

Third, large, multilineage villages will be produced if tribal movements, war, or other factors dislocate the bands or lineages from their territories or villages causing them to intermingle in the same locality, or if, in an increasing population, newly founded lineages fail to move away from the parent group.

Fourth, it is not inevitable that these intermingled unilateral groups become clans. They will do so, however, if possession of a group name, common ceremonies, or other factors create solidarity and prevent loss of recognition of kinship in succeeding generation; or, to put it differently, if the fiction of kinship is preserved after the known connection is no longer traceable.

Fifth, in the course of these transformations, political autonomy passes from the localized lineage to a larger group, and a higher level of sociocultural integration appears — the Pueblo village, the Yuman nation.

The presence of patrilineal sibs among the Yuman tribes of the Colorado River is more easily explained in these terms than by the theory that they diffused from the Pueblo area, that descent was reversed, and that all basic features were transformed. The archaeological data of Pueblo history are entirely in harmony with the theory of local amalgamation of previously independent lineages. This theory does not preclude diffusion, but it assumes that diffusionist explanations need not be applied on so great a scale as in the past and suggests that diffusionists must prove the borrowing of the unilateral groups, not the "arbitrary" concomitants of them.

This chapter has emphasized developmental processes in the formation of multilineage and multiclan societies rather than distinctions between types of such societies. Such distinctions can best be made on the basis of cross-cultural comparison. On this basis Chapter 7 has shown that the patrilineal band is a type which is found in many parts of the world. Very possibly, such bands have been drawn together in post-white times to constitute multilineage communities. The transformation of patrilineal bands into nonlocalized clans among the Colorado River Yuman peoples is assumed to have followed the introduction of agriculture and the rise of warfare. Since the agriculture was carried on predominantly on the flood plains, an ecological adaptation very different from that of the Pueblo was involved. The Basket Maker–Pueblo developmental sequence differs from the remainder of the Southwest in several respects. There is no evidence that a patrilineal band was its antecedent, as in southern California. If the Great Basin people throw any light on Basket Maker II society, the latter had a bilateral family, which was the more likely adaptation to a seed-gathering economy. Agriculture led to localized matrilineal lineages, which finally amalgamated into multiclan communities under the influence of cultural-historical factors. No doubt other parts of the world show developmental types like those of the Yuman tribes and the Western Pueblo.

10

Variation in Ecological
Adaptation: The Carrier Indians

The method of cultural ecology differs from that of environmental determinism or economic determinism in that it makes the question of how the employment of a particular technology in a particular environment an open question; but it does not prejudge the answer one way or another. In the case of the loose family aggregates of the Shoshoni, the patrilineal hunting bands, and the composite hunting bands, the ecological adaptations determine the main structure of the societies. These cases, however, do not constitute an a priori conclusion that ecological processes inevitably produce a fixed and predetermined type of society. Each case must be judged on its own merits, and broad generalizations will be possible only when an adequate taxonomy of sociocultural types has been developed and when the cultural ecology of each has been analyzed. The following analysis illustrates an instance in which the cultural ecology allowed considerable latitude in sociopolitical types and diffusion caused a change of the basic pattern.

West of the continental divide in the interior of British Columbia and Alaska there lives a group of Athabaskan tribes who are linguistically and culturally similar to the peoples of the Mackenzie Basin of northern Canada. Both groups were once divided into simple hunting bands (Chapter 8), but some of the Western Athabaskans had replaced their bands with a system of matrilineal moieties in prehistoric times and others were in the process of doing so at the time of white contact. As neither the habitat nor technology had changed during this succession of social types, it is clear that the cultural ecology allowed a certain latitude in the range of possible types.

The Mackenzie Basin and Western Athabaskans had substantially similar exploitative technologies. They used bows and arrows, traps, and deadfalls to take game and hooks, nets, and weirs to take fish. They traveled with dogsleds in winter and in bark canoes in summer. The environment of both groups is similar in that it has extreme winters, considerable precipitation, a vegetation which ranges from coniferous forests in the south to subarctic and arctic muskegs in the north and a variety of large herbivors, small fur-bearing carnivors and fish. There is a crucial difference in resources, however, in that the country west of the continental divide lacked large herds of caribou but possessed salmon streams of some importance. These characteristics of the Western Athabaskan habitat permitted the tribes to adopt from the coastal peoples a system of moieties and social stratification, a type of society which differed fundamentally from that of the northern Athabaskans and which the latter could not adopt, as historical evidence proves.

The cultural ecological factors underlying the sociopolitical change among the Western Athabaskans are best illustrated by the Carrier Indians of Stuart Lake and upper Skeena River in British Columbia, who have been the subject of special study from this point of view.[1] The subsistence pattern of the Carrier Indians represented a rhythm of complementary activities that were carried on during the summer and winter, respectively. In summer, people remained in permanent villages near their fisheries on the lakes and rivers, where they caught considerable quantities of salmon and other fish. The largest villages were at sites where the community could co-operate in the construction of weirs. In the fall, families traveled alone or in small groups to the streams and forests to hunt deer, bear, and caribou and to trap beaver, muskrat, mink, fox, and other fur-bearing animals. They

---

[1] Only two brief articles have been published on a considerable body of material: Julian H. Steward, "Recording Culture Changes Among the Carrier Indians of British Columbia," *Explorations and Field Work of the Smithsonian Institution in 1940* (1941), pp. 83-90; Steward, "Determinism in Primitive Society," *Scientific Monthly*, 1941, pp. 491-501.

remained within easy access of their villages, however, because hunger might compel them to return to their stores of smoked salmon.

The original type of Carrier society was some kind of simple hunting band. There is insufficient evidence to know whether it was composite or patrilineal. During the historic period, caribou had decreased and moose had increased in the territory. As the former occur in much larger herds than the latter, it is possible that the aboriginal band had been composite for the same reasons as among the northern Athabaskans. In any event, the Carrier society differed from the northern Athabaskan bands in that its territories were comparatively small and its villages fairly permanent, for the salmon surpluses were anchor points from which the people did not dare wander too far.

Long before the advent of the white man, the Haida, Tlingit, and other tribes of the coast had developed a society which combined social classes, strong chieftainship, and a matrilineal moiety organization. This society was made possible by an unusually ample food supply. Great quantities of salmon and other marine fauna together with plant and animal foods from the mainland supported a very dense population and even afforded a surplus. This surplus was controlled by hereditary nobles who periodically distributed it to their rivals in competitive ceremonial feasts called potlatches. The titles of nobility were inherited within the clan and passed from a man to his sister's son. Common clansmen and lesser nobles were obligated to help the potlatching chief accumulate sufficient goods for their ceremonies, and they gained a kind of vicarious pleasure from the success of their chief who symbolized the clan.

These Northwest Coast patterns had spread up the Skeena River among the Tsimshian, where they were strongly developed, and they finally crossed the divide from the Skeena to the Fraser River into Carrier territory. Adoption of the moiety-potlatch pattern meant a major revolution in Carrier society, but it did not, so far as I can ascertain, require any changes in exploitative technology. The land was divided among hereditary nobles, each holding title to a well-defined territory in the name of his moiety. The common people lived, hunted, and fished as before, but from time to time they had to hand over the surplus to their moiety chief for a potlatch ceremony. These potlatches were poor affairs compared with those of the coast. Whereas a coastal noble might not only distribute quantities of food and hundreds of blankets but also kill a slave or burn a large canoe in wanton abandon, the potlatching Carrier could only give each guest a bit of food, perhaps a pair of moccasins or leggings, and a quarter or a sixth of a blanket. It was said that a man who had been potlatched often might receive enough pieces of blanket to sew them together into a whole blanket.

The Carrier pattern of moieties, nobles, and potlatches was a rather shabby imitation of the Northwest Coast system. Nevertheless, it was a pattern which required some surplus wealth, however slight, for the nobles could validate their titles only through potlatches. This wealth came from salmon, which, though far less abundant in Carrier territory at the headwaters of the rivers entering the Pacific than nearer the coast, made the difference between the western Athabaskans and the people of the Mackenzie Basin. The Sekani, just across the continental divide east of the Carrier, attempted to borrow the Carrier pattern but they could not make it work and after a few years they gave it up. Lack of surpluses for potlatches was the principal difficulty.

Other Athabaskans of the Western Cordillera were similar to those of Stuart Lake in that they had a fairly dense population and settled life owing to the presence of excellent fishing streams (Morice, 1909: 583), and many of them had a system of castes, potlatching, and matrilineal clans and moieties.[2] The Babine had matrilineal clans and matrilocal residence (Morice, 1910), the Chilcotin had a somewhat obscure system of clans with the addition of social stratification (Jenness, 1932:362), the Tsetsaut had matrilineal moieties. The Tahltan had moieties, each subdivided into three clans, which are said formerly to have claimed distinctive territory but now share land communally (Jenness, 1932:369-70, 372-73). The Nahani (Jenness, 1932:396-99) and Kutchin or Loucheux (Jenness, 1932:399-404; Osgood, 1931) had, in addition to independent bands, matrilineal moieties, the relationship of which to the economic system is not clear. It is not certain that the Northwest Coast pattern was present in full strength among these tribes, but it seems clear that the cultural ecology permitted sufficient latitude in the basic social structure to make diffusion a major determinant.

The system of potlatching, nobility, and moieties was introduced in late pre-white times among the Stuart Lake Carrier, and it was still

[2] Diamond Jenness, *Canada Department Mines National Museum* Bulletin 65 (1932), pp. 365-67; A. G. Morice, *Anthropos*, V (1910), 135, speaks of fishing places among the Carrier and Babine which are owned by "families or groups of related families."

spreading among the Carrier farther south at the time of white penetration of the area. The first Europeans among the Carrier were fur traders, and the initial effect of their activities was to intensify the existing moiety pattern. Their trade goods, especially Hudson's Bay blankets, augmented the wealth used in potlatching. In the course of time, however, the concept of individual wealth grew in importance. Knives, pots, traps, axes, and other crucial items that did not lend themselves to potlatching but became necessities to each individual led men to trade directly with the fur company. The importance of the individual was enhanced when more intimate contacts with whites gradually introduced European social ideals, while the adoption of Christianity undermined native belief which had sanctioned the older system.

At Stuart Lake, a pattern of individual trapping territories, much like that found elsewhere in Canada (Chapter 8), was introduced about two generations ago. The chiefs and nobles, who had previously held title to large tracts on behalf of their moieties, divided the land among their own children both male and female instead of passing it on to their sister's sons according to the former matrilineal principle. Owing to the inheritance of fur tracts by both sexes, to the collapse of social classes, and to the extensive intermarriage between all families in each area nearly every person or family in the general region of Stuart Lake now owns a well-defined fur territory. These territories are registered in the Provincial game warden's office, and they are protected against poaching by the government warden who regularly patrols them.

11

Development of Complex Societies:

Cultural Causality and Law: A Trial

Formulation of the Development of Early

Civilizations[1]

METHODOLOGICAL ASSUMPTIONS

It is about three-quarters of a century since the early anthropologists and sociologists attempted to formulate cultural regularities in generalized or scientific terms. The specific evolutionary formulations of such writers as Morgan (1877) and Tylor (1871, 1865) and the functional or sociological formulations of Durkheim and others were largely repudiated by the twentieth-century anthropologists, especially by those of the so-called "Boas" school, whose field work tested and cast doubt on their validity. Today, despite an enormous and ever-

---

[1] This chapter appeared as an article in the *American Anthropologist* in 1949. It is virtually unchanged except for certain regrouping of developmental periods in Table 4 and modifications of dating in Table 5 to conform with several new carbon 14 dates. A symposium of specialists who re-examined some of the hypotheses of this chapter at the meetings of the American Anthropological Association at Tucson, Arizona in 1953, will be published in both Spanish and English in *Ciencias Sociales*. Contributions are by Karl Wittfogel on China, Robert Adams on the Near East, Angel Palerm on Meso-America, Donald Collier on Peru, and myself on the general implications of the foregoing.

An important consideration brought out by the symposium is that irrigation may not have been used until fairly late times in Meso-America. This raised the possibility that surplus production of luxury goods and central control of trade may have led to theocratic state controls.

increasing stockpile of cultural data, little effort has been made to devise new formulations or even to develop a methodology for doing so, except as White and Childe have kept alive the tradition of Morgan, as Radcliffe-Brown and Redfield have continued in the spirit of Durkheim, and as Malinowski has attempted to reconcile diverse schools of anthropology through a "scientific theory of culture."

Reaction to evolutionism and scientific functionalism has very nearly amounted to a denial that regularities exist; that is, to a claim that history never repeats itself. While it is theoretically admitted that cause and effect operate in cultural phenomena, it is considered somewhat rash to mention causality, let alone "law," in specific cases. Attention is centered on cultural differences, particulars, and peculiarities, and culture is often treated as if it developed quixotically, without determinable causes, or else appeared full-blown.

It is unfortunate that the two approaches are so widely thought of as theoretically irreconcilable rather than as expressions of different purposes or interests. The nineteenth-century writers had the perfectly legitimate purpose of making scientific generalizations from what they considered recurrent cultural patterns, sequences, and processes in different cultures, while the more recent school has the equally legitimate purpose of examining the distinctive or nonrecurrent features of cultures. As all cultures, though unique in many respects, nonetheless share certain traits and patterns with other cultures, an interest in either or both is entirely defensible. In fact, the analyses of cultural particulars provide the data necessary for any generalizations. If the nineteenth-century formulations were wrong, it was not because their purpose was inadmissible or their objective impossible, but because the data were inadequate and insufficient, the methodology weak, and the application of the schemes too broad.

In spite of a half century of skepticism concerning the possibility of formulating cultural regularities, the conviction is widely held that the discovery of cultural laws is an ultimate goal of anthropology to be attained when fact-collecting and detailed analyses of particular cultures and sequences are sufficiently advanced. White (1943) has already offered some general formulations concerning the relationship of energy to cultural development, and he has argued for the importance of formulations of all kinds. Even some members of the so-called "Boas" school expressly advocate a search for regularities. Lowie, for example, remarks that cultural phenomena "do point toward certain regularities, and these it is certainly our duty to ascertain as rigor-

ously as possible" (Lowie, 1936). Lesser cites several trial formulations
of regularities, which have been made by various persons, including
Boas, and calls for more explicit statement of the regularities which,
in the course of his work and thinking, every social scientist assumes
to exist (Lesser, 1939). The author has attempted to formulate
regularities pertaining to the occurrence of patrilineal bands among
hunting and gathering tribes (Steward, 1936) and has suggested
others that may occur in the origin and development of clans (Steward, 1937). In reality, hundreds of formulations appear in the literature — for example, correlations of kinship terminologies with forms
of social organization — and the possibility of recognizing the general
in the particular is implicit in the very terminology of anthropology.
The routine use of such concepts, or typological categories, as "clans,"
"castes," "classes," "priests," "shamans," "men's tribal societies,"
"cities," and the like are tacit recognition that these and scores of
other features are common to a large number of cultures, despite the
peculiarities of their local patterning.

The present need is not to achieve a world scheme of culture
development or a set of universally valid laws, though no doubt many
such laws can even now be postulated, but to establish a genuine
interest in the scientific objective and a clear conceptualization of
what is meant by regularities. It does not matter whether the formulations are sequential (diachronic) or functional (synchronic), on a
large scale or a small scale. It is more important that comparative
cultural studies should interest themselves in recurrent phenomena
as well as in unique phenomena, and that anthropology explicitly
recognizes that a legitimate and ultimate objective is to see through
the differences of cultures to the similarities, to ascertain processes
that are duplicated independently in cultural sequences, and to recognize cause and effect in both temporal and functional relationships.
Such scientific endeavor need not be ridden by the requirement that
cultural laws or regularities be formulated in terms comparable to
those of the biological or physical sciences, that they be absolutes and
universals, or that they provide ultimate explanations. Any formulations of cultural data are valid provided the procedure is empirical,
hypotheses arising from interpretations of fact and being revised as
new facts become available.

Three requirements for formulating cultural regularities may be
stated in a rough and preliminary way as follows:

(1) *There must be a typology of cultures, patterns, and institutions.*

Types represent abstractions, which disregard peculiarities while isolating and comparing similarities. To use Tylor's classic example, the mother-in-law taboo and matrilocal residence, though in each case unique in their local setting, are recurrent types, the cause and effect relationships of which may be compared and formulated. Anthropological terminology demonstrates that hundreds of types of culture elements, patterns, and total configurations are recognized, despite the peculiarities attaching to each in its local occurrence.

(2) *Causal interrelationship of types must be established in sequential or synchronic terms, or both.* Any reconstruction of the history of a particular culture implies, though it may not explicitly state, that certain causes produced certain effects. Insights into causes are deeper when the interrelationships of historical phenomena are analyzed functionally. Functional analysis of archaeological data has not been lacking, though archaeology has used an atomistic and taxonomic approach (Steward and Setzler, 1938) far more than has conventional history. Gordon Childe (1934, 1946) is exceptional in his effort to treat archaeological materials functionally. Wittfogel (1935, 1938, 1939) has been outstanding in his use of historical data to make functional-historical analyses of the socioeconomic structure of early civilizations.

Where historical data are not available, only the synchronic approach to cause and effect is possible. Radcliffe-Brown, Redfield, and Malinowski, despite important differences in their thinking, are distinctive for their functional analyses.

(3) *The formulation of the independent recurrence of synchronic and/or sequential interrelationships of cultural phenomena is a scientific statement of cause and effect, regularities, or laws.* The particularists, though conceding that such formulations are theoretically possible and even desirable, are inclined to hold that in practice it is virtually impossible to isolate identifiable cause-and-effect relationships that operate in independent cases. Similarities between cultures are interpreted as the result of a single origin and diffusion, provided the obstacles to diffusion do not seem too great. If the obstacles are very great, differences are emphasized. Thus, most American anthropologists explain similarities between the early civilizations of the New World as a case of single origin and diffusion, but, impressed by the obstacles to transoceanic culture contacts, they stress the dissimilarities between the civilizations of the Old and New Worlds. Some writers, however, like Elliot-Smith, Perry, and Gladwin (1947) rec-

ognize the similarities between the two hemispheres and, unimpressed by barriers to diffusion, use the similarities as proof of a single world origin.

The use of diffusion to avoid coming to grips with problems of cause and effect not only fails to provide a consistent approach to culture history, but it gives an explanation of cultural origins that really explains nothing. Diffusion becomes a mechanical and unintelligible, though universal, cause, and it is employed, as if in contrast to other kinds of causes, to account for about 90 percent of the world's culture. One may fairly ask whether each time a society accepts diffused culture, it is not an independent recurrence of cause and effect. Malinowski (1944:214-15) states: "Diffusion . . . is not an act, but a process closely akin in its working to the evolutionary process. For evolution deals above all with the influence of any type of 'origins'; and origins do not differ fundamentally whether they occur by invention or by diffusion" (see also Wittfogel, 1939:175-76). For example, the civilizations of the Andes and Mexico were based on dense, sedentary populations, which in turn were supported by intensive irrigation farming. In both cases, the early societies were integrated by a theocratic hierarchy, which controlled communal endeavor and enlisted labor for the construction of religious centers. It is not sufficient to say that the agricultural, social, and religious institutions merely diffused as a unit, for that would be merely stating distributions in historical terms but failing to explain process. Incipient farming appeared first, and it diffused before the other complexes developed. The latter have a functional dependence on intensive farming. They could not have been accepted anywhere until it developed, and in the course of its development similar patterns would undoubtedly have emerged, whether or not they were diffused. The increasing population and the growing need for political integration very probably would have created small states in each area, and these states would almost certainly have been strongly theocratic, because the supernatural aspects of farming — for example, fertility concepts, the need to reckon seasons and to forecast the rise and fall of rivers, and the like — would have placed power in the hands of religious leaders. Diffusion may have hastened the development of theocratic states, but in each case the new developments were within determinable limits, and independently involved the same functional or cause-and-effect relationships.

It is true, of course, that many peculiar features common to New

World civilizations do not represent a logical outgrowth of basic patterns and that they can be disposed of with the superficial explanation that they diffused. Thus, the wide distribution of such concepts as the plumed serpent or the jaguar god, or of such constructions as terraced pyramids, may be explained in this manner, though deeper analysis might reveal the reasons for their wide acceptance. In general, it is the rather arbitrary, specific, or stylized features, that is, those features which have the least functional dependence on the basic patterns, that provide the greatest evidence of diffusion. These, in other words, are the particulars, which distinguish tribes or areas and obscure regularities.

Another means of denying the possibility of isolating cultural regularities is to stress that the complexity or multiplicity of the antecedents or functional correlates of any institution makes it virtually impossible to isolate the true causes of the institution; convergent evolution rather than parallel evolution is generally used to explain similarities that seem not to be the result of diffusion. The answer to this is simply that in dealing with cultural phenomena, as in dealing with all the complex phenomena of nature, regularities can be found only by looking for them, and they will be valid only if a rigorous methodology underlies the framing of hypotheses.

It is not necessary that any formulation of cultural regularities provide an ultimate explanation of culture change. In the physical and biological sciences, formulations are merely approximations of observed regularities, and they are valid as working hypotheses despite their failure to deal with ultimate realities. So long as a cultural law formulates recurrences of similar interrelationships of phenomena, it expresses cause and effect in the same way that the law of gravity formulates but does not ultimately explain the attraction between masses of matter. Moreover, like the law of gravity, which has been greatly modified by the theory of relativity, any formulation of cultural data may be useful as a working hypothesis, even though further research requires that it be qualified or reformulated.

Cultural regularities may be formulated on different levels, each in its own terms. At present, the most promising possibilities lie largely in the cultural or superorganic level, for anthropology's traditional primary concern with culture has provided far more data of this kind. Moreover, the greater part of culture history is susceptible to treatment in cultural terms. Both sequential or diachronic formulations and synchronic formulations are superorganic, and they may be functional to the extent that the data permit. Redfield's tentative formulation (Redfield, 1941) that urban culture contrasts with folk culture in being more individualized, secularized, heterogeneous, and disorganized is synchronic, superorganic, and functional. Morgan's evolutionary schemes (Morgan, 1877) and White's formulations concerning the relationship of energy to cultural development (White, 1943) are sequential and somewhat functional. Neither type, however, is wholly one or the other. A time-dimension is implied in Redfield's formulation, and synchronic, functional relationships are implied in White's.

Cultural formulations do not, of course, provide the deeper insights concerning human behavior that may come from a psychological level or a biological level. Research on these latter levels may profitably run concurrently with the other, but for the present their formulations will be more applicable to synchronic, functional studies than to sequential ones. Thus, to advocate search for regularities in cultural terms is not at all in conflict with those who state that "culture does not exist apart from the individual, its human carrier." The latter represents a different problem and level of discourse. Basic and ultimate explanations of behavior that will interrelate cultural, psychological, neurological, physiological, and even physical phenomena would require very different formulation. In view of anthropology's traditional and primary concern with culture, it is both admissible and necessary to deal in restricted terms.

The present statement of scientific purpose and methodology rests on a conception of culture that needs clarification. *If the more important institutions of culture can be isolated from their unique setting so as to be typed, classified, and related to recurring antecedents or functional correlates, it follows that it is possible to consider the institutions in question as the basic or constant ones, whereas the features that lend uniqueness are the secondary or variable ones.* For example, the American high civilizations had agriculture, social classes, and a priest-temple-idol cult. As types, these institutions are abstractions of what was actually present in each area, and they do not take into account the particular crops grown, the precise patterning of the social classes, or the conceptualization of deities, details of ritual, and other religious features of each culture center. The latter are secondary and variable so far as the institutions in question are concerned. In a more comprehensive analysis, however, they would serve to distinguish subtypes, which would require more specific formulations.

This conception of culture is in conflict with an extreme organic view, which regards culture as a closed system in which all parts are of equal importance and are equally fixed. It holds that some features of culture are more basic and more fixed than others and that the problem is to ascertain those which are primary and basic and to explain their origin and development. It assumes that although the secondary features must be consistent and functionally integrated with the primary ones, it is these latter that are more susceptible to fortuitous influences from inside or outside the culture, that change most readily, and that acquire such a variety of aspects that they give the impression that history never repeats itself.[2]

For the present, it is not necessary to state criteria for ascertaining the primary features. In general, they are the ones which individual scientists are most interested in studying and which the anthropological record shows to have recurred again and again in independent situations. A procedure which attempts to give equal weight to all features of culture amounts to a negation of typing and of making formulations, for it must include all the unique features, which obscure similarities between cultures.

ERAS IN THE DEVELOPMENT OF EARLY CIVILIZATIONS

The present section deals with the development of early agricultural civilizations in Northern Peru (the sequences are longest and best known in this part of Peru, thanks to the Viru Valley project of the Institute of Andean Research), Meso-America (Mexico and the Maya area), Mesopotamia, Egypt, and China. These areas were chosen because they were the cradles of civilization and because their exploitation by a pre-iron technology seems to have entailed similar solutions to similar problems and consequently to have caused similar developmental sequences. The environments are arid or semiarid, which, contrary to a common belief, did not impose great difficulties and thereby stimulate cultural development. Instead, they facilitated

---

[2] This proposition has been developed in detail in Julian H. Steward, "Native Cultures of the Intermontane (Great Basin) Area," *Essays in Historical Anthropology of North America. Smithsonian Miscellaneous Collection,* C (1940), 479-98; Steward, *Bureau of American Ethnology Bulletin 120,* 1938, pp. 1-3, 230-62.

Since this concept of primary traits (now called core features) and secondary or variable traits was devised, it has become evident that many if not most of the latter may be secondary in a formal but not a functional sense. This point is implicit throughout these chapters, but it could be made explicit only by elaboration of the *form-function* concept.

culture growth because they were easily tilled by digging-stick and irrigation farming. The tropical rain forests, the northern hardwood forests, and the sodded plains areas, on the other hand, were exploited only with the greatest difficulty by people who lacked iron tools.

The procedure to be followed is first to establish a tentative developmental typology or sequence in which the smaller periods are grouped into major eras, which have similar diagnostic features in each area. This requires considerable revision of current terminology, for no two authors use quite the same criteria for major stages of development. Americanists, who have discussed some of these problems together, are now using such terms as Formative, Developmental, Classical, Florescent, and Empire and Conquest, and they are attempting to reach an understanding about the cultural typology implied by these terms. Old World writers still cling largely to such entrenched terms as Mesolithic, Neolithic, Chalcolithic, Ceramolithic, Bronze, and Dynastic, thereby emphasizing technological features of minor developmental significance. Gordon Childe's use of Neolithic Barbarism, Higher Barbarism of the Copper Age, Urban Revolution, and Early Bronze Age, which incorporate some terms from L. H. Morgan, indicates that his thinking is somewhat closer to that of the Americanists, but his terminology and his period markers still fail to be very comparable to those of the latter. Braidwood has developed a somewhat different terminology for grouping periods of the Near East, but his interest in process is very similar to that of Americanists. His three major divisions are Food-Gathering (Hunting and Gathering), Food-Producing (farming), and Civilization. Whereas the present chapter utilizes the emergence of new levels of organization as the criterion of eras (farm villages or Incipient Agriculture, amalgamation of villages into small States or Formative, the state being achieved by the end of the era, Regional Florescent States, and multi-state Empires based on conquest), Braidwood is more interested in the peasant-urban contrast. This view is not in conflict with that presented here; indeed, it offers supplementary criteria which, in a more detailed comparison of the irrigation areas, could well serve to reveal new interrelationships of phenomena and to distinguish smaller periods. For Iraq, Braidwood's sequence runs from Food-Gathering through Incipient Agriculture to an "era of primary peasant efficiency" under Food-Production, with permanent villages, pottery, metal, and weaving. This is followed by "established peasant efficiency" with market-towns and temples, which grades into "incipient urbanization." These eras are grouped in the present scheme under the Formative and Regional

Florescent Eras, because they represent the establishment of basic technologies and the gradual formation of local states, which achieved some esthetic excellence in production. Braidwood's final era of Civilization, with a formal state, cities, laws, social classes, writing, and other features corresponds to our eras of Empire, Dark Ages, and Cyclical Imperial Conquests (Braidwood, 1952, 1948).

It will be noted that the present taxonomy of developmental periods makes little use of technological features. Diffusion might carry many features from one area to another, but our criterion of their importance is their functional effect upon the society. Since our interest is primarily in sociolcultural systems, specific techniques are significant only if they affected the nature of cultural ecological adaptations in an area. Thus, the absence of bronze in Meso-America and the presence of iron in China have minor importance. The methods of irrigation agriculture had little use for metals. The possession of iron could not convert peasant-like folk communities in China into larger systems. Only improved farming and population growth could accomplish this.

The second step in the procedure (p. 181) is to suggest cause-and-effect relationships between the cultural phenomena of the successive eras and to formulate as basic regularities those relationships which are common to all areas. These formulations are offered primarily as an illustration of the generalizing approach to cultural data. Tentative and preliminary, they will be revised again and again as long as research continues and as long as scholars probe for a deeper understanding of the basic processes of cultural development. Even if these formulations were entirely scrapped, they would have served their purpose if they stimulated students of culture development to interest themselves in the same problems, to use comparable methods, and to present their findings in comparable terms — in short, to talk one another's language.[3]

---

[3] Cultural historical data are from the following sources, unless otherwise cited.

Northern Peru: Wendell C. Bennett, "The Andean Highlands: An Introduction," *Handbook of South American Indians,* ed. Julian H. Steward, *Bureau of American Ethnology Bulletin 143,* II (1946), 1-60; A. L. Kroeber, "The Present Status of Americanistic Problems," *The Maya and Their Neighbors* (New York, 1940), pp. 460-87; A. L. Kroeber, "Peruvian Archaeology in 1942," *Viking Fund Publication Anthropology,* No. 4 (New York, 1944); W. D. Strong, "Finding the Tomb of a Warrior-God," *National Geographic Magazine,* April, 1947, pp. 453-82; Gordon R. Willey, *New World Cultures* (Byron Cummings Anniversary Volume, 1948).

Meso-America: Pedro Armillas, "A Sequence of Cultural Development in Meso-America," *A Reappraisal of Peruvian Archaeology,* ed. Wendell C. Bennett, *Society for American Archaeology,* Memoir 4, 1948; Alfred Kidder, Jesse Jennings, and Edwin Shook, *Excavations of Kaminaljuyú,* Carnegie Institution

Table 4 groups the periods of each center into eras that have the same general features. Periods in the same relative position, consequently, were similar but were not contemporaneous. Table 5 places the eras of each center on an absolute time-scale, which is fairly precise for the periods of written history but much less accurate for the early periods. The margin of error in dating these early periods does not, however, greatly affect the functional analysis of cultural development.

In the following characterization of eras it must be stressed that the diagnostic features appeared by the end of each era, not in the beginning. An interpretation similar to ours might appear very different if the classification of periods were such that each era began when the key traits appeared.

Pre-Agricultural Era

This era includes all the Old World paleolithic and mesolithic periods, which lacked farming, and the New World pre-agricultural periods. To judge by the simple remains of these periods as well as by the recent hunting and gathering cultures, the technologies were devoted principally to satisfying biological needs for food, clothing, and shelter. Pottery, basketry, loom-weaving, metallurgy, permanent houses, and boat and animal transportation were probably absent until

of Washington, Publication No. 561 (1946); Sylvanus Morley, *The Ancient Maya* (Stanford University Press, 1946); Eric Thompson, "A Trial Survey of the Southern Maya Area," *American Antiquity,* IX (1943), 106-34; Eric Thompson, "A Survey of the Northern Maya Area," *American Antiquity,* XI (1945), 2-24; George Vaillant, *The Aztecs of Mexico* (New York, 1944).

Mesopotamia and Egypt: V. Gordon Childe, *New Light on the Most Ancient East* (New York, 1934); V. Gordon Childe, *What Happened in History* (New York, 1946); William F. Albright, *From the Stone Age to Christianity* (Baltimore, 1946); Robert Braidwood, "Prehistoric Men," *Chicago Natural History Museum Popular Series, Anthropology,* No. 37 (1948); Robert Braidwood, *The Near East and the Foundations for Civilization,* Oregon State System of Higher Education (Eugene, Oregon, 1952).

China: C. W. Bishop, *Origin of the Far Eastern Civilizations,* Smithsonian Institution War Background Studies, No. 1 (1942); H. G. Creel, *The Birth of China* (New York, 1937); H. G. Creel, *Studies in Early Chinese Culture* (Baltimore, 1937); Karl A. Wittfogel, "The Foundations and Stages of Chinese Economic History," *Zeitschrift für Sozial forschung* (Paris), IV (1935), 26-60; Karl A. Wittfogel, "Die Theorie der Orientalischen Gesselschaft," *Zeitschrift für Sozial forschung* (Paris), Vol. VII, Nos. 1-2 (1938), pp. 90-122; Karl A. Wittfogel, "The Society of Prehistoric China," *Studies in Philosophy and Social Science,* VIII (1939), 138-86; Karl A. Wittfogel and Feng Chia-Sheng, "General Introduction [to History of Chinese Society, Liao]," *American Philosophical Society, Transactions,* XXXVI (1946), 1-35.

Table 4. ARCHAEOLOGICAL AND HISTORICAL PERIODS GROUPED IN MAJOR ERAS

Eras	Mesopotamia, Syria, Assyria	Egypt	China	Meso-America Mexico	Meso-America Maya Area	Northern Peru
Industrial Revolution	Euro-American 19th and 20th century economic and political empires.					
Iron Age Culture	Influences from Greece, Rome; later from north and central Europe. In New World Spanish conquest destroys native empires.					
Cyclical Imperial Conquests	Kassites Hammurabi Dynastic Accad	Hyksos New Empire	Ming Sui, T'ang, Ch'in, Han			Inca
Dark Ages	Invasions	First Intermediate	Warring states			Local states
Initial Empire	Royal tombs Ur Early Dynastic Sumer	Pyramid Age Early Dynastic	Chou	Aztec Toltec Chichimec?	Mexican "Absorption"	Tiahuanaco
Regional Florescent States	Jedmet Nasr Warkan-Tepe Gawram Ubaid	Gerzian Amratian Badarian	Shang "Hsia"	Teotihuacán	"Initial Series" Glyphs or Classical	Mochica Gallinazo
Formative (Peasant communities to states)	Halafian Hassunan-Matarrah Jarmo	Merimdean Fayumian	Yang Shao Pre-Yang Shao	Archaic or Middle Periods (Zacatenco)	Formative or Old Empire Mamóm	Salinar Chavín-Cupisnique
Incipient Agriculture	Karim Shahir?		Plain Pottery?	?	?	Cerro Prieto
Hunting and Gathering	Natufian Paleolithic and "Terminal Food-Gathering"			Pre-Agriculture		

Table 5. ABSOLUTE CHRONOLOGY OF MAJOR AREAS[a]

(years)	Mesopotamia	Egypt	N. China	N. Peru	Meso-America
2000 A.D.					
1000 A.D.					Cyclical Conquests
A.D. / B.C.	Cyclical Conquests	Cyclical Conquests	Cyclical Conquests	Cyclical Conquests	Regional Florescent
1000 B.C.			Dark Ages	Regional Florescent	
			Initial Empire		Formative
2000 B.C.	Dark Ages	Dark Ages	Regional Florescent	Formative	Incipient Agriculture?
			Formative	Incipient Agriculture	
3000 B.C.	Initial Empire	Initial Empire	Incipient Agriculture		Hunting and Gathering
	Regional Florescent	Regional Florescent	Hunting and Gathering	Hunting and Gathering	
4000 B.C.	Formative	Formative			
	Incipient Agriculture	Incipient Agriculture			
5000 B.C.	Incipient Agriculture	Hunting and Gathering			
6000 B.C.	Hunting and Gathering				
7000 B.C.					
8000 B.C.					
9000 B.C.					

[a] These dates have been revised on the basis of Braidwood's estimates for the Near East (*The Near East and the Foundations for Civilization*, Eugene, Oregon, 1952) and of radiocarbon dates for the Near East and America. These new dates place the origin of agriculture about 2,000 years more recent than was formerly believed in the Near East and about 2,000 years earlier in the Andes. Period dates for India and China are revised to fit the Near East dates, but still presumably show a time lag. (New World dates are taken from *Radiocarbon Dating* (Assembled by Frederick Johnson), Memoir of the Society for American Archaeology, *American Antiquity*, Vol. XVII, No. 1, 1951).

they were borrowed to a limited degree from higher centers. Social patterns were based on kinship, age, and sex, but they varied greatly as they became adapted to local conditions. Warfare was restricted to blood feuds, revenge for witchcraft, and perhaps in some areas retaliation against trespass.

Incipient Agriculture

This era cannot be dated exactly, and it is known through very few finds. It must have been very long, passing through several stages, which began when the first cultivation of plant domesticates supplemented hunting and gathering, and ended when plant and animal breeding was able to support permanent communities. To judge by what are the earliest-known evidences of domestication in Mesopotamia and Peru, technologies made little advance over those of the previous era until settled village life was fully achieved.

PERU: Cerro Prieto.

Culture: Farming based on Canavalia beans, calabash, and cotton; twined weaving; ceramics absent; semisubterranean houses.

MESO-AMERICA: As the earliest-known agricultural periods of Meso-America appear to have had technologies and temple mounds, which elsewhere characterized the Formative Era, it is generally believed (Morley [1946] excepted) that the cultures of these periods were introduced full-blown from elsewhere. Theoretically, however, it would seem that remains of simpler agricultural peoples should antedate the fairly developed theocratic communities in Meso-America.

MESOPOTAMIA: Karim Shahir?

Culture: Probably domesticated wheat, barley, peas, sheep, goat, pig, ox; adobe houses; ceramics (late); mortars; ground stone axes; unbaked clay figurines. Villages on the "hilly flanks."

EGYPT:

Culture: Possibly domesticated plants. Pottery present.

CHINA: Period of Plain Pottery. This period is considered to be the first phase of neolithic China, though the presence of domesticated plants or animals is doubtful.

Formative Era of Basic Technologies and Folk Culture

The Formative Era is so named because the principal technologies — basketry, pottery, weaving, metallurgy, and construction — appeared and the patterns of community culture took form at this time. It was an era of population growth, area expansion of cultures and peoples, comparative peace, and wide diffusion of culture between centers of civilization.

The principal domesticated plants were by now brought under intensive cultivation, and irrigation was begun on a community scale. In the Old World, the more important domesticated animals, except the horse, were present from early in the era. In the New World, the absence of suitable wild species for domestication limited such animals to the dog, and, in the Andes, to the llama and alpaca.

Food production was on a subsistence basis, except as a share was provided for the ruling class. Increasingly efficient farming released considerable labor for the satisfaction of socially derived needs; that is, craft production of finer goods and construction of religious edifices for the theocracy made rapid progress during each period.

The sociopolitical unit seems to have been the small local community, but by the end of the era local, multicommunity states appeared. The clustering of rooms in house units suggests that lineages or kin-groups were the basis of society. One to several such units were associated with a ceremonial center, which served as the nucleus and integrating factor of a dispersed community. Control of irrigation, which was on a local scale, was one of the more important practical functions of the religious leaders. Warfare was probably limited to raids and contributed little either to social structure or to expansion of the state.

PERU: Chavín-Cupisnique, Salinar.

Technologies: Domesticated maize, manioc, beans, gourds, peanuts; small-scale irrigation; llamas. Pottery; metallurgy in gold, copper (?); loom-weaving in cotton; twined baskets; surface adobe houses; balsa (reed bundle) boats.

Social features: Dispersed communities, evidently centering in religious mounds and temples. Feline, condor, and serpent deities. Theocratic control of society; rulers accorded status burial.

MESO-AMERICA: Armillas' (1948) and Kidder's (1945) Formative; in Mexico, Vaillant's (1944) Middle Periods; in Yucatan, Thompson's (1943, 1945) Formative and Morley's (1946) Pre-Maya. These include Zacatenco and Ticomán in highland Mexico, Lower Tres Zapotes on the east coast, Mamóm and Chicanel in lowland Guatemala, Miraflores in highland Guatemala, and Playa de los Muertos in Honduras.

Technologies: Probably domesticated maize, manioc, and other plants; local irrigation. Pottery; loom-weaving, probably in cotton; basketry (?); no metallurgy. Wattle-and-daub houses in Guatemala.

Social features: Small, scattered settlements. Female figurines suggest a fertility cult. Temple mounds; funerary architecture; and beginnings of intellectual development, as evidenced by calendrical stelae of the Maya area, which appeared at the end of the era.

MESOPOTAMIA: Childe's (1946) Higher Barbarism of the Copper Age and beginnings of his Urban Revolution; beginnings of Albright's (1946) Chalcolithic; Braidwood's (1952) "era of primary peasant efficiency." In Mesopotamia: Jarmo Sialk I, Hassunan, Samarran, and Halafian.

Technologies: Domesticated plants, probably wheat, barley, millet, and others; cattle, sheep, goats, pigs; some irrigation. Pottery; loom-weaving, probably in flax; basketry; metallurgy in gold and copper; possibly the wheel. Rectangular, adobe houses.

Social features: Villages have local shrines. Religion involves female and animal figurines; male and female gods are represented.

EGYPT: Fayumian, Merimdean.

Technologies: Wheat, barley; cattle, pigs, sheep, goats. Pottery; metallurgy in gold and copper; loom-weaving in linen; coiled basketry. Semisubterranean, circular houses. Balsa (papyrus bundle) boats.

Social features: Clans or kin groups (?); captive slaves (?); female and animal figurines in religion; dog-sacrifice in burials.

CHINA: Neolithic (Pre-Yang Shao, Yang Shao).

Technologies: Millet, sorghum (?), rice, wheat; pigs; probably well-and-ditch irrigation. Pottery; loom-weaving in hemp (?); basketry; metallurgy in copper.

Social features: Small, semipermanent settlements of circular pit-houses, possibly based on matrilineal lineages. Religion evidenced by pottery phalli; possibly human sacrifice and cannibalism.

Era of Regional Development and Florescence

This era was marked by the emergence and florescence of regionally distinctive cultures. No new basic technologies were invented, but irrigation works were enlarged, thus releasing a larger portion of the population to develop arts and crafts and to further intellectual interests. Multicommunity states arose.

States were still strongly theocratic, but interstate competition and state expansion seem to have entailed some militarism. A class-structured society, which was foreshadowed in the previous era, now became fully established. The ruling class appears to have been predominantly theocratic, but it was likely that some status was accorded successful warriors. The priesthood now had sufficient leisure to develop astronomy, mathematics, and writing (these were little developed in Peru). The largest religious edifices were built, and the finest art and manufactures of any era were produced toward the end of this era, each region producing distinctive styles. These products were made by special artisans and were dedicated principally to the upper classes and to the temples. Trade attained important proportions, and improved transportational devices were introduced.

PERU: Willey's (1948) Regional Classical; Strong's (1947) Late Formative and Florescent; Bennett's (1946) late Early Periods. Gallinazo and Mochica (Nazca in south Peru).

Technologies: Maize, manioc, potatoes, sweet potatoes, calabashes, pumpkins, peanuts; llamas, alpacas. Inter-valley irrigation.

Social features: Large communities; population maximum; largest mounds, temples; fanged deity, and gods of agriculture, fishing, celestial phenomena, and places. Ruler was warrior-god. Hilltop forts were built. Regional states (entire valley or several valleys?). War captives, human sacrifice, human trophies. Status burial for the upper class. Trade.

Transportation: Roads; probably llama-packing; ocean-going balsa boats with sails (?).

Intellectual and esthetic traits: Ideographic writing on beans (?); quipus. Finest art of all eras.

MESO-AMERICA: Armillas' (1948) Florescent; Kidder's (1945) Classical; Thompson's (1943, 1945) Initial Series; Morley's (1946) Old Empire. These include: Middle and Upper Tres Zapotes on the east coast; Teotihuacán and Monte Albán II and III in Mexico; Esperanza in highland Guatemala; and Tsakol and Tepeu in lowland Guatemala.

Technology: Local irrigation, chinampas, and terracing in agriculture.

Social features: Dispersed settlements; local theocratic states that controlled all settlements of a valley or other natural regions. Population maximum (?) (Cook, 1947). Largest mounds and temples. Priestly hierarchy. Gods of rain, water, jaguar, serpent, quetzal. Child sacrifice (?); possibly ancestor worship (as evidenced by figurine portraits in Mexico, status burial in Guatemala). Militarism evidently restricted to raids, with some captive-taking.

Transportation: Roads and causeways; widespread trade; (toy wheel).

Intellectual and esthetic traits: Phonetic writing, mathematics, astronomy. Finest art of all eras.

MESOPOTAMIA: Latter part of Albright's (1946) Chalcolithic; Childe's (1946) Urban Revolution and Eary Bronze; Braidwood's (1952) "era of established peasant efficiency" and "Proto-Literate phase." These include: Obeidian (Al'Ubaid), Warkan-Tepe Gawra, and Jedmet Nasr.

Technologies: Wheat, barley, millet, date palm, figs, grapes, sesame, onions, garlic, lettuce, melons, chick peas, horse beans; drained fields, large-scale irrigation. Wheel-made ceramics.

Social features: Urbanization began with riverine settlements. Multicommunity states, which were essentially theocratic, though rulers had also war power. Large palace-temples. Gods of agriculture. Some pressures of infiltration by foot-nomads. Widespread trade.

Transportation: Horse (?), chariot and four-wheeled wagon; balsa (reed bundle) boats.

Intellectual traits: Pictographic writing, mathematical systems, astronomy.

EGYPT: Badarian, Amratian, Gerzian.

Technologies: Farming as in Formative Era, though probably increased irrigation. Rectangular, above-ground, adobe houses.

Social features: Tendency to urbanization; multicommunity states, each with an associated animal god and under the rule of heads of principal lineages (?). Some warfare implements expansion of state. Status burial shows a cult of the dead. Considerable trade.

Transportation: Sailing vessels; ass.

Intellectual traits: Beginnings of writing; calendrical and numerical systems.

Possibly the Semainian period and the beginnings of the Early Dynastic periods should be included in the Era of Regional Florescence in Egypt, for the temple cult appeared, class differentiation became definite, and phonetic writing, a calendrical system, and mathematics were developed. These features, however, continued to develop with little interruption into the era of Conquest and Empire.

CHINA: "Hsia" (Black Pottery period) and Shang Dynasty.

Technologies: Wheat, millet, rice, pig, cattle, sheep, in north; buffalo and chicken in south. Beginnings of public works in form of dikes; otherwise, local well-and-ditch irrigation were practiced. Bronze manufactures. Horse and chariot. Weaving in silk.

Social features: Local state, Wittfogel's "Feudal" type, under which serfs cultivated the local ruler's land. Divine monarch; status burial in deep grave. Use of oracle bones to forecast rain and for other divination; dragon deity; human and animal sacrifice. Warfare arising from conflict over grazing lands (Creel, 1937b:184) and from pressure of herding nomads.

Intellectual and esthetic traits: Picture and ideographic writing. Finest esthetic expressions, especially in bronzes.

Cyclical Conquests

The diagnostic features of this era are the emergence of large-scale militarism, the extension of political and economic domination over large areas or empires, a strong tendency toward urbanization, and the construction of fortifications. In the social structure, priest-warriors constituted the ruling groups, usually under a divine monarch, whose importance is revealed in elaborate status burial. Social classes now tended to become frozen into hereditary classes, in contrast to society of the previous era, which probably permitted individuals some upward mobility through personal achievements. Gods of war became prominent in the pantheon of deities.

There were no important technological changes. Bronze appeared in Peru, Mesopotamia, and Egypt, and was used for weapons and ornaments, but it contributed little to the production of food or other goods. Iron, though not an iron-age culture, appeared in China. The principal change in manufactures was a strong trend toward standardization and mass production, with a concomitant sacrifice of esthetic freedom and variety. Large-scale trade within the empires, and even beyond, brought the beginnings of a special commercial class, but coinage and an efficient monetary system were not yet developed.

PERU: Willey's Expansion and Conquest; Strong's Fusion and Imperial periods; Bennett's Tiahuanaco, Late Periods, and Inca.

Technologies: As before, except that bronze was used for ornaments, weapons, and a few tools. By the Inca period, there was standardized, mass production.

Social features: Planned urban centers were constructed, and they drew off much population from the local communities. Under the Inca, social classes were finally frozen in a caste system, headed by the divine royal family. A priesthood and bureaucracy ruled the state and placed levies on the commoners, but the local folk culture persisted. An ancestor cult occurred along with agricultural, place, and animal gods. The state was enlarged by wars of conquest, which perhaps started in the previous era and originated from population pressures. Populations were moved from place to place by imperial command.

MESO-AMERICA: Armillas' Militaristic Period (in Mexico, Toltec, Aztec, Monte Alban V, Tzintzuntzan Tarascan; and, in Yucatan, Mexican Absorption). Thompson's Mexican Period and Morley's New Empire in Yucatan. Kidder's Amatle and Pamplona in highland Guatemala.

Technologies: As before, except that metallurgy in copper and gold appeared, being used mainly for ornaments. There was extensive trade, and money, in the form of cacao beans, was used during the Aztec period.

Social features: The population was increasingly concentrated in defensible sites, and special forts were constructed. Larger and larger areas were drawn into empires, and wealth was concentrated through tribute in the hands of the ruling classes. The king-priest had great military power. There were military classes, warrior societies, and slaves. Great population movements are evident in the inroads of Chichimecs into the Valley of Mexico, the Nahuatl migrations to Central America, and the Mexican invasion of Yucatan. Warfare was intensified, gods of war entered the pantheon, and human sacrifice became a major feature of religion.

MESOPOTAMIA: Early Dynastic Sumerians to Dynasty of Accad. Braidwood's "Civilization."

Technologies: Bronze was used for weapons, ornaments, and a few tools. There was standardized mass production, especially of goods used by commoners, and widespread trade, mainly for luxury items.

Social features: Urban communities attained great size and served as military, political, religious, and commercial centers. The king combined religious and military leadership and controlled multi-community states. Statuses were strongly differentiated: the king, representing the god (sometimes a war god), was supreme; priests and nobles tended to have hereditary status; farmers, artisans, and wage-earners were either attached to the temple or else worked on privately-owned lands; captives became slaves. Soldiers sometimes gained status. Gods included agricultural and local deities; the cult of the dead attained some importance, as shown in status burials.

EGYPT: Early Dynasties, I-IV.

Technologies: Bronze was used for weapons and ornaments, and there was evidence of mass production and extensive trade.

Social features: Planned cities were built. The god-king became the military and political head of large states, which were expanded through warfare, and he eclipsed the power of the priesthood. Social structure became rigid, hereditary nobles controlling great wealth. Warfare, probably originating in population pressures and dislocations throughout the Near East, was waged to create empires and to ward off invasions.

Theology was based on a pantheon of general gods, such as the Sun, on local animal gods, and on a cult of the dead. The last, combined somewhat with the first two, became predominant, as evidenced by the divine power of the king and by his status burial in pyramids.

CHINA: The Chou through Ming Dynasties. The culture center shifts south from the Yellow River to the Yangtze River (Ch'ao-Ting Chi, 1936), while conquests, starting with the Chou Dynasty, culminate in Wittfogel's (1935) type of oriental absolute state by the T'ang Dynasty.

Technologies: Irrigation and water works develop under state control and become large-scale under the Warring States; plow and fertilizer. Iron, glass, and other technologies diffuse from the west.

Social features: The Chou Dynasty initiates the era of conquests. A divine ruler and bureaucracy control a state which is stratified into hereditary nobles with military and economic power, merchants, serfs, and some slaves. Cities develop as administrative, religious, and commercial centers.

TRIAL FORMULATION OF DEVELOPMENTAL REGULARITIES OF EARLY CIVILIZATIONS

At the present time the difficulties in making any formulation of the development of early civilizations in the five principal centers of the world are obviously very great. Data on early periods are incomplete, not only because research has been limited but also because it has been directed toward special and restricted problems. Archaeology has, until recently, paid comparatively little attention to settlement patterns, demographic trends, and sociological implications of its materials. Historians on the whole are more interested in the fate of particular societies than in culture and its development, and anthropologists have made comparatively little use of the data of written history. These difficulties mean primarily that any present formulation must be highly tentative.

The successive eras in each of the five principal centers of early civilizations appear to have had similar diagnostic features which, arranged chronologically, might be considered as a superficial formulation of regularities. Such a formulation, however, would fail to provide a satisfactory and generally valid functional explanation of cause-and-effect relationships between phenomena. To provide deeper explanations, it is necessary to make cause-and-effect relationships as explicit as possible and to test the explanations offered for the sequence in each center by the data of other centers. This purpose is consistent with the comparative approach of anthropology, and it is far more important to find a common problem than to construct enduring formulations.

The formulation here offered excludes all areas except the arid and semiarid centers of ancient civilizations. In the irrigation areas, environment, production, and social patterns had similar functional and developmental interrelationships. The productivity of farming was limited only by the amount of water that could be used in irrigation. Metal tools and animal-drawn plows, though essential to maximum efficiency of farming in forest or grassland areas, could not increase the yield of irrigation areas beyond the limits imposed by water supply.

Early civilizations occurred also in such tropical rain-forest areas as southern Asia and Yucatan. Yucatan appears to fit the formulation made for the more arid areas to the extent that its sequences were very similar to those of Meso-America generally. Farming in Yucatan, however, required slash-and-burn rather than irrigation techniques, and the rural population must have been very scattered. It is possible, therefore, that the Maya were able to develop a high civilization only because they enjoyed an unusually long period of peace; for their settlement pattern would seem to have been too vulnerable to warfare. Yucatan, consequently, should perhaps be excluded from the present formulation. In southeastern Asia, the environment is extremely humid, presenting the difficulties of rain forests and also requiring large drainage projects. And in both areas, the civilizations appear to have been later than, and in part derived from, those of the irrigation areas.

The era of Incipient Agriculture in the irrigation centers is very little known, but evidence from Peru and Mesopotamia suggests that it lasted a much shorter time than had once been supposed. Farming was at first supplementary to hunting and gathering, and the social groups were consequently small and probably seminomadic. Technologies differed little from those of the earlier hunting and gathering periods. By the end of this era, farming supported permanent communities, and new technologies began to appear.

A local community, "folk" or "peasant," culture[4] took form during the next era. Nearly all the principal crops and animals were by now brought under domestication, but irrigation was undertaken only on a small, local scale. In subsequent eras, agricultural production increased as irrigation works were developed, the only limit being available land and water, especially the latter. The animal-drawn plow, which appeared in the Old World much later, during the era of Cyclical Conquests, and which was unknown in prehistoric America, no doubt released a certain portion of the population from farm work, but neither it nor iron tools, which appeared still later, could increase production beyond the limits of water supply. Population consequently increased as irrigation works were developed to their maximum. For this reason, the Old World possession of draft animals and the plow does not affect the present formulation.

During the Formative Era, all centers of civilization developed ceramics, loom-weaving, basketry, metallurgy (except Meso-America), and the construction of houses and religious edifices. These technologies soon came to be used for two kinds of goods: first, objects that served the simple, domestic — that is, essentially biological — needs of the common folk; second, highly elaborate, stylized goods that served the socially derived needs as well as the more basic needs of the theocratic class. In simple form, some of these technologies spread beyond the areas of irrigation.

Subsequent to the Formative Era, no very important technological advances were made until the Iron Age. Metallurgy ran through similar sequences everywhere (except in Meso-America), starting with work in copper and gold and finally achieving bronze. Copper and tin were so rare that the use of bronze was largely limited to ornaments and weapons, while tools of stone, bone, wood, and shell were used for daily chores. Improvement in the other technologies consisted of

---

[4] As a developmental level, this may be considered to have had the general characteristics of Robert Redfield's "Folk Society." See "The Folk Society," *American Journal of Sociology,* LII (1947), 293-308.

embellishments and refinements that enhanced their esthetic qualities and produced varied products; but there were no important new inventions.

Transportation improved in successive eras. Domesticated animals were first probably used for packing in all centers except in Meso-America, which lacked species suitable for domestication. Wheeled vehicles appeared in the Old World during the era of Regional Florescence. The wheel was evidently used on toys during the same era in Meso-America (Ekholm, 1946), but its failure to be used in transportation perhaps may be explained by the absence of draft animals. The importance of transportation increased as states grew larger and as trade expanded. Although draft animals and wheels, which were used on war chariots before they were used on carts and wagons, gave the Old World some technical advantage, every New World center developed roads, boats, and canals to a degree of efficiency which enabled them to achieve states as large as those of the Old World.

The general sequence of social, religious, and military patterns ran a similar course in each center of civilization, and a generally valid formulation is possible. Certain problems which cannot yet be answered will be stated subsequently.

In the era of Incipient Agriculture it is reasonable to suppose that sociopolitical groups were as varied in nature as they are today among the hunting and gathering peoples of arid areas.

At the beginning of the Formative Era, the sociopolitical unit was a small house cluster, which probably consisted of a kin group or lineage. As population increased, new clusters evidently budded off and established themselves in unsettled lands. In Mesopotamia, the Formative Era villages were on what Braidwood calls the "hilly flanks," where rainfall permitted farming, rather than along the river. This raises the question of whether the riverine flood plains were the principal habitat in any of the areas at this time. In the course of time, as flood plains became densely settled and as need arose to divert water through canals to drier land, collaboration on irrigation projects under some co-ordinating authority became necessary. That the need was met by the rise to power of a theocratic class is shown by the appearance toward the end of the Formative Era of evidence of religious domination of society, for example, ceremonial centers, such as mounds and temples, and a large number of religious objects. Farming required careful reckoning of the seasons, considerable ritual, and worship of agricultural gods, tasks which necessitated a special priest-hood. During the Formative Era, a small number of house clusters were dispersed around a ceremonial center and were ruled by a priesthood. The priesthood provided centralized control of irrigation and new patterns of group religion. Society became differentiated into theocratic and common classes. Thus, society became organized on a higher level than that of the localized lineage.

In the Formative Era, state warfare was probably of minor importance. There is little archaeological evidence of militarism, and it is likely that warfare was limited to raids. As long as there was ample land for the expanding population, competition for terrain cannot have been important. Because pastoral nomads during this era were unmounted and probably had not become very numerous, they cannot have been a great threat. In the Near East, they probably had asses, cattle, sheep, and goats, but did not ride horses and camels until the Iron Age (Albright, 1946:120-23), and horse riding did not appear in China until the era of Dark Ages or Warring States.

The precise patterning, content, and history of religion, which supplied the socially integrating factor, varied with each center of civilization. In some centers, such as Egypt, China, Peru, and Guatemala, elaborate burials for certain individuals suggest a cult of the dead or ancestor worship, which elevated these persons to the status of god-priests while living and to the status of gods after death. Other kinds of gods are represented by animal, place, and fertility deities. In some instances, the priesthood may have developed from an earlier class of shamans.

The particular religious patterns of each center arose from complex factors of local development and diffusion, and they gave local distinctiveness to the cultures. In terms of the present formulation, however, these differences are secondary in importance to the fact that in all cases a national religion and a priestly class developed because increasing populations, larger irrigation works, and greater need for social co-ordination called upon religion to supply the integrating factor. The very great importance of religion at the end of the Formative Era is proved by the effort devoted to the construction of temple mounds, temples, palaces, and tombs, and to the special production of religious ornaments, sculpture, and various material appurtenances of the priesthood and temples. It was the priesthood which, devoting full time to religious matters, now laid the foundations of astronomy, writing, and mathematics in all centers.

The era of Regional Florescence fulfilled the potentialities of the Formative Era. Communities were welded into small states, which, however, continued to be essentially theocratic, for archaeological remains of this era are predominantly of a religious nature. The largest mounds, temples, and tombs (mortuary pyramids and burial mounds) of any eras were constructed. Intellectual trends were fulfilled in the development of phonetic writing, numerical systems, and accurate calendars. Even Peru, which never developed phonetic writing, may have used an ideographic system at this time (Hoyle, 1946). Ceramics, metallurgy, weaving, work in precious stones, and sculpture attained their highest peak of esthetic expression and their most distinctive local stylization.

The relation of militarism to the enlargement of irrigation works and the expansion of states during the era of Regional Florescence is not clear. Population, irrigation works, and states all increased in size until the end of the era. In Meso-America, it is generally believed (Armillas, 1948; Kidder, Jennings, and Shook, 1946; Morley, 1946) that the states were peaceful and theocratic, and Cook (1947) believes that population reached its maximum at this time, decreasing in the subsequent era. In this case, a priesthood without the backing of armed force was able to create multicommunity states, though the extent of irrigation works at this time is not well known. In other areas, it appears that some militarism was present in the era of Regional Florescence, and that without warfare the rulers could not have increased the size of states and thereby of irrigation works. In northern Peru, warfare was definitely present in the era of Regional Florescence, and in China, warfare, arising from conflicts over grazing lands enabled local rulers to extend their authority over subject states (Bishop, 1942:20), perhaps facilitating the enlargement of irrigation works. Irrigation, however, did not attain maximum size in China until true empires appeared in the following era of Cyclical Conquests (Ch'ao-Ting Chi, 1936; Wittfogel, 1938, 1939). Thus, in China the population maximum came only when militarism achieved empire-wide irrigation projects. In Mesopotamia and Egypt, warfare also appeared during the era of Regional Florescence, and it was no doubt instrumental in enlarging states, but true kingdoms or empires did not appear until the following era. The relation of irrigation and population to warfare and state size in Egypt is not clear, but if Childe (1946) is correct in believing that warfare resulted from competition for lands as well as from the pressures of nomads, it would seem that population limits may have been reached.

This seeming contradiction cannot be resolved at present, but it may be suspected either that Meso-America had unusually powerful priests or else that the population maximum was not really reached until after the era of Regional Florescence, when militarism increased the size of states and consequently of irrigation works. In all centers, a temporary decrease of population probably followed the initiation of large-scale warfare.[5]

Social structure seems to have been very similar in all centers of civilization. The local community retained its folk culture, that is, its social structure, local shrines, agricultural practices, and the like, and its members constituted the commoners. Rulers were predominantly priests, though they began to acquire some military functions. It is possible that war achievements gave status to special individuals and that war captives formed a slave class, but as the existence of true economic slavery in native America is in doubt, the social role of captives and the problem of the origin and nature of slavery are open problems which are excluded from consideration here.

The era of Cyclical Conquests was one of comparatively few culture changes, except those produced by warfare. It initiated a succession of empires and then local states or dark ages that alternated in a fairly stereotyped pattern until the Iron Age and Industrial Era brought cultural influences from other areas. In each center, large-scale warfare, which probably originated from internal population pressures, from competition for resources, and from the pressures of outside nomads, was an instrument in creating true empires and starting dynasties. As the empires grew, irrigation works were increased to the limits of water supply and population also increased. After reaching a peak, marked by a temporary florescence of culture, population pressure and abuse of the common people brought rebellion, which destroyed the empires and returned society to local states and a period of dark ages. Irrigation works were neglected and population decreased. New conquests initiated another cycle.

The cyclical phenomena are strikingly illustrated in China (Wittfogel, 1938, 1946) where, during 1,500 years of the era of Cyclical Conquests, each of the four major peaks of empires and dynasties

---

[5] Robert Rands, in a study of the classical Maya, found considerable pictorial evidence of militarism but no definite indication that it was nationalistic in the sense of furthering state purposes (Rands, 1952).

coincided with a population peak (Ta Chen, 1946). These were separated by periods of internal strife and local autonomy. The series of empires in the Near East, which began in Mesopotamia with the early Dynasty of Sumer and in Egypt with the Dynastic period, ran through cycles generally comparable with those of China and lasted until the northern Mediterranean states of the Iron Age brought portions of the Near East under periodic conquests. In Peru, the widespread Tiahuanaco culture and the later Inca Empire probably represent two cycles of empire growth, while in Mexico, the first cycle, that of the Aztec conquests, had not run its course when the Spaniards conquered America.

In the era of Conquest, militarism produced several important social changes. Braidwood and Childe properly stress urbanization as a characteristic of this era. It should be noted, however, first that cities are but one aspect of state and imperial levels of sociocultural integration and second that the nature of cities changed in each era. Towns, which previously had been ceremonial, administrative, production and trading centers, now became large walled cities, and special forts were built to afford refuge to the dispersed farm settlements. A true military class appeared in the social hierarchy, and warrior-priests ruled the states and empires. War gods became prominent in the pantheons of state deities.

In this era, all aspects of culture were increasingly regimented at the expense of creative effort. There were sharpened differences in social classes, such as nobles, priests, warriors, commoners, slaves, and stronger differentiation of occupational groups. Laws were codified, learning was systematized (astronomy, theology, mathematics, medicine, writing), art became standardized, and goods were mass-produced by specialists.

Specialized production of commodities and widespread trade laid a basis for commercialism, but a free commercial class, factory production, and wage labor could not emerge until economy achieved a strong monetary basis, private property, and specialized cash crops, and until trade was disengaged from the system of state tribute and freed from state control. Though foreshadowed everywhere, this did not occur in the Near East until the Iron Age. In China, the development of private property in land and a system of money and taxation was not sufficient to free economy from the control of powerful states, which existed by virtue of grain taxes which their water works made possible (Wittfogel, 1935, 1939). In the New World, this era was not reached until the Spanish conquest.

The developments of the Iron Age and the Industrial Era are beyond the scope of the present inquiry. Iron appeared in China in the era of Cyclical Conquests, but it did not revolutionize the patterns of basic production and social structure as it did in the forested areas of the northern Mediterranean.

SUMMARY AND CONCLUSIONS

The above analysis may be briefly summarized.

In arid and semiarid regions, agriculture may be carried on by means of flood-plain and irrigation farming, which do not require metal tools. In Mesopotamia, farming began in the higher altitudes with rainfall some distance from the rivers. Whether or not this was true everywhere, there is no question that maximum production in these areas of critical and minimal precipitation required irrigation, and that in proportion as irrigation works develop, population will increase until the limits of water are reached. Social or political controls become necessary to manage irrigation and other communal projects. As early societies were strongly religious, individuals with supernatural powers — lineage heads, shamans, or special priests — formed a theocratic ruling class, which first governed multihouse-cluster communities of Formative Era "peasants" and later multicommunity states.

The increasing productivity of farming released considerable labor from subsistence activities, and new technologies were developed — basketry, loom-weaving, pottery, metallurgy, domestic and religious construction, and transportational facilities. Products made for home use were simple and utilitarian; those made for the theocratic class and for religious purposes became increasingly rich and varied, and they required an increasing proportion of total productive efforts.

When these societies reached the limits of agricultural productivity set by their water supply, population pressures developed within each state and states began to compete with one another for resources and products. At first, interstate conflict was probably instigated by the ruling groups; for it seems that once a trend toward concentration of wealth and power in any society is initiated it continues under its own momentum. Empire-building meant, therefore, that any local state which was intent on conquest and wished to exact goods and services from other states had to subordinate the rulers of those states.

But empire-building also affected the basic population, the peasant communities, of the states; for they were subjected to increased tribute in goods or services while their per capita productive capacity decreased. In each area, therefore, there came a critical point at which the relationship of population to food and goods fell below the biological or culturally conceived optimum — when the standard of living decreased and the death rate increased to the point that local populations were willing to support revolutions against imperial authority. The crumbling of empires was probably accompanied by deterioration of irrigation works, decrease of food production, decline of population, return of local states to power, and loss of certain cultural achievements. After a "Dark Age" the process of empire-building was begun anew either by a local state or a predatory nomadic group.

The culture of the empires differed from that of the Regional Florescent states in several respects. Extreme militarism brought about the formation of armies, the installation of warrior-leaders, and in some cases the development of classes of warriors. Social life was regimented by strong political controls backed by legal systems and sanctioned by state religion. Few intellectual or technological innovations were made, but goods were produced in quantity and in standard forms.

The Iron Age gave the Old World a revolutionary technology, but as iron tools cannot increase water supply, the irrigation areas were little affected, except as they fell under the empires of the north Mediterranean. Iron Age cultures developed in the forested areas of Europe, which had been exploited only with difficulty under the old technology. The New World never reached an Iron Age in pre-Columbian times. The Spanish conquest brought it an Iron Age culture from the Old World, and native culture development was abruptly ended just after it had entered the era of Cyclical Conquests.

Table 5 showing the absolute chronology of the developmental eras in each center of civilization has been revised for this collection of essays on the basis of recent dates, especially radiocarbon or carbon 14 dates. While these are still subject to revision and while the place of certain prehistoric periods in major eras is by no means clear, an interesting feature has emerged from this revised chart. Previously, it was supposed that culture developed in a rather smooth and ever-rising curve. Incipient farming was thought to have lasted many thousands of years, while the Formative Era and subsequent periods became shorter and shorter. This seems not to have been the case.

Apparently, the potentialities of a revolutionary technology such as "food production" or agriculture were quickly realized. In both hemispheres, irrigation-based empires, which we assumed to have represented the sociocultural limits under the given technology, developed within about three thousand years. After this, they endured for an equal or even longer period until the areas were brought under the influence of European sociopolitical systems. In America, the duration of empires was briefer since they were cut short by the Spanish conquest.

The above formulation is rough, cursory, and tentative. It applies only to the early centers of world civilization. The eras are not "stages," which in a world evolutionary scheme would apply equally to desert, arctic, grassland, and woodland areas. In these other kinds of areas, the functional interrelationship of subsistence patterns, population, settlements, social structure, co-operative work, warfare, and religion had distinctive forms and requires special formulations.

The principal grounds for questioning the present formulation will, I suspect, be that diffusion between the centers of civilization in each hemisphere can be demonstrated. The relative chronology of the eras (Table 5) fits a diffusionist explanation perfectly. The essential question, however, is just what diffusion amounts to as an explanation. There is no doubt about the spread of domesticated plants and animals and little doubt about the diffusion of many technologies, art styles, and details of both material and nonmaterial culture. Proof of diffusion, however, lies in the unique qualities of secondary features, not in the basic types of social, economic, and religious patterns — the features of the cultural core. These features could be attributed to diffusion only by postulating mass migration or far-flung conquests.

If people borrow domesticated plants and agricultural patterns, it is evident that population will increase in favorable areas. How shall dense, stable populations organize their sociopolitical relations? Obviously, they will not remain inchoate mobs until diffused patterns have taught them how to live together. (And even diffused patterns had to originate somewhere for good and sufficient reasons.) In densely settled areas, internal needs will produce an orderly interrelationship of environment, subsistence patterns, social groupings, occupational specialization, and over-all political, religious, and perhaps military integrating factors. These interrelated institutions do not have unlimited variability, for they must be adapted to the requirements of subsistence patterns established in particular environments; they involve a cultural ecology. Traits whose uniqueness is proof of their diffusion are acceptable if they are congruent with the basic socio-economic institutions. They give uniqueness and local color, and they may help crystallize local patterns in distinctive ways, but they cannot per se produce the underlying conditions of, or the need for, greater social and political organization. It is therefore possible to concede wide diffusion of particulars within the hemispheres and even between the hemispheres without having to rely upon diffusion as the principal explanation of cultural development.

We have attempted here to present a conception of culture and a methodology for formulating the regularities of cultural data which are consistent with scientific purpose. The data are those painstakingly gathered and arranged spatially and temporally by culture history. Thorough attention to cultural differences and particulars is necessary if typology is to be adequate and valid, but historical reconstructions need not be the sole objective of anthropology. Strong observed that "the time is coming when the rich ethnological and archeological record of the New World can be compared in full detail and time perspective with similar records from Europe, Egypt, Mesopotamia, India, China, and Siberia. When such comparative data are in hand the generalizations that will emerge may well revolutionize our concept of culture history and culture process over the millennia" (Strong, 1943). Any generalizations or formulations must be subject to frequent revision by new data, for, as Kroeber (1940:477) remarks, "Detailed case-by-case analyses are . . . called for if interpretations are not to become vitiated over-generalizations which more and more approach formulas." At the same time, it is obvious that the minutiae of culture history will never be completely known and that there is no need to defer formulations until all archaeologists have laid down their shovels and all ethnologists have put away their notebooks. Unless anthropology is to interest itself mainly in the unique, exotic, and nonrecurrent particulars, it is necessary that formulations be attempted no matter how tentative they may be. It is formulations that will enable us to state new kinds of problems and to direct attention to new kinds of data which have been slighted in the past. Fact-collecting of itself is insufficient scientific procedure; facts exist only as they are related to theories, and theories are not destroyed by facts — they are replaced by new theories which better explain the facts. Therefore, criticisms of this paper which concern facts alone and which fail to offer better formulations are of no interest.

12

Analysis of Complex Contemporary
Societies: Culture Patterns of Puerto Rico[1]

This essay will deal primarily with the culture patterns or life-ways of certain classes or segments of the Puerto Rican people, with special attention to how the processes of industrialization have modified a predominantly agrarian population. The term "industrialization" used in connection with rural people refers rather broadly not only to their involvement in a system of cash crop production and of consumption of mass manufactured commodities, but also, at least in the Western world, to the development of political democracy, an augmented role of the state in controlling and directing change and in providing services to its people, religious freedom, and other patterns which have accompanied technological progress and the growth of economic free enterprise.

[1] The present chapter is a résumé of a forthcoming study, to be published by the University of Illinois Press, that was written not only by the present author but by those who did the field research in Puerto Rico: Robert A. Manners, Sidney Mintz, Elena Padilla, Raymond L. Scheele, and Eric Wolf. My co-workers should share full credit and responsibility for the analyses herein offered. The whole chapter is a republication of an article by the same name which first appeared in "Puerto Rico: A Study in Democratic Development," ed. Millard Hansen and Henry Wells, *The Annals of the American Academy of Political and Social Science,* Vol. 285 (1953), pp. 95-103.

In Puerto Rico, industrialization has produced certain general trends which provide a kind of common denominator to all classes of people. These trends began during the nineteenth century, but they were greatly accelerated during the twentieth century after the island came under United States sovereignty. Industrialization in Puerto Rico today is developing rapidly, and it involves not only general tendencies but certain economic patterns, a political ideology, a legal and governmental system, and other features specific to the United States.

URBAN CHANGES

All segments of the Puerto Rican population have been influenced by industrialization, but the town and urban centers have responded most uniformly. Urbanization, itself a major trend, has entailed a number of characteristic changes. Not only do towns become much larger and comprise an ever greater percentage of the total population, but their functions and internal composition are being altered. The local communities mediate the national institutions to the countryside by serving as centers for marketing, wholesaling, retail trade, and credit; for governmental administration and for education, farm extension, health, and other public services; for the servicing and building trades and the transportational workers; for local political parties and labor unions, for religious and recreational functions; and for the distribution of certain media of mass communication.

While these new urban functions tend to create greater similarity between towns, they also differentiate the population within each town into special segments, classes, or sociocultural groups: wealthy commercial and professional personnel; civil servants, transportational workers, and servicing and building trades groups; and skilled and unskilled laborers. Most characteristic of these are the new middle classes of varied occupation and income. They represent a new trend, a new set of values which ascribes major importance to the symbols of personal achievement and wealth. Upward mobility in the socioeconomic hierarchy becomes a crucial goal; and individual effort, thrift, education, and utilization of governmental services and opportunities become means to the goal.

RURAL CHANGES

The rural population also is affected by these industrial trends. Cash crops or wage labor provides money with which to purchase desired items in the rising tide of manufactured goods offered by the town merchants, and to maintain a standard of living that carries prestige. The farm population is acquiring a cash-oriented value system, which is supplanting the older rationale of personal relations and services. The traditional patterns of labor exchange between small farmers, of personal favors and perquisites between landowners and laborers, and of kinship and ritual kinship duties and obligations are disappearing or being seriously modified.

However, the sociocultural groups created in the rural areas by industrialization are less uniform than those in the urban centers. Each rural region has a distinctive environment and therefore particular crop potentials. In each region the productive arrangement — the kind of crop, mechanization in field production or in processing, land tenure, capitalization and credit, and the nature of labor and of owner-worker relations — has created distinctive subcultures among the people involved. The present article is primarily concerned with the subcultures of the rural workers.

PUERTO RICAN CULTURE AND SUBCULTURES

In order to understand the cultural patterns of contemporary Puerto Rico, it is necessary to view the processes of industrialization against the background of the cultural tradition of the island. For four centuries the culture was essentially Hispanic, both in its national institutions and in its folk aspects. Early in the island's history there were probably important subcultural differences between landowners, ecclesiastical and lay officials, craftsmen, merchants, subsistence farmers, and other groups. For an undetermined period there were probably also differences between ethnic groups — Indians native to Puerto Rico and from the continent, Africans, and Europeans of various origins and classes. But true ethnic minorities are not now important. The Hispanic heritage, however, was the basis of Puerto Rican culture and subcultures, and, despite the effects of industrial trends, many features of the tradition survive today: the Spanish language, certain familial patterns, religious practices, forms of recreation, food habits, and others.

Today, the Puerto Rican subcultures, or special regional and class groups, represent distinctive interactions between the Hispanic patterns, the local productive arrangements, the effects of industrialization, and the specific influence of Americanization. The subcultures are many and varied. Only certain of the more important types were selected for analysis: a representative *municipio* of the small farmers of subsistence crops and tobacco in the mountains, the so-called *jíbaro*, who are in the tradition of the isolated and independent farmers of the island; the growers of coffee, both landlords and workers, who are of interest because they exemplify the traditional Hispanic paternalistic pattern of two closely interrelated classes; the sugar-cane workers on a corporate plantation and on a government-owned, profit-sharing plantation, both groups of whom comprise a rural proletariat; and the insular upper class, which consists of a few hundred families who live in San Juan, the capital, who represent United States commercial enterprises, and who are by far the most Americanized of any segment of the population.

In spite of these subcultural differences there is an over-all Puerto Rican culture, in that the Hispanic heritage provides a common background, the processes of industrialization are creating insular-wide trends, and most of the Puerto Rican people feel a sense of common origin and destiny. But the cultural common denominator can be overemphasized. The following pages will be concerned with the more important subcultures which have emerged from Puerto Rico's complex historical background.

THE SMALL FARMERS

The mountain farmers who grow their own foods as well as a cash crop of tobacco are of interest not only because they are numerically important but because they exemplify the adaptation of a formerly self-sufficient, isolated, and independent folk society to the demands of modern industrialization. During much of its history, Puerto Rico was somewhat distinctive among Spanish possessions in lacking important mineral wealth and in having little access to markets for such crops as it could grow. Until the nineteenth century the country was underpopulated, and there was ample opportunity for squatter farmers of Indian, Negro, and white ancestry to clear lands in the interior where they lived in comparative self-sufficiency and isolation from the state, the church, and the currents of world economy.

During the last century, however, world trends began to reach these farmers. Improved communications drew them more into the orbit of national affairs. The lure of manufactured goods stimulated their desire for cash, which they obtained primarily through growing tobacco. Tobacco can be grown at little risk, it can be rotated with other crops on small plots, and it requires no expensive field or processing machinery. Moderate credit facilities will carry the producer over a year. Neither losses nor profits can be great. Owing to market restrictions, Puerto Rican tobacco production has not run to large plantations. It is the small farmer's source of cash income, whether he be landowner or sharecropper.

Our study of a tobacco *municipio* shows that certain changes have accompanied the introduction of the cash crop. As the people still grow their own food, subsistence is not so vital a problem as it is in the monocrop sugar area, where all food must be purchased from wages. But cash goals have led to individualization of landownership, and, since population has increased beyond the agricultural resources, farms tend to be divided among heirs to the extent that individual holdings are often insufficient to support the family. This individualization of landownership has been a major factor in disrupting the extended family. Duties and obligations to the extended kin group have become secondary to responsibility for the immediate family.

The trends in land use and landownership have reduced the functional household and familial unit to the nuclear family. The somewhat patrilineal and patrilocal traditional Hispanic family has been modified in that residence and affiliation tend to follow lines of property, which may be inherited on either side of the family. The nature of the marital union, moreover, is affected by economic and social considerations. Where property or social status is involved, marriage. is usually religious or civil; where neither counts, it tends to be consensual.

These tobacco farmers have a new value orientation based on monetary standards and the importance of individual effort. It is known that upward mobility in the socioeconomic scheme can be achieved, and the people are eager to take advantage of all aids: education, farm extension services, health facilities, and the like. Simultaneously, interfamily relations based on labor exchange and other services lacking a monetary standard have declined. The goal of upward mobility has been facilitated by the constant fragmentation of landholdings, for it is possible for a thrifty and successful small farmer or sharecropper to purchase small parcels of land. Although few persons can acquire great wealth, there is considerable opportunity for upward as well as downward mobility in the socioeconomic hierarchy.

Social, Political, Religious Features

The socioeconomic mobility in the tobacco region has influenced social relations. Class lines cannot be sharp, even though there are differences in wealth and corresponding differences in social participation, recreation, standard of living, and other features. Comparative equality is manifest in various ways, including the nature of the *compadrazgo*. *Compadres* (coparents, that is, godparents of one's children) are selected from among one's economic superiors and inferiors as well as among one's equals.

Political ideology of the tobacco farmers is consistent with other aspects of their culture. They are independent in their political as well as economic and social attitudes. Since they are actual or potential landowners, they stand to gain less than the proletariat of the sugar areas from a political program designed to benefit landless workers. The greatly expanded governmental services have been to their advantage, and they have utilized them perhaps more than any other rural group. But in the 1948 election, a much larger portion of the tobacco farmers than of any other rural group voted for the rather militant *Independentistas* rather than for the dominant Popular Democratic party which has stood for rural and social reform.

The small mountain farmers are traditionally and nominally Catholic, but Protestant sects have begun to penetrate the area. It is perhaps too early to appraise this trend, but a factor which appears to favor the new faiths is the ideal of individual initiative and the concept of individual responsibility — the "Protestant ethic," which is part and parcel of the new socioeconomic trends. Another aspect of religious change is that the Catholic festivals, although still observed, have assumed a recreational rather than religious character.

THE COFFEE HACIENDA CULTURE

The coffee haciendas are of interest less because they involve large numbers of persons today than because they still exemplify in many ways a typically Hispanic pattern which once characterized much of the sugar area as well as the coffee area. The earlier pattern has been perpetuated through several factors.

First, coffee cannot be the poor man's cash crop, for it requires a fairly large capital outlay. Unlike tobacco, which can be grown on plots of any size and during brief periods, coffee requires a fairly large acreage in order to justify the processing equipment; and, since it does not bear for several years after planting, the owner must have resources to carry him over. There are a few small and medium coffee farms, but the tendency is toward large holdings which are worked by peasants or landless laborers. Because needed capitalization for coffee production has increased, coffee haciendas tend to become fewer and larger.

Second, since coffee production can be carried on profitably in isolated areas which lack improved roads and communications, the farm population tends to remain socially and culturally isolated from the urban centers. Public services, political ideologies, and the effects of media of mass communication have been slow to reach the coffee workers.

Owner-Worker Relations

The productive arrangements of the large haciendas set the framework for the survival of the traditional culture. The owners are largely Spaniards, often third or fourth generation, and they constitute a well-defined upper class of highly educated and sophisticated persons who maintain close ties with the town. The laborers, both peasants and landless workers, are mostly native Puerto Ricans. The relationship between owner and worker is typically paternalistic, personal, face to face, and variable, as compared with the impersonal wage-based and legalized relationship in sugar production. Between owner and laborer there is a mutual dependency, a system of personal understandings and perquisites. The laborer is paid in wages, but since work is seasonal he is also granted favors in lieu of wages, such as a subsistence plot on which to grow foods, or the chance to burn charcoal on shares. The owner takes a personal interest in him, advising him in his affairs and looking to his welfare. In return, the worker renders unpaid services to his landlord and may even supply daughters as servants in the landlord's household.

The culture of the workers and peasants reflects the isolation and traditionalism perpetuated by the productive arrangement. The family is strongly paternalistic. The father manages its property and income, directs the labor of all its members, including the children, who usually perform useful tasks, and dictates the social behavior and marriages of his offspring.

Solidarity and reciprocity within the working class are manifest in many traditional ways. There is labor exchange based on reciprocity rather than on monetary standards; there is visiting and participation in socioreligious events; there is choice of *compadres;* and there is intermarriage.

Between owners and workers, relations are reciprocal but unequal. They include the system of favors and services already mentioned. The workers seek *compadres* among the owners in order to strengthen their position, but the reverse is not true. They look to the owners for leadership in political as well as economic and social affairs. They are not yet sufficiently sophisticated to recognize the program of the Popular Democratic party as their own. They have too little economic opportunity to place value on individual effort, too little access to and use for education to recognize it as a means of upward mobility, and too little chance to utilize governmental services to feel that these are vital to them. They depend upon their landlord rather than upon unions, political parties, or the government.

Religion

The coffee workers are perhaps the most thoroughly Catholic of all farm people, but their Catholicism is not wholly orthodox. Partly because of limited contact with the church and the priests, the religion tends to center in a cult of saints. Formal church rites and priestly administrations are secondary to a system of household and village saints which constitute the principal supernatural functionaries. These saints receive prayers and supplications, and if they fail to respond they may be punished. At the same time, certain church rites such as baptism sanctioned *compadre* relationships and hence have great sociological importance. Moreover, the many religious festivals provide a traditional form of recreation, in contrast to other regions, where social dancing and sports have become popular.

SUGAR PLANTATION CULTURES

The sugar regions of Puerto Rico exhibit the most pronounced effects of industrialization upon the rural cultures. Since sugar is produced competitively for an outside market, it is necessary that the most modernized methods be used in field production and processing. The mills cost a half-million dollars or more, and in order for them to operate at maximum efficiency, cane from a vast acreage must be fed into them. Sugar, therefore, tends to be monocrop, and subsistence farming, which is so vital to the rural people of other areas, is virtually eliminated.

Earlier in Puerto Rican history, when sugar plantations had ox-driven mills and simple steam boilers, they were family owned. At one time they depended partly upon slave labor; later upon free labor. The productive and social arrangement was the family hacienda type. As technology advanced and the necessary capital outlay increased, there became fewer and larger mills and plantations. Less opulent families, which could not afford mills, contracted to have their cane ground at the large plants. On the arid south coast, however, where cattle ranching had prevailed and where irrigation projects were essential to sugar expansion, the costs were best met by corporate credit. Meanwhile, through its program of land reform, the government finally bought up many production units and made them into profit-sharing mills and plantations.

The Corporate Sugar Plantation

The corporate community on the south coast consists almost entirely of a very homogeneous group of workers who have a considerable Negro admixture, having descended in part from slaves. There is no upper class today, for the private owners have sold out and moved away. Their economic functions have been taken over by a handful of managers representing the American corporation. The middle classes of the community are small, for many of the services they would normally perform are carried out by the corporation.

The working class differs profoundly from that of the tobacco and coffee regions. It consists entirely of wage-earners, whose employment is seasonal and whose income is barely adequate for survival. There are no subsistence plots, and there is no system of personal favors between owner and worker, as on the family hacienda. The workers even have difficulty finding dwellings. They live in clusters of houses on small plots on some of the older hacienda centers, along public highways, and on the beach.

There is remarkable similarity among all members of this class, since opportunities for advancement are absent, and the position of everyone is fixed by a uniform system of wages and agreements. The ideal of self-improvement which characterizes the tobacco farmers is absent. Escape from the fixed socioeconomic status can be achieved only through out-migration or through winning a stake in illegal gambling or bootlegging, both of which would be regarded by the highland people as unwarranted risks rather than as opportunities.

The sugar workers place little value on individual initiative. Their hope is not to achieve upward mobility through education, thrift, or effort, for the job hierarchy holds no place for them. Instead, they seek common goals through the collective means of the labor union, which not only is used to bargain with management but which is a political instrument that lends mass support to the Popular Democratic party in its legislative struggle for improvement of wages, hours, and working conditions.

In the typical labor-class family, all members who are old enough work for wages, which gives a measure of independence to each individual. Since neither property nor considerations of religious orthodoxy are important, marriage unions are likely consensual. Because divorce is frequent and children generally remain with the mother, the family has a matrilineal and matriarchal character. The *compadrazgo* has proliferated among the sugar workers, and a person may have thirty to forty *compadres. Compadres* are always chosen within the working class, however, for the American managerial staff will have no part in such arrangements. Ritual kinship, therefore, instead of binding together members of different socioeconomic classes as in the tobacco and coffee areas, serves as a surrogate for extended kin ties and as a means of furthering the security of the individual within his class.

The homogeneity and solidarity of the working group is also expressed to some extent in religion. Here more than anywhere else on the island, evangelical sects of Protestantism have made considerable progress. This seemingly reflects in part the traditional association of orthodox Catholicism with the ruling upper-class whites, and in part the need for a common emotional outlet which such religions frequently provide insecure groups. Despite the large Negro element in this community, no religious beliefs or practices of unquestioned African provenience were found.

The Profit-Sharing Sugar Plantation

The culture patterns and the attitudes of the workers on the government-owned, profit-sharing sugar plantations are very similar to those of the corporation employees. The workers do not have a sense of proprietorship and participation in plant affairs, because they do not manage the plant. In fact, they speak of it as "the corporation." The line of authority from worker to mill runs a devious course. The worker belongs to a union and supports the Popular Democratic party through the local organization. The party controls the government, which in turn appoints the plantation managers. The workers bargain directly with the managers through their union.

Two features distinguish the profit-sharing plantations from the corporate ones, but these have made little difference in the lives of the workers. First, the workers receive proportional benefits, but this provision has been counterbalanced by the need to spread work as widely as possible, so the labor force is several times as large as it need be, and individual income is very low. Second, subsistence plots have been provided the workers, but since little value is attached to owning land and growing one's own food, the people turn during the "dead" season to activities which yield cash, and make slight use of their plots.

Fixed essentially in a proletariat class, the workers constitute a fairly homogeneous sociocultural group. The processes of industrialization have not affected them as deeply as on the corporate plantation, for they were fairly recently on family haciendas, and the older patterns survive in slight degree. But the nature of the family, life goals, economic activity and union organization, and political attitudes are substantially the same as under the corporation.

The greatest difference between government and corporation workers is in religion. The saint cult survives in some strength among the former, and there is considerable fear of witchcraft. A plausible explanation of witchcraft is that the general insecurity of the people has led them to channel hostility toward competitors — in this case especially migrants from the highlands seeking jobs — into a fear of supernatural measures rather than to express it overtly.

THE UPPER CLASS

The Puerto Rican upper class is limited to a few hundred families which are distinguished by their wealth, their social prominence, and their extreme Americanization. Their income is usually over $10,000 a year. Most of them are engaged in commerce, especially as representatives of United States business firms, although some also derive income from the land. Unlike the wealthy agrarian families, such as the coffee growers, the primary economic allegiance of these families to the United States has been a major factor in their Americanization.

The necessity of carrying out business activities on American terms has profoundly affected the lives of the upper-class people. Children are indoctrinated at an early age in the status and role they will assume. They become accustomed to luxurious housing, automobiles, servants, and other evidences of a very high standard of living. They are educated in American social customs and business practices. Many of them are sent to the United States for their high school education and most of them for college education, which is taken in the business and professional fields. As adults, they are largely business executives.

Cultural characteristics of the Hispanic heritage are rapidly disappearing among upper-class families. They are bilingual, but it can hardly be said that they are bicultural. The nuclear family of man, wife, and children is acquiring independence of the extended kin ties, just as it is in the United States. There is a great love of children, but the number of children has decreased despite prevalent Catholicism which disapproves of birth control.

These families must deal with Puerto Ricans in their business activities, and consequently they understand Puerto Rican behavior. But to a large extent they force their own terms upon business associates and thus become an acculturating influence.

In their relationship to one another, the upper-class families constitute a strong in-group which moves in restricted circles. They belong to highly exclusive social clubs, and their patterns of visiting and entertainment involve only their equals. Social and recreational activities have assumed a predominantly American character. Political attitudes are conservative. The upper class has been opposed to the program of the Popular Democratic party, but since the latter seems to have moderated its social reform program, most of the class has supported it. These classes may also be described as conservative in religion, in that Catholic orthodoxy continues to characterize them.

SOME CONCLUSIONS

The acculturation of the upper-class families has resulted not only from the general processes of industrialization but also from conscious borrowing of the patterns of upper-class business families of the United States. These Puerto Rican families, however, have played only a minor role in acculturating other local groups. They have, no doubt, strongly influenced the lower echelons of the business classes with whom they have direct contact, but their subculture presupposes an economic basis and opportunities which are absent among the workers, the peasants, and the small farmers.

The tobacco farmers and the sugar workers are similar in many respects to their counterparts in the United States, but the similarities are less the result of borrowing (these groups have had little contact

222   THEORY OF CULTURE CHANGE

with one another) than of the industrial trends which have introduced national institutions of a North American type into Puerto Rico. Many North American culture elements, such as manufactured goods, clothes, sports, and motion pictures, have also spread very widely in Puerto Rico, but they have been incorporated in local subcultures which are patterned quite differently.

This article has emphasized the subcultural differences, the distinctive life-ways, found among certain segments of the rural population, rather than the common denominator of Puerto Rican culture. There is, of course, much that all Puerto Ricans share. All groups speak Spanish, and they have in common something of the Hispanic tradition of familial patterns, the Catholic religion, the *compadrazgo*, music, dancing, and recreation. They were all once under Spanish political, economic, and religious domination, and they have been under United States sovereignty for a half-century.

The new goals, values, and patterns created by industrialization have been mediated specifically by the United States, but they would undoubtedly have been much the same under any other sovereignty. They have set up new currents of political, social, economic, and religious activity. Fundamental and rapid change is always disturbing. Most Puerto Ricans quite understandingly react to some degree against these trends; that is, they exhibit evidences of insecurity. Some are openly antagonistic to the United States, which they hold responsible for what is happening to them. If Puerto Rico can be said to manifest nationalism, however, it is a form of cultural rather than overtly political nationalism. It is the spontaneous and inevitable reaction of all segments of the population to profound changes brought about by a set of institutions which has been imposed upon them from the outside.

bibliography

Adams, C. C.

1935. "The Relations of General Ecology to Human Ecology," *Ecology,* XVI, 316-35.

1940. "Introductory Note to Symposium on Relation of Ecology to Human Welfare," *Ecological Monographs,* X, 307-11.

Albright, William F.

1946. *From the Stone Age to Christianity.* Baltimore: Johns Hopkins Press.

Alihan, Milla Aissa

1938. *Social Ecology.* New York: Columbia University Press.

Armillas, Pedro

1948. "A Sequence of Cultural Development in Meso-America," in *A Reappraisal of Peruvian Archaeology.* Ed. Wendell C. Bennett. Society for American Archaeology, Memoir, Vol. XIII, No. 4.

Bates, Marston

1953. "Human Ecology," in *Anthropology Today: An Encyclopedic Inventory.* Ed. A. L. Kroeber. Chicago: University of Chicago Press. Pp. 700-13.

Beals, R. L.

1932a. "Unilateral Organizations in Mexico," *American Anthropologist,* n.s., Vol. XXXIV, No. 3, pp. 467-75.

1932b. "The Comparative Ethnology of Northern Mexico Before 1750," *Ibero-Americana* (University of California), II, 116-21.

Beerbohn, Julius

1881. *Wanderings in Patagonia or Life Among the Ostrich-Hunters.* London.

Benedict, Ruth

1934. *Patterns of Culture.* Boston: Houghton Mifflin Company.

1946. *The Chrysanthemum and the Sword.* Boston: Houghton Mifflin Company.

Bennett, Wendell C.

1946. "The Andean Highlands: An Introduction," *Handbook of South American Indians.* Ed. Julian H. Steward. *Bureau of American Ethnology Bulletin 143,* II, 1-60.

1948. "The Peruvian Co-Tradition," in *A Reappraisal of Peruvian Archaeology.* Ed. Wendell C. Bennett. Society for American Archaeology, Memoir, Vol. XIII, No. 4, Part 2, pp. 1-7.

Bennett, Wendell C., and Junius B. Bird

1949. "Andean Culture History," *American Museum of Natural History Handbook Series,* No. 15.

Bingham, Harold C.

1932. *Gorillas in a Native Habitat.* Joint Expedition of 1929-1932 by Yale University and Carnegie Institution of Washington . . . to Parc National Albert in the Belgian Congo, Africa. New Haven: Yale University Press.

Birket-Smith, Kaj

1930. "Contributions to Chepewyan Ethnology," *Report of the Fifth Thule Expedition, 1921-1924* (Copenhagen), Vol. IV, No. 3.

Bishop, C. W.

1942. *Origin of the Far Eastern Civilizations.* Smithsonian Institution War Background Studies, No. 1.

Braidwood, Robert J.

1948. "Prehistoric Men," *Chicago Natural History Museum Popular Series, Anthropology,* No. 37.

1952. *The Near East and the Foundations for Civilization.* Oregon State System of Higher Education. Eugene, Oregon.

Ch'ao-Ting Chi

1936. *Key Economic Areas in Chinese History.* London: G. Allen and Unwin.

Chapple, Eliot Dismore, and Carleton Stevens Coon

1942. *Principles of Anthropology.* New York: H. Holt & Company.

Childe, V. Gordon

1934. *New Light on the Most Ancient East.* New York: Appleton-Century Company.

1946. *What Happened in History.* New York: Pelican Books.

1951. *Social Evolution.* London and New York: H. Schuman.

Colton, M. R. F., and H. S. Colton

1918. *The Little-Known Small House Ruins in the Coconino Forest.* American Anthropological Association, Memoir 5, No. 4.

1932. "A Survey of Prehistoric Sites in the Region of Flagstaff, Arizona," *Bureau of American Ethnology Bulletin 104.*

Cook, S. F.

1947. "The Interrelation of Population, Food Supply, and Building in Pre-Conquest Central Mexico," *American Antiquity,* XIII, 45-52.

Coon, Carlton S.

1948. *A General Reader in Anthropology.* New York: H. Holt & Company.

Cooper, John M.

1942. "Areal and Temporal Aspects of Aboriginal South American Culture," *Primitive Man,* Vol. XV, Nos. 1 and 2, pp. 1-38.

Coulborn, Rushton (Ed.)

1950. "Conference on Feudalism." Mimeographed summary of conference held at Princeton University, under the sponsorship of the American Council of Learned Societies, Oct. 31 to Nov. 1, 1950.

Creel, H. G.

1937a. *The Birth of China.* New York: Reynal and Hitchcock.
1937b. *Studies in Early Chinese Culture.* Baltimore: Waverly Press.

Daifuku, Hiroshi

1952. "A New Conceptual Scheme for Prehistoric Cultures in the Southwestern United States," *American Anthropologist,* LIV, 191-200.

Davidson, D. Sutherland

1928. "The Family Hunting Territory in Australia," *American Anthropologist,* n.s., XXX, 614-32.

Dornan, S. S.

1925. *Pygmies and Bushmen of the Kalahari.* London.

Dunn, E. J.

1931. *The Bushman.* London.

Eggan, Fred

1950. *The Social Organization of the Western Pueblo.* Chicago: University of Chicago Press.

Ekholm, Gordon F.

1946. "Wheeled Toys in Mexico," *American Antiquity,* XI, 222-27.

Embree, John

1939. *Suye Mura, A Japanese Village.* Chicago: University of Chicago Press.

Fewkes, J. Walter

1909. "Antiquities of Mesa Verde National Park: Spruce Tree House," *Bureau of American Ethnology Bulletin 41.*
1911a. "Preliminary Report on a Visit to the Navajo National Monument, Arizona." *Bureau of American Ethnology Bulletin 50.*
1911b. "Antiquities of Mesa Verde National Park: Cliff Palace," *Bureau of American Ethnology Bulletin 51.*

Ford, James

1954. "On the Concept of Types," *American Anthropologist,* LVI, 42-54.

Forde, C. Daryll

1931a. "Ethnography of the Yuman Indians," *University of California Publications in American Archaeology and Ethnology,* Vol. XXVIII, No. 4, pp. 142-46.
1931b. "Hopi Agriculture and Land Ownership," *Journal of the Royal Anthropological Institute,* LXI, 357-405.
1949. *Habitat, Economy and Society.* London: Methuen and Company.

Gifford, E. W.

1918. "Clans and Moieties in Southern California," *University of California Publications in American Archaeology and Ethnology*, XIV, 155-219.

1926. "Miwok Lineages and the Political Unit in Aboriginal California," *American Anthropologist*, n.s., XXVIII, 389-401.

1931. "The Kamia of the Imperial Valley," *Bureau of American Ethnology Bulletin 97*.

1932. "The Southeastern Yavapai," *University of California Publications in American Archaeology and Ethnology*, Vol. XXIX, No. 3, pp. 177-252.

1933. "The Cocopa," *University of California Publications in American Archaeology and Ethnology*, Vol. XXXI, No. 5, pp. 257-334.

Gifford, E. W., and R. H. Lowie

1928. "Notes on the Akwa'ala Indians of Lower California," *University of California Publications in American Archaeology and Ethnology*, Vol. XXIII, No. 7, pp. 339-52.

Gladwin, Harold S.

1947. *Men Out of Asia*. New York: Whittlesey House.

Gusinde, Martin

1931. "Die Feuerland Indianer. Band I. Die Selk'nam. Verlag der Internationalen Zeitschrift," *Anthropos*, pp. 302-06.

Hargrave, L. L,

1933. "Pueblo II Houses of the San Francisco Mountains, Arizona," *Museum of Northern Arizona* (Flagstaff, Arizona), Bulletin 4, pp. 15-75.

Harrington, John P.

1917. "Work Among the Indians of California and Arizona," *Smithsonian Miscellaneous Collections*, LXVI, 111-13.

Harris, J. S.

1940. "The White Knife Shoshoni of Nevada," in *Acculturation in Seven American Indian Tribes*. Ed. Ralph Linton. New York.

Hawley, Amos H.

1950. *Human Ecology: A Theory of Community Structure*. New York: The Ronald Press.

Hewett, Edgar L.

1906. "Antiquities of the Jemez Plateau, New Mexico." *Bureau of American Ethnology Bulletin 32*.

Hollingshead, A. B.

1940. "Human Ecology and Human Society," *Ecological Monographs*, X.

Hoyle, Rafael Larco

1946. "A Culture Sequence for the North Coast of Peru," in *Handbook of South American Indians*. Ed. Julian H. Steward. *Bureau of American Ethnology Bulletin 143*, II, 149-73.

Huxley, Julian S.

1952. "Biological Evolution and Human History" (brief on a paper presented at supper conference, Wenner-Gren Foundation, June 8, 1951), *American Anthropological Association News Bulletin 6,* pp. 15-16.

Jenness, Diamond

1932. "The Indians of Canada," *Canada Department of Mines National Museum,* Bulletin 65.

Judd, Neil M.

1926. "Archaeological Observations North of the Rio Colorado," *Bureau of American Ethnology Bulletin 82.*

Kidder, A. V.

1924. *An Introduction to the Study of the Southwestern Archaeology.* New Haven: Yale University Press.

1945. "Excavations at Kaminaljuyu, Guatemala," *American Antiquity,* XI, 65-75.

Kidder, A. V., and S. J. Guensey

1919. "Archaeological Explorations in Northeastern Arizona," *Bureau of American Ethnology Bulletin 65.*

Kidder, Alfred, Jesse Jennings, and Edwin Shook

1946. *Excavations of Kaminaljuyu,* Carnegie Institution of Washington, Publication No. 561.

Klineberg, Otto

1950. "Tensions Affecting International Understanding," *Social Science Research Council Bulletin* No. 62 (New York).

Kluckhohn, Clyde

1949. *Mirror for Man.* New York: Whittlesey House, McGraw-Hill Book Company.

1953. "Universal Categories of Culture," in *Anthropology Today: An Encyclopedic Inventory.* Ed. A. L. Kroeber. Chicago: University of Chicago Press. Pp. 507-23.

Kniffen, Fred, Gordon MacGregor, Robert McKennan, Scudder McKeel, Maurice Meek (ed. A. L. Kroeber)

1934. *Walapai Ethnography,* American Anthropological Association, Memoir 42.

Koppers, Wilhelm

1921. *Die Anfänge des menschlichen Gemeinschaftslebens.* Vienna.

Kroeber, A. L.

1917. "Zuñi Kin and Clan," *American Museum of Natural History, Anthropological Papers 18,* No. 2.

1925. "Handbook of the Indians of California," *Bureau of American Ethnology Bulletin 78.*

1928. "Native Culture of the Southwest," *University of California Publications in American Archaeology and Ethnology,* Vol. XXIII, No. 9.

1934. "Native American Population," *American Anthropologist,* n.s., Vol. XXXVI, No. 1, pp. 1-25.

1939. "Cultural and Natural Areas of Native North America," *University of California Publications in American Archaeology and Ethnology,* XXXVIII, 1-242.

1940. "The Present Status of Americanistic Problems," in *The Maya and Their Neighbors.* New York: Appleton-Century Company. Pp. 460-87.

1944. "Peruvian Archaeology in 1942," *Viking Fund Publication Anthropology* (New York), No. 4.

1948. *Anthropology.* New York: Harcourt, Brace and Company.

Kroeber, A. L., and Clyde Kluckhohn
1952. "Culture: A Critical Review of Concepts and Definitions," *Papers of the Peabody Museum of American Archaeology and Ethnology,* Harvard University, Vol. XLVII, No. 1.

Leacock, Eleanor
1954. "The Montagnois 'Hunting Territory' and the Fur Trade," *American Anthropologist,* Vol. LVI, No. 5, Part 2, Memoir No. 78.

Lesser, Alexander
1939. "Research Procedure and Laws of Culture," *Philosophy of Science,* VI, 345-55.

Linton, Ralph
1936. *The Study of Man.* New York: Appleton-Century Company.

Lothrop, Samuel K.
1948a. "Archaeology of Panama," in *Handbook of South American Indians,* Ed. Julian H. Steward. *Bureau of American Ethnology Bulletin 143,* Vol. IV.

1948b. "The Circum-Caribbean Tribes," in *Handbook of South American Indians.* Ed. Julian H. Steward. *Bureau of American Ethnology Bulletin 143,* IV, 143-67.

Lowie, Robert
1925. *Primitive Society.* New York: Liveright.

1934. "Some Moot Problems in Social Organization," *American Anthropologist,* n.s., Vol. XXXVI, No. 3, pp. 321-30.

1936. "Cultural Anthropology: A Science," *American Journal of Sociology,* XLII, 301-20.

1940. *An Introduction to Cultural Anthropology.* New York: Farrar and Rinehart.

1946. "Evolution in Cultural Anthropology: A Reply to Leslie White," *American Anthropologist,* XLVIII, 223-33.

Malinowski, Bronislaw

1944. *A Scientific Theory of Culture.* Chapel Hill: University of North Carolina Press.

Man, H. R.

1882. "On the Aboriginal Inhabitants of the Andaman Islands," *Journal of the Royal Anthropological Institute,* Vol. XII.

Martin, Paul

1929. "The 1928 Archaeological Expedition of the State Historical Society of Colorado," *The Colorado Magazine,* Vol. VI, No. 1, The State Museum, Denver.

Martin, Paul S., and John B. Rinaldo

1951. "The Southwestern Co-Tradition," *Southwestern Journal of Anthropology,* VII, 215-29.

Mindeleff, Victor

1891. "A Study of Pueblo Architecture," *Bureau of American Ethnology, Annual Report,* VIII, 13-228.

Morgan, Lewis H.

1877. *Ancient Society, or Researches in the Lines of Human Progress from Savagery, through Barbarism to Civilization.* New York: H. Holt and Company.

1910. *Ancient Society.* Chicago: Charles H. Kerr and Company.

Morice, A. G.

1906. "The Great Déné Race," *Anthropos* I, 229-78, 483-509, 695-730.

1907. "The Great Déné Race," *Anthropos,* II, 1-34, 181-96.

1909. "The Great Déné Race," *Anthropos,* IV, 582-606.

1910. "The Great Déné Race," *Anthropos,* V, 113-42, 419-43, 643-53, 969-90.

Morley, Sylvanus

1946. *The Ancient Maya.* Stanford: Stanford University Press.

Morss, Noel

1927. *Archaeological Exploration in the Middle Chinlee,* American Anthropological Association, Memoir.

Murdock, George Peter

1949. *Social Structure.* New York: Macmillan Company.

1951. "The South American Culture Areas," *Southwestern Journal of Anthropology,* VII, 415-36.

Musters, George C.

1873. *At Home with the Patagonians. A Year's Wandering over Untrodden Ground from the Straits of Magellan to the Rio Negro.* London.

Northrop, F. S. C.

1947. *The Logic of Science and the Humanities.* New York: Macmillan Company.

Olson, R. L.

1933. "Clan and Moiety in Native America," *University of California Publications in American Archaeology and Ethnology,* Vol. XXXIII, No. 4, pp. 351-422.

Osgood, Cornelius B.

1931. "The Ethnography of the Great Bear Lake Indians," *National Museum of Canada Annual Report.*

1933. "The Ethnography of the Great Bear Lake Indians," *National Museum of Canada Annual Report.*

Outes, Felix F., and Carlos Bruch

1910. *Los Aborigines de la República Argentina.* Buenos Aires.

Parsons, E. C.

1929. *The Social Organization of the Tewa of New Mexico,* American Anthropological Association, Memoir 36.

1932. "Isleta, New Mexico," *Bureau of American Ethnology Annual Report.*

Passarge, S.

1907. *Die Buschmanner der Kalahari.* Berlin.

Phillips, Philip, James A. Ford, and James B. Griffin

1951. "Archaeological Survey in the Lower Mississippi Alluvial Valley, 1940-47," *Papers of the Peabody Museum of American Archaeology and Ethnology,* Harvard University, Vol. XXV.

Prudden, T. M.

1918. *A Further Study of Prehistoric Small House Ruins in the San Juan Watershed,* American Anthropological Association, Memoir 5 (1).

Putnam, Patrick

1948. "The Pygmies of the Ituri Forest," in Carleton S. Coon, *A General Reader in Anthropology.* New York: H. Holt and Company. Pp. 322-42.

Radcliffe-Brown, A. R.

1922. *The Andaman Islanders.* Cambridge University Press.

1930a. "Former Numbers and Distribution of the Australian Aborigines," *Official Yearbook of the Commonwealth of Australia* No. 23, pp. 671-96.

1930b. "The Social Organization of Australian Tribes, I," *Oceania,* I, 34-63.

1930c. "The Social Organizations of Australian Tribes, II," *Oceania*, I, 204-46.

1931. "The Social Organization of Australian Tribes, III," *Oceania*, I, 426-56.

Rands, Robert L.

1952. "Some Evidence of Warfare in Classic Maya Art." Unpublished Ph.D. dissertation, Columbia University. University of Michigan Microfilm Publication No. 4233.

Redfield, Robert

1941. *The Folk Culture of Yucatan*. Chicago: University of Chicago Press.

1947. "The Folk Society," *American Journal of Sociology*, LII, 293-308.

Roberts, Frank H. H., Jr.

1929. "Shabik'eshchee Village: A Late Basket Maker Site in the Chaco Canyon, New Mexico," *Bureau of American Ethnology Bulletin 92*.

1930. "Early Pueblo Ruins in the Piedra District, Southwestern Colorado," *Bureau of American Ethnology Bulletin 96*.

1931. "The Ruins at Kiatuthlanna, Eastern Arizona," *Bureau of American Ethnology Bulletin 100*.

1932. "The Village of the Great Kivas on the Zuñi Reservation, New Mexico," *Bureau of American Ethnology Bulletin 111*.

1933. "Some Early Pueblo Remains in Eastern Arizona," *Smithsonian Institution Exploration and Field Work in 1932*, pp. 65-68.

Roth, H. Ling

1899. *The Aborigines of Tasmania*. Halifax (England): F. King and Sons.

Russell, Frank

1908. "The Pima Indians," *Bureau of American Ethnology Annual Report 3*.

Schapera, I.

1926. "A Preliminary Consideration of the Relationship between the Hottentots and the Bushmen," *South African Journal of Science*, XXIII, 833-66.

1930. *The Khoisan Peoples of South Africa*. London.

Schebesta, Paul

1929. *Among the Forest Dwarfs of Malaya*. London.

1931. "Erste Mitteilungen über die Ergebnisse meiner Forschungsreise bei den Pygmäen in Belgisch-Kongo," *Anthropos*, XXVI, 1-17.

Scheele, Raymond

1947. "Warfare among the Iroquois and Their Neighbors." Unpublished Ph.D. dissertation, Columbia University.

Schmidt, P. W.

1910. "Die Stellung der Pygmaenvölker in der Entwicklungsgeschichte des Menschen," *Studien u. Forschungen zur Menschen- u. Völkerkunde.* Stuttgart.

Serrano, Antonio

1930. *Los Primitivos Habitantes del Territorio Argentino.* Buenos Aires.

Skeat, W. W., and C. O. Blagden

1900. *Pagan Races of the Malay Peninsula.* London and New York: The Macmillan Company.

Speck, Frank G.

1915a. *Family Hunting Territories and Social Life of Various Algonkian Bands of the Ottawa River Valley,* Canada Geological Survey, Memoir 70.

1915b. "The Family Hunting Band as the Basis of the Social Organization of the Algonkian," *American Anthropologist,* n.s., XVII, 289-305.

1917a. "The Social Structure of the Northern Algonkian," *Publication of the American Sociological Society,* XII, 82-100.

1917b. "Game Totems among the Northeastern Algonkians," *American Anthropologist,* n.s., XIX, 9-18.

1922. "Beothuk and Micmac," *Museum of American Indian, Heye Foundation, Indian Notes and Monographs,* No. 22.

1923. "Mistissini Hunting Territories in the Labrador Peninsula," *American Anthropologist,* n.s., XXV, 452-71.

1927. "Family Hunting Territories of the Lake St. John Montagnais and Neighboring Bands," *Anthropos,* XXII, 387-403.

1928. "Land Ownership Among Hunting Peoples in Primitive America and the World's Marginal Areas," *Twenty-second International Congress of Americanists* (Rome), II, 323-32.

Spier, Leslie

1922. "A Suggested Origin for Gentile Organization," *American Anthropologist,* n.s., XXIV, 487-89.

1928. "Havasupai Ethnography," *American Museum of Natural History, Anthropological Papers 29,* pp. 209-35.

1933. *Yuman Tribes of the Gila River,* Chicago: University of Chicago Press.

"Statement on Human Rights," *American Anthropologist,* XLIX (1947), 539-43.

Steward, Julian H.

1933. "Ancient Inhabitants of Western Utah: Mounds and House Types," *University of Utah Bulletin 23,* No. 7.

1936. "The Economic and Social Basis of Primitive Bands," in *Essays in Honor of A. L. Kroeber.* Berkeley, California: University of California Press.

1937. "Ecological Aspects of Southwestern Society," *Anthropos*, XXXII, 87-104.

1938. "Basin-Plateau, Sociopolitical Groups," *Bureau of American Ethnology Bulletin 120*.

1940a. "Recording Culture Changes Among the Carrier Indians of British Columbia," *Explorations and Field Work of the Smithsonian Institution in 1940*, pp. 83-90 (1941).

1940b. "Native Cultures of the Intermontane (Great Basin) Area," *Essays in Historical Anthropology of North America, Smithsonian Miscellaneous Collection*, C, 479-98.

1941a. "Archaeological Reconnaissance of Southern Utah," *Bureau of American Ethnology Bulletin 128*.

1941b. "Determinism in Primitive Society," *Scientific Monthly*, pp. 491-501.

1946-48. *The Handbook of South American Indians*. Ed. Julian H. Steward. *Bureau of American Ethnology Bulletin 143*, Vols. I-IV.

1949. "Cultural Causality and Law: A Trial Formulation of the Development of Early Civilizations," *American Anthropologist*, LI, 1-27.

1950. "Area Research: Theory and Practice," *Social Science Research Council Bulletin*, No. 63 (New York).

1951. "Levels of Sociocultural Integration: An Operational Concept," *Southwestern Journal of Anthropology*, VII, 374-90.

1953. "Evolution and Process," in *Anthropology Today: An Encyclopedic Inventory*. Ed. A. L. Kroeber. Chicago: University of Chicago Press. Pp. 313-26.

1954. "Types of Types," *American Anthropologist*, LVI, 54-57.

Steward, Julian H., and Frank M. Setzler

1938. "Function and Configuration in Archaeology," *American Antiquity*, IV, 4-10.

Stewart, O. C.

1939. "Northern Paiute Bands," *Anthropological Records* (Berkeley, California: University of California Press), Vol. II, No. 3, pp. 127-40.

Stout, David

1938. "Culture Types and Culture Areas in South America," *Papers of the Michigan Academy of Science, Arts, and Letters*, XXIII, 73-86.

1948. "The Cuna," in *Handbook of South American Indians*. Ed. Julian H. Steward. *Bureau of American Ethnology Bulletin 143*, IV, 257-68.

Stow, George W.

1905. *The Native Races of South Africa*. New York.

Strong, W. D.

1927. "An Analysis of Southwestern Society," *American Anthropologist*, n.s., XXIX, 1-61.

1929. "Aboriginal Society in Southern California," *University of California Publications in American Archaeology and Ethnology*, XXVI, 1-358.

1943. "Cross Sections of New World Prehistory," *Smithsonian Miscellaneous Collection*, Vol. CIV, No. 2.

1947. "Finding the Tomb of a Warrior-God," *National Geographic Magazine*, April, pp. 453-82.

Ta Chen

1946. *Population in Modern China.* Chicago: University of Chicago Press.

Thompson, Eric

1943. "A Trial Survey of the Southern Maya Area," *American Antiquity*, IX, 106-34.

1945. "A Survey of the Northern Maya Area," *American Antiquity*, XI, 2-24.

Tolstoy, L. P.

1952. "Morgan and Soviet Anthropological Thought," *American Anthropologist*, LIV, 8-17.

Trilles, R. P.

1932. "Les Pygmees de la Forêt Equatorial," *Anthropos*, III, 1-530.

Tylor, E. B.

1865. *Researches into the Early History of Mankind and the Development of Civilization.* London: John Murray.

1871. *Primitive Culture.* London: John Murray.

1881. *Anthropology.* London: Watts and Company.

1899. *Anthropology: An Introduction to the Study of Man and Civilization.* New York: Appleton and Company.

Vaillant, George

1944. *The Aztecs of Mexico.* New York: Doubleday, Doran and Company.

Vanoverbergh, Morice

1925. "Negritos of Northern Luzon," *Anthropos*, XX, 148-99, 399-443.

1930. "Negritos of Northern Luzon," *Anthropos*, XXV, 25-71, 527-65.

Wagley, Charles

1953. *Amazon Town. A Study of Man in the Tropics.* New York: Macmillan Company.

White, Leslie A.

1943. "Energy and the Evolution of Culture," *American Anthropologist*, XLV, 335-56.

1949. *The Science of Culture.* New York: Farrar, Strauss.

Willey, Gordon R.

1948. *New World Cultures.* Byron Cummings Anniversary Volume.

Wissler, Clark

1922. *The American Indian.* New York and London: Oxford University Press.

1923. *Man and Culture.* New York.

Wittfogel, Karl A.

1935. "The Foundations and Stages of Chinese Economic History," *Zeitschrift für Sozial forschung* (Paris), IV, 26-60.

1938. "Die Theorie der Orientalischen Gesselschaft," *Zeitschrift für Sozial forschung* (Paris), Vol. VII, Nos. 1-2, pp. 90-122.

1939. "The Society of Prehistoric China," *Studies in Philosophy and Social Science,* VIII (1940), 138-86.

Wittfogel, Karl A., and Feng Chia-Sheng

1946. "History of Chinese Society, Liao: General Introduction." *American Philosophical Society Transactions,* XXXVI, 1-35.

1951. "The Influence of Leninism-Stalinism on China," *Annals of the American Academy of Political and Social Science,* September, pp. 22-34.

Zuckerman, S.

1932. *The Social Life of Monkeys and Apes.* New York: Harcourt, Brace and Company.

index